THEATER IN THE AMERICAS

A Series from
Southern
Illinois
University
Press
ROBERT A.
SCHANKE
Series Editor

Other Books in the Theater in the Americas Series

Unfriendly Witnesses

Unfriendly Witnesses

GENDER, THEATER, AND FILM
IN THE McCARTHY ERA

Milly S. Barranger

Southern Illinois University Press / Carbondale

Copyright © 2008 by the Board of Trustees,
Southern Illinois University
All rights reserved
Printed in the United States of America

11 10 09 08   4 3 2 1

Library of Congress Cataloging-in-Publication Data
Barranger, Milly S.
  Unfriendly witnesses : gender, theater, and film in
the McCarthy era / Milly S. Barranger.
     p. cm. — (Theater in the Americas)
  Includes bibliographical references and index.
  ISBN-13: 978-0-8093-2876-5 (pbk. : alk. paper)
  ISBN-10: 0-8093-2876-3 (pbk. : alk. paper)
  1. Actresses—United States—Political activity.
2. Blacklisting of entertainers—United States—
History—20th century. 3. Women dramatists,
American—20th century—Political activity.
4. Blacklisting of authors—United States—History—
20th century. 5. United States. Congress. House.
Committee on Un-American Activities. I. Title.

PN1590.B5B33 2008
792.082'09045—dc22   2007040920

Printed on recycled paper. ♻
The paper used in this publication meets the minimum
requirements of American National Standard for Information Sciences—Permanence of Paper for Printed
Library Materials, ANSI z39.48-1992. ♾

For Vera Mowry Roberts

Contents

Illustrations

Preface

Not since the Salem witch trials had civil agencies in the United States branded citizens as subversives until the twentieth century when the U.S. Congress established investigative committees on un-Americanism. Salem's historical shadow looms large over the shameless period in U.S. political history that goes by the name of *McCarthyism* and infected the life not just of a single village but of a nation.

My examination of gender issues inherent in the show business investigations of the House Committee on Un-American Activities, Joseph McCarthy's Senate Investigative Subcommittee on Government Operations, and Pat McCarran's Senate Internal Security Subcommittee reveals the experiences—public and private—of artists and writers during the anti-Communist crusades that swept our nation between 1947 and 1962. The majority of witnesses were men who in many instances cooperated as friendly witnesses with the committees in the naming of names. Women were in the minority as witnesses and appeared largely as *unfriendly*, a designation for those individuals who chose not to cooperate with the committees. The political histories of creative women as victims of the witch-hunts during the McCarthy period have been largely ignored, dismissed, or lost to memory. In truth, the left-wing politics of the period have been viewed as a male experience with the exception of Lillian Hellman's challenge to both conservative and liberal establishments with her much-contested book *Scoundrel Time*.

This book on *McCarthy's women*, a means of labeling a collective experience that took place within the political cauldron of the fifties, is an act of restoration of the political histories, the damaged careers, the heartbreaks and triumphs of the uncooperative witnesses of stage and film during the congressional hearings of the forties and fifties. The women of Hollywood and Broadway celebrity with links to "front" groups and the Communist Party—USA shared their experiences with their male cohorts, including Philip Loeb, Canada Lee, John Garfield, J. Edward Bromberg, Morris Carnovsky, and Zero Mostel. In tandem, the histories of the women and the men bring into focus the scope of the federal investigations of creative artists of stage and film and the blacklisting that stymied careers. Nevertheless, for over fifty years, the women's experiences and testimonies as congressional witnesses have not been collected as part of historical or cultural records. The experiences of the seven women profiled here span the professional and political experiences of witnesses called before various congressional and state investigative committees. It is my purpose here to examine the role of creative women in a complicated period of American political history that goes by the name of *McCarthyism*.

Critical questions had to be asked in the exploration of the case histories, especially of the principal women—actors, directors, and playwrights—who dissented in the congressional game of denounce-and-survive. For example, how did the feminine sensibility play out in tandem with the defiance of Arthur Miller and Paul Robeson before the committees on the one hand and the informing of Larry Parks, Edward G. Robinson, Elia Kazan, José Ferrer, and Lee J. Cobb on the other? How did the tough-mindedness of Anne Revere and Lillian Hellman inform their responses to the House Committee on Un-American Activities? How did moral courage shape the choices of Judy Holliday, Margaret Webster, and Kim Hunter? Why did the women arrive in the political cauldron as *unfriendly* witnesses while the male majority, with few exceptions, walked the corridors of power as cooperative or friendly witnesses? Moreover, how did the complex weave of relationships—public and private, male and female, aesthetic and ideological—play out within an artistic community during one of the nation's most divisive periods in modern history?

The answers to these questions are found in the struggles of creative artists of both sexes who were marginalized by the unchecked agendas of government committees, ambitious politicians, and conservative groups. The collective experiences of the unfriendly women who wrote *The Children's Hour*, starred in *Born Yesterday*, and staged *Saint Joan* with the blacklisted actress Uta Hagen span the three permanent investigative committees authorized by the U.S. Senate and the U.S. House of Representatives. The women's political histories along with those of their male cohorts highlight a dark chapter of fear, humiliation, financial loss, and even fatal illness in the long political debacle that touched so many lives in mid-twentieth-century America.

I have been asked how the women differed from the men in the crucible of the congressional hearings. In truth, the women shared with the men their roles as scapegoats, liars, victims, dupes, and fellow travelers. Some had been Communist Party members in earlier times. Nevertheless, there were differences. The women dressed stylishly for their congressional appearances, used feminine guile to distract the committeemen, gave performances in the congressional hearing rooms, and generally engaged in tough-minded banter with the committee chairmen. The committees expected the women to be attractive, scattered, and submissive. Their behavior did not always conform to congressional expectations, and they frequently surprised, irritated, and embarrassed the congressmen. Nevertheless, the women categorically *refused to name names*. Larry Parks, José Ferrer, Clifford Odets, Lee J. Cobb, and Elia Kazan could not say as much. Anne Revere's defiance was worthy of her revolutionary ancestors who damned the British authorities to hell, and Lillian Hellman skillfully parsed her words to avoid ending her career as a screenwriter and her future on Broadway. When asked why he did not send Lillian Hellman to jail, the chauvinistic Chairman John Wood of HUAC responded, "Why cite her for contempt? After all, she's a woman."[1]

Ten years before the rise of the women's movement, these women of stage and film made "appearances," exhibited strength in adversity, and frequently confounded the committeemen. To paraphrase J. Parnell Thomas of the first Un-American committee in respect to Hallie Flanagan Davis, national director of the Federal Theatre Project, professional women were "tough" witnesses—to be avoided whenever possible. To say it another way, the women were often viewed as "more trouble than they were worth" in congressional hearings.

As viewed from the vantage point of millennial America, I am encouraged to believe that by remembering how political repression a half century ago took hold of an artistic community, we can avoid a replay of a time that former blacklisted actress Phoebe Brand described to me as "killingly horrific." With the exception of Hallie Flanagan's *Arena: The History of the Federal Theatre*, Lillian Hellman's *Scoundrel Time*, and Margaret Webster's chapter "Of Witch Hunting" in her memoir *Don't Put Your Daughter on the Stage*, the women published few accounts of their experiences. The blacklisted Uta Hagen included a single paragraph in her memoir *Sources* about "political involvement," and Kim Hunter masked her experience with recipes in a cookbook-memoir called *Loose in the Kitchen*. Even those women interviewed on the subject were terse. Anne Revere dismissed the "bloody era" as contriving to make witnesses who took the Fifth "dead in the business."[2]

Nonetheless, Arthur Miller in *Time-Bends* and Elia Kazan in *A Life* set down their encounters with McCarthyism. Director and critic Harold Clurman wrote *The Fervent Years: The Story of the Group Theatre in the Thirties*, and blacklisted screenwriter Dalton Trumbo, one of the Hollywood Ten, reprised his experience in *The Time of the Toad: A Study of Inquisition in America*. In *Fear on Trial*, talk show host John Henry Faulk described his libel trial resulting from his blacklisting by CBS. More recently, playwright and screenwriter Arthur Laurents recorded his memories of the decade in *Original Story By: A Memoir of Broadway and Hollywood*.

The difference between the genders during McCarthyism can be found in the autobiographies written and interviews granted by congressional witnesses. For the most part, the women were *silenced* by the experience. Even though Dorothy Parker shouted defiantly at a rally for the defense of composer Hanns Eisler that HUAC was a "bunch of fools," she failed to translate her bitterness and disgust into her writing.[3] In true fashion, Pat McCarran's stand-in, Senator

Arthur Watkins of Utah, extracted a promise from actress Judy Holliday not to reveal details of her private hearing. She kept her promise to remain silent rather than "dig my own grave."

The politics of tyranny that infected the cultural landscape at mid-twentieth-century reminds us of the potential for a return to wholesale abridgements of civil liberties and for the abuse of government power that effectively suppressed dissenting voices fifty years ago. Moreover, those artists of stage and film that defied congressional committees on un-American activities remind us of the personal, artistic, and cultural costs to an America enthralled by extremism.

Acknowledgments

This book could not have been written without the support and generosity of the theater and film community. Many artists and managers talked with me about the McCarthy years and shared their memories about the political maelstrom of the fifties. Others recalled coworkers whose lives and careers were jolted from unexpected quarters—the U.S. Congress.

I am grateful to the following for sharing their experiences, their memories of friends and associates, and their insights into Broadway and Hollywood during that period. They are lyricists, agents, critics, actors, directors, writers, composers, managers, friends, husbands, wives, and daughters: Richard Adler, Eloise Armen, Hartney Arthur, Eric Bentley, Melvin Bernhardt, Phoebe Brand Carnovsky, Margaret Croyden, Nancy Da Silva, Kathryn Emmett, Mitchell Erickson, Lenore DeKoven, Leticia Ferrer, Madeleine Lee Gilford, George Grizzard, Uta Hagen, Barbara Hogenson, Joseph Hardy, William Herz, Jeff Hunter, Kim Hunter, Floria V. Lasky, Biff Liff, Sloane Shelton, Ann Shepard Sheps, Gina Shields, Diana Raymond, Timothy d'Arch Smith, Max Steele, Berenice Weiler, and Liz Woodman.

I have benefited from the efforts of biographers, researchers, historians, legal scholars, theater critics, and friends, most particularly, Thomas P. Adler, Brooks Atkinson, Laurence G. Avery, K. Kevyne Baar, Joanne Bentley, Jackson Breyer, Oscar G. Brockett, Richard Brown, Michael C. Burton, Marion Capron, Gary Carey, Larry Ceplair, Helen Krich Chinoy, Martha Coigney, Alan Deptula, Martin B. Duberman, Pam Ebel, Helen Epstein, Steven Englund, John Henry Faulk, Jesse Feiler, Leslie Frewin, Pat Galloway, Carol Gelderman, Walter Goodman, Martin Gottfried, Paul M. Green, Robert Griffith, Mel Gussow, Allean Hale, Mary C. Henderson, W. Kenneth Holditch, Will Holtzman, Rhona Justice-Malloy, Stefan Kanfer, Lauren Kessler, Alice Kessler-Harris, Arthur F. Kinney, Marion Meade, Joan Mellen, Tice L. Miller, Ted Morgan, Mary N. Morrow, Brenda Murphy, Victor S. Navasky, Robert P. Newman, Bobbi Owen, Daniel H. Pollitt, Vera Mowry Roberts, Alice M. Robinson, Carl Rollyson, Robert A. Schanke, Ellen Schrecker, Marian Seldes, Helen Sheehy, Richard Schickel, Hugh Southern, Sam Tanenhaus, Howard Taubman, Robert Vaughn, Daniel J. Watermeier, Peter Webb, Albert Wertheim, Don B. Wilmeth, Barry Witham, William Wright, Michael J. Ybarra, and Glen Young.

Something must also be said about the importance of the writings of Harold Clurman, Cheryl Crawford, John Henry Faulk, Uta Hagen, Lillian

Hellman, Elia Kazan, Arthur Laurents, Arthur Miller, and Margaret Webster. In their memoirs and autobiographies, they set forth personal responses to the entanglements of the McCarthy period and describe the repercussions upon their careers, families, friends, and coworkers.

My thanks also to Alice L. Birney, Literary Manuscript Historian, Library of Congress, who steered me through the Margaret Webster and Eva Le Gallienne archives; Alan J. Pally, Program Series Producer, the New York Public Library for the Performing Arts, for aiding in the cross referencing of the Margaret Webster, Cheryl Crawford, and Uta Hagen archives; Donald A. Ritchie, Associate Historian, U.S. Senate, for advising on the testimonies of Joseph McCarthy's Senate Permanent Subcommittee on Investigations of the Committee on Government Operations; Dean M. Rogers, Special Collections, Vassar Library, for making available the Hallie Flanagan Davis archives; Thomas Lisanti of the New York Public Library and Marguerite Lavin of the Museum of the City of New York for assistance with their respective photographic collections; K. Kevyne Baar, project archivist for the Tamiment Library, Robert F. Wagner Labor Archives, at New York University, for guiding me through the Actors' Equity Association archives and for sharing her thoughts on Actors' Equity and blacklisting; Bonnie Nelson Schwartz, producer of "Who Killed the Federal Theatre?" and Ira H. Klugerman of the Educational Film Center for providing the image of Hallie Flanagan; Robert S. Dalton and Thomas J. Nixon, Reference Librarians, Davis Library of the University of North Carolina, Chapel Hill, for enabling my research into newsletters, periodicals, and government records of the period; James Sherwood, Reference Librarian, Law Library of the University of North Carolina, Chapel Hill, for guidance in the search for the court testimony of Kim Hunter; Nancy Horan and William Gorman, New York State Library, Albany, for making available the court testimonies of Dorothy Parker; and Joan Franklin of Cinema Sound, Ltd., New York City, for providing access to an audiotape interview with Parker.

Finally, my research on the political activities of these stage and film artists would have been incomplete without access to government documents made available through the Freedom of Information Act.

Once again, I want to thank Vera Mowry Roberts for her friendship and encouragement over the span of years that I have been writing on theater. I dedicate this book to her.

Unfriendly Witnesses

It is hard to have a witch-hunt without witches.
—Ellen Schrecker, *The Age of McCarthyism*

1 McCarthyism

Taking its name from the U.S. senator, *McCarthyism* was a period of widespread political repression against the threat of Communism in the United States. The fate of the Federal Theatre Project lead by the intrepid Hallie Flanagan Davis in the thirties was a mere tip of the iceberg for the future of the entertainment industry and government-sponsored programs in the forties and fifties.

Anti-Communist political repression of Americans antedates the four years of McCarthy's reign in the U.S. Senate that began in 1950 with the senator's speech before the Women's Republican Club of Wheeling, West Virginia. He announced that he held in his hand the names of 205 Communist sympathizers in the State Department. For the version published in the *Congressional Record,* he changed the number to fifty-seven.[1] The same year, FBI director J. Edgar Hoover told a New York audience that a half million fellow travelers and sympathizers were ready to do the Communist bidding.[2]

Historians agree that McCarthyism existed in its dictionary definition long before the senator, as evidenced by the political practice of publicizing accusations of disloyalty or subversion without regard to evidence and in the use of dubious methods of investigation in order to suppress opposition.[3] In the early fifties, the senator's voice became the clarion call for a coalition of politicians, bureaucrats, right-wing journalists, and conservative activists crusading against dissent and subversion in American life. In turn, opponents branded the anti-Communist crusade that gripped the nation for more than a decade as Red-baiting, witch-hunting, scoundrel time, plague years, and so on.

Under McCarthyism, investigative spotlights were turned on the entertainment industry, educational institutions, and U.S. information agencies and libraries abroad. Known as the "McCarthy Committees," the House Committee on Un-American Activities (HUAC) was Congress's best known anti-Communist investigating arm, with its powerful chairmen—Martin Dies,

1

J. Parnell Thomas, John S. Wood, and Francis E. Walter—as desirous of press coverage as Senator McCarthy. McCarthy's own base of operations was the Senate Government Operations Committee, with its Permanent Subcommittee on Investigations, and Pat McCarran's watchdog committee was the Senate Internal Security Subcommittee (SISS), designed to insure that no Eastern European subversives immigrated into the country.

Only HUAC became a household word, while McCarthy himself, in Lillian Hellman's estimation, became "a very inaccurate name for a shameless period." "McCarthy only summed up the angers and fears of a great many people," she told a reporter for *Rolling Stone*.[4] Nevertheless, HUAC was the star chamber conducting the Hollywood Ten hearings and subsequent investigations into Hollywood and New York City that captured the public's attention more so than any individual congressman.

It was the Committee, as HUAC was popularly known, that remained in the limelight for a decade by means of its extensive show business hearings of 1951 and 1952, labeled "Investigations into Communist Activities in the Los Angeles Area" and later "Investigations into Communist Activities in the New York Area." Although McCarthy grabbed the headlines, the impact of the Committee's investigations—and the industry blacklist that proceeded from those deliberations—on the Hollywood community and film and television artists sent shockwaves throughout the entertainment industry that eventually reached Broadway.

Those writers and artists showcased by the investigative committees usually had star status to generate the headlines so dear to the congressional committeemen and to their constituencies, made up of ultra-conservatives, right-wing activists, and ambitious politicians. In terms of stage and film celebrity, the names of Anne Revere, Judy Holliday, and Lillian Hellman along with Clifford Odets, Elia Kazan and Arthur Miller, resonated with the press and the committees.

The witch-hunters of the McCarthy era knew where to look for witches in American society. They sought out civil rights activists, left-wing labor leaders, "front" group adherents, left-leaning celebrities of stage and film, and socially minded individuals who attended rallies and collected money for the Spanish Republic and its refugees, held Communist Party—USA cards, circulated petitions against nuclear war, allowed their names to be used on letterhead stationery for fundraising purposes, and took part in peace conferences and marches.

In the same round of hearings that ensnared stage director Margaret Webster, McCarthy questioned composer Aaron Copland on the grounds that he had gone to Italy on a government-funded Fulbright professorship in 1951. "I spend my days writing symphonies, concertos, ballads," Copland protested. "I'm not a political thinker."[5] Nevertheless, the composer allowed his name to be used by a number of front groups on petitions for dismissal of charges against the Smith Act defendants, and on committees for world peace conferences. He was in the same leaky boat as Anne Revere, Lillian Hellman, Dorothy Parker, and Margaret Webster. Copland's defense was that his artistic impulses as a composer were connected to his concerns for the plight of humanity: "A musician, when he writes his notes, he makes his music out of emotions and you cannot make your music unless you are moved by the events."[6]

The political and the apolitical, actors and composers, screenwriters and playwrights, film and television artists, were targets of the Cold War crusade to eradicate Communism from American culture and society. The collective zeal of the McCarthyites created a powerful network of anti-Communist organizations and methods: congressional committees, government agencies, professional witnesses, confidential informants, blacklists, indexes of security risks and "front" organizations, "loyalty-security" programs, and coalitions of right-wing newspapers and journalists.[7] *National security* became the rationale for loyalty oaths and unwarranted invasions of privacy. Moreover, anti-Communist campaigns were as diverse as their mechanisms. Communist threats were perceived, naturally, among members of the Communist Party—USA. The obsession over the Red threat to national security spread to left-wing labor unions, Jewish "radicals," New Deal supporters, civil rights groups, naturalized citizens, and foreign aliens. Left-wing activists were viewed as targets to be exorcised by vigilant employers, watchful journalists, FBI agents, government hearings, and court trials.

McCarthyism pervaded the American landscape for forty years and did not end with the Senate's censure of the Wisconsin senator in December of 1954. The sporadic harassment of Communists and suspected Communists continued unchecked until 1957. McCarthy died in May of that pivotal year, and the U.S. Supreme Court, known as the Warren court for its Chief Justice, Earl Warren, struck at the foundations of McCarthyism. The previous year, the Supreme Court had limited the scope of the federal loyalty programs, but, on June 17, 1957, the Court restricted the power of congressional investigations to write new laws. The legitimate need of Congress to pass new laws, Earl Warren wrote, "cannot be inflated into a general power to expose where the predominant result can only be an invasion of the private rights of the individual."[8] As Ted Morgan summarized, "Thus Warren limited the power of the committees in two crucial ways: the questions they asked had to be pertinent to the development of new legislation; and there was to be no prying into the personal affairs of witnesses for the sake of prying."[9]

Eric Bentley pointed further to the radical opposition against another war—Vietnam—that finally intimidated and restrained the congressional committees. Strong, vocal, outrageous, and disconcerting, the halls of Congress were shaken by the challenges to HUAC when witnesses answered the sixty-four-dollar question ("Are you now, or have you ever been, a member of the Communist Party?") in a proud affirmative.[10] The new militancy stunned and distracted the investigative committees who had been used to the meek, the frightened, the intimidated, and the quietly sullen for a period of forty years.

Early Showcase

Before McCarthy arrived to give the witch-hunts a name, Hallie Flanagan, national director of the Federal Theatre Project, stood before the Special House Committee on Un-American Activities in 1938, chaired by Martin Dies of Texas. She was one of the first women associated with the theater to be spotlighted in Congress's search for pro-Communist activities in government agencies.

A small, dark-haired woman of fashionable conservative dress highlighted by a brightly colored scarf volunteered to testify before the Dies committee to answer allegations that the four-year-old Federal Theatre Project was employing Communists and producing Communistic plays. On December 6, 1938, she took her place in the witness chair. Seated at the end of one of two long tables that stretched out in the form of a "T," Flanagan (the only woman at the table) faced members of the committee seated cross-wise at the opposite end. At parallel tables on either side of the "T" were stenographers, reporters, and photographers. Exhibits from the Federal Theatre Project and the Federal Writers' Project lined the walls around the hearing room. Overhead in the high-walled chamber, great chandeliers beamed down fragments of light from crystal teardrops onto the proceedings.

Flanagan's feminine demeanor belied her tough-minded and spirited defense of the government-sponsored theater project and her leadership of it. She set down a marker for the women who followed her in similar quasi-judicial hearings sponsored by the U.S. Congress.

Already in place by 1938 were the rituals of intimidation: the preliminary questions (name, residence, education, profession), the pre-set agendas, the denial of due process, and the quashing of political debate. Prepared for the question about her appointment by the Roosevelt administration, Flanagan related that Harry Hopkins, head of the Federal Emergency Relief Administration, named her to the post of national director of the Federal Theatre Project in the Works Progress Administration. Her response to the chairman's question about the nature of her duties surprised Martin Dies. "Since August 29, 1935," she replied, "I have been concerned with combating un-American inactivity."[11]

"I refer to the inactivity of professional people," she explained, "who, at the time when I took office, were on the relief rolls." Hastening to regain control of the hearing, J. Parnell Thomas asked her to explain a trip she had taken to

4

Russia. She told the committee that she taught at Vassar College, had traveled to Europe and Russia on a Guggenheim Foundation Fellowship, and had written a book on the Russian theater, called *Shifting Scenes*.

Throughout the morning, she parried questions about the "Communist propaganda" circulated by the project in its productions. Flanagan was fully prepared for the question about "theater as a weapon for propaganda." "We have done plays," she explained, "which were propaganda for democracy." The reference to *democracy* riveted the committee's attention, and they wanted to know more about propaganda plays for democracy. Again, Flanagan was prepared. She cited works of "the Living Newspaper," a documentary form that integrated factual data taken from newspapers and the *Congressional Record* with vignettes about current social problems: "Well, let us say first, *One Third of a Nation* [a play about slum housing]. In that the definite propaganda was for better housing for American citizens."

Although neither the chairman nor any member of the committee had seen a production by the Federal Theatre Project (and none ever did), their staffers had researched newspaper reviews and the pro-Communist *Daily Worker* for information on the productions. Parnell Thomas asked about *Power* (a play about rural electrification). Flanagan was quick to reply:

MRS. FLANAGAN: Yes, I would say that *Power* was propaganda for better understanding of the derivation and the scientific means of power and for its wide use—

MR. THOMAS: Was it for public ownership of power?

MRS. FLANAGAN: —that portrayed as effectively as possible both sides of that controversy, and quoted both sides.

At one point in the proceeding, Joe Starnes of Alabama quoted from an article written by Flanagan for *Theatre Arts Monthly*, called "A Theatre Is Born," in which she made reference to "Marlowesque madness." "You are quoting from this Marlowe," Starnes remarked. "Is he a Communist?"

Surprised into laughter along with the spectators in the balcony, Flanagan quickly apologized to the congressman. "I am very sorry," she said. "I was quoting from Christopher Marlowe."

MR. STARNES: Tell us who Marlowe is, so we can get the proper reference, because that is all that we want to do.

MRS. FLANAGAN: Put in the record that he was the greatest dramatist in the period immediately preceding Shakespeare.

In response to Starnes's later assertion that she was sympathetic with Communistic doctrines, she defended her patriotism and set a precedent for future witnesses.

MRS. FLANAGAN: I am an American, and I believe in American democracy. I believe the Works Progress Administration is one great bulwark of that democracy. I believe the Federal Theater, which is one small part of that large pattern, is honestly trying in every possible way to interpret the best interests of the people of this democracy. I am not in sympathy with any other form of government in this country.

When the committee adjourned for lunch, it was clear that they had no further interest in Flanagan's testimony. She asked Martin Dies if she could return to make a final statement for the record. "We will see about it after lunch," he responded.

"We never saw about it after lunch," Flanagan recalled. There was no afternoon session.[12] Nor was she placated by Parnell Thomas's attempt to be jovial as the hearing recessed. "You don't look like a Communist," he said to her. "You look like a Republican!"[13]

Pressing her point, she requested to return in the afternoon to convince the committee that neither she nor the Federal Theatre Project was Communistic. "We don't want you back," Thomas laughed. "You're a tough witness and we're all worn out."[14]

In January, the Dies committee filed a report with the House of Representatives. After six months of sensational charges, the substance of the report came down to one short paragraph.

We are convinced that a rather large number of the employees on the Federal Theatre Project are either members of the Communist Party or are sympathetic with the Communist Party. It is also clear that certain employees felt under compulsion to join the Workers' Alliance [a union of unemployed relief workers reputed to be under Communist control] in order to retain their jobs.[15]

So, on June 30, 1939, the House Appropriations Committee ended funding to the Federal Theatre Project, and the country's first and only national theater was out of business.

Martin Dies's celebrated investigation of the Federal Theatre Project was the first anti-Communist showcase staged by a special House committee to investigate un-American activities on behalf of the U.S. Congress. In Hallie Flanagan's view, the affair was a "badly staged courtroom scene."[16]

Hallie Flanagan, the featured witness, participated in a congressional showcase held ostensibly to undermine the New Deal. The 1938 hearing was prelude to the spectacle that was to come in the next decade. Flanagan's performance was spirited and remarkable. She was not a witness shaken by fear and paranoia. She did not engage in dodgings and weavings with the First and Fifth Amendments as later witnesses were inclined to do. Moreover, she experienced no personal repercussions, such as unemployment or ill-health. At age forty-nine, Hallie Flanagan returned to her faculty position at Vassar College and wrote her memoir (*Arena: The History of the Federal Theatre*). Throughout her career, she never lost her vision of theater as a life force and as a vibrant social institution that at its most courageous addressed present problems touching American life.

Performing Gender

Hallie Flanagan's skillfully controlled performance in defense of the Federal Theatre Project raises questions, in general, about the presence of professional women before the all-male congressional committees, and, in particular, about the appearance of women tutored in theatrics, role-playing, and public performance. As the director of a national arts group and an appointee of the Roosevelt administration, Flanagan had the star power to attract press coverage for the committee's anti-Communist agenda. With the ferocity of a lioness, she gave a spirited defense of her duties to combat un-American inactivity. A small, well-educated woman, she was not expected to parry and thrust, to give as good as she got from the committeemen, oftentimes putting them on the defensive.

In the male-dominated congressional committees, women were recognized as a social class bringing sexual difference to the halls of Congress. Considered the weaker sex, they entered the witness chair as fictional constructs of femininity. They were expected to be intimidated, even cowed, by the authority and brilliance of their male interlocutors. Even the configuration of the seating in the hearing rooms signaled the dominance of the men and the lone subservience of the witness. Witnesses were seated "below the salt," as the saying goes. Moreover, the comparatively small number of women subpoenaed to appear before the committees was expected to soften the image of the men controlling the discourse. The women were needed to show the broad influence of Communism in American life—how Communists had infiltrated not only the stages and movie screens of Broadway and Hollywood but the bedrooms and kitchens of America. However, the committees called notable professional women, such as Hallie Flanagan, Anne Revere, and Lillian Hellman, who forcefully challenged them. Because these professional women were not suitably intimidated, they were soon dismissed as more trouble than they were worth. As he dismissed Hallie Flanagan, Parnell Thomas brusquely confessed that she had been a tough witness.[17] In time, other women were excused as dupes and fellow travelers but none was jailed.

Secure in their power to punish with subpoenas and contempt citations, and their ability to harm through insinuation and headlines, the committeemen failed to take into account the unique professionalism of the creative women called to the hearings. McCarthy's women, the label given here to the women of film and stage who became congressional witnesses in the fifties, were celebrated actresses and nationally known playwrights and screenwriters experienced in generating publicity photos and headlines in the advancement of their careers. Approaching the witness chair, they might masquerade as vulnerable women, but they emerged as fierce protectors of their names, careers, and economic security.

For their appearances before the committees, the women dressed smartly, fully prepared their defense, and used any and all stratagems to ensure survival. The most famous masquerade was played out before SISS by comedienne Judy Holliday in the guise of Billie Dawn, the dumb-blonde character in Garson Kanin's *Born Yesterday*. The actress's appearance before Pat McCarran's Senate Internal Security Subcommittee brought the gender masquerade into the courtroom and played out as a new political phenomenon: *stage performance meets congressional theatrics.*

Now I don't say "yes" to anything except cancer, polio, and cerebral palsy, and things like that.

—Judy Holliday

2 Billie Dawn Goes to Washington: Judy Holliday

Judy Holliday was the best-known stage and film celebrity called before the Senate Internal Security Subcommittee. In the spring of 1952, Philip Loeb, Sam Levenson, Burl Ives, and Judy Holliday were subpoenaed to appear before McCarran's subcommittee of the Senate Judiciary Committee to testify on subversion in the entertainment industry.

Senator Pat McCarran, the silver-haired chairman of the Senate Judiciary Committee, was a vocal anti-Communist who also chaired the Internal Security Subcommittee. In 1950, he authored the Internal Security Act, requiring the registration of all Communist-action and "Communist-front" organizations with the U.S. government. The McCarran Act, as it was known, further established the Subversive Activities Board to oversee "internal security emergencies" and the "detention of subversives" during national emergencies. Prior to the McCarran Act, the U.S. House of Representatives passed the 1948 Mundt-Nixon bill, sponsored by congressmen Karl E. Mundt and Richard M. Nixon, requiring the registration of all Communists.[1]

Like other powerful committee chairmen, Pat McCarran, a conservative Democrat from Nevada, was also interested in creating headlines. Created in December of 1951, his Internal Security Subcommittee (SISS), authorized to investigate subversive activities, focused on the State Department and made few incursions into what he considered the minor field of show business. In the new year, he looked toward Hollywood and Broadway to ensure the passage of legislation restricting immigration into the United States.[2] His Immigration and Naturalization Act, soon to be known as the McCarran-Walter Act, tightening immigration restrictions against subversives and easing procedures whereby to revoke the citizenship of naturalized citizens, passed Congress in June of 1952, two months after Judy Holliday appeared on the congressional stage. Well-known for his anti-Semitic views, the chairman set about establishing that there was a susceptibility to Communism among entertainers of Middle European background. Judy Holliday's celebrity as stage and film star of *Born Yesterday* consolidated McCarran's twin aims. The Oscar-winning actress guaranteed headlines; moreover, she was a descendent of Middle European immigrants. In a word, she was Jewish.

Early Years

Born Judith Tuvim in New York City in 1921, Judy Holliday's American-born mother, Helen Gollomb, was of Russian-Jewish descent. Holliday's maternal grandfather had manufactured epaulets and military braid for the czar's guards in St. Petersburg. In 1888, there were rumors that a series of pograms were to be enacted, and the Gollomb family joined the mass migration of Russian Jews to Ellis Island and eventually to New York City's Lower East Side.[3]

Life on the Lower East Side, with its low wages and crushing poverty, soon proved a disappointment to the new arrivals. Gollomb found work as a tailor but died prematurely, leaving his wife with four children (three sons and a daughter) to care for. Determined not to be beaten down by an unwelcoming new world, Rachel Gollomb worked at menial jobs to feed and educate her children. Her ordeal increased her devotion to socialism, and she reached out to like-minded groups who shared her beliefs. Her daughter, Helen, was indoctrinated into her mother's socialist politics and met her future husband, Abraham Tuvim, at a group meeting. The darkly handsome Abe Tuvim became a successful fundraiser for Jewish organizations. The couple married in 1920, and their daughter was born the following year.

Judith Tuvim grew up in Sunnyside Gardens, Queens, where she scored an impressive 172 on the Otis Intelligence test at P.S. 150, which placed her in the genius category. A family friend remembered her as a shy, reserved, and quiet adolescent with a high-pitched voice.[4]

During her years at Julia Richman High School in Manhattan, Tuvim decided that she wanted a career in the theater as a writer or director, and, upon graduation in 1938, she applied to the Yale Drama School but was one year short of the minimum age requirement for admission. She found a summer job as a telephone operator at the Mercury Theatre, run by John Houseman and Orson Welles. Also that summer, she met Adolph Green, a young man from the Bronx, who provided theatricals for resorts in the Catskills. She reconnected with Green at a coffeehouse in Greenwich Village, called the Village Vanguard, which was run by Max Gordon. She soon became a member of the Revuers, an offbeat satirical group headed by Green with Betty Comden, Alvin Hammer, and John Frank. Comden and Green would later make their Broadway careers as librettists, lyricists, and featured performers with *On the Town, Wonderful Town, Bells Are Ringing, On the Twentieth Century,* and *Singin' in the Rain.*

From their Village Vanguard base, the Revuers performed at benefits for wartime causes. As it would later turn out, some of these benefits were promoted by Communist-front organizations. Although Tuvim marched in parades and joined left-wing demonstrations, the Revuers did little politically engaged satire. In contrast, *Pins and Needles,* the famous musical revue first sponsored in 1936 by the International Ladies Garment Workers Union, satirized labor and other left-wing topics for over one thousand performances on Broadway.

It can be said that all members of the Revuers were inclined politically to the left, as indeed were most theater people in the 1930s. Nonetheless, Rachel Gollomb's granddaughter was actively involved in more social causes than the others with the possible exception of Alvin Hammer.

By the spring of 1939, the Revuers had been discovered, and a talent agent persuaded the group to come to Hollywood and test for a film version of the popular radio show *Duffy's Tavern.* They arrived in Hollywood in the summer of 1943 only to learn that the film had been cancelled but that they had been booked into the Trocadero. The Los Angeles press gave the Revuers sensational reviews, but film offers were for Judith Tuvim alone. She signed a contract with Twentieth Century Fox that included one film, *Greenwich Village,* with nightclub sketches by the Revuers. The sketches were deleted from the film's final cut.

When Comden and Green returned to New York, Tuvim, legally obligated to Fox, stayed in Hollywood where she was "made-over" by the studio for Hollywood stardom. She was given softer makeup, a more flattering hair style, and a new name. Since Tuvim sounded too Jewish for Hollywood success in the forties, she was redubbed *Holliday,* a translation of her Hebraic family name. Tuvim came from *toyvim,* the most common transliteral spelling of the Hebrew word for *holidays.* The second "l" was added to avoid confusion with the blues singer Billie Holiday.[5] Despite supporting roles in *Something for the Boys,* based loosely on the Dorothy Fields and Cole Porter stage musical, and in the film version of Moss Hart's Broadway play *Winged Victory,* directed by George Cukor, Fox did not renew her contract.

A Broadway Career

Upon her return to New York, Holliday found Comden, Green, Leonard Bernstein, and Jerome Robbins collaborating on a new musical called *On the Town.* One afternoon, Green invited Holliday to lunch at Sardi's, where he introduced her to the highly regarded Broadway director and producer Herman Shumlin, who remembered her from the Vanguard, where he had gone at Lillian Hellman's insistence to see the Revuers. It is likely that Green knew that Shumlin was looking for an actress to play a small part and hoped to help his friend land a job. "I'm casting a play at the moment," Shumlin told her, "and there's a part that might be right for you. If you'd like to audition, stop by my office on Forty-second Street anytime this week."[6]

Shumlin cast Holliday in *Kiss Them for Me*, an adaptation of Frederic Wakeman's bestselling novel *Shore Leave*, about three navy pilots on a four-day leave following months in the South Pacific. Holliday played the good-hearted dumb blond and sometime prostitute with all of the clever lines.[7] New York critics greeted *Kiss Them for Me* at the Belasco Theatre in March 1945 with little enthusiasm except for Holliday's dumb blond, who appeared in a scarlet dress with Joan Crawford shoulder pads and purple pumps and got laughs out of lines not written to be funny.[8]

She won the prestigious Clarence Derwent Award for best supporting performance by a nonfeatured player in the 1944–45 season. She turned down offers to play other "dumb blonds" to avoid type-casting only to learn that producer Max Gordon had a show in difficulty out-of-town and was looking for a replacement for Jean Arthur. The show was *Born Yesterday*.

Garson Kanin's *Born Yesterday* tells the story of Harry Brock (played by Paul Douglas), a junkyard tycoon, who goes to Washington to pull off a congressional swindle. He brings along his mistress, Billie Dawn, an ex-showgirl who is beautiful, tough, and seemingly a dim-wit. Predictably, in this variation of George Bernard Shaw's *Pygmalion*, Billie turns out not to be as dumb as she appears. By the final curtain, she has shed her minks and diamonds for horn-rimmed glasses and snared her love interest (played by Gary Merrill).

Holliday settled into the long run of *Born Yesterday* and a film career that included *Adam's Rib* with Katharine Hepburn and Spencer Tracy, *Born Yesterday* with Broderick Crawford and William Holding, and *The Marrying Kind* with Aldo Ray and Madge Kennedy. Nevertheless, by 1947, she was on record supporting left-wing political causes, including the Stop Censorship Committee, the Civil Rights Congress, and the World Federation of Democratic Youth. She marched for peace, campaigned for Henry Wallace, the Progressive candidate in the presidential election, and supported organizations that promoted the freedoms of the First Amendment and fostered civil rights.[9]

Between 1947 and 1950, Holliday was attacked in the conservative press for her left-wing activities. Moreover, her name appeared in *Red Channels: The Report of Communist Influence in Radio and Television*, published in 1950 by Vincent W. Hartnett and former FBI associates who called themselves American Business Consultants. The 213 pages spotlighted 151 "pro-Communist" artists working ostensibly in radio and television and identified 149 organizations and publications as Communist or pro-Communist "fronts" with data attributed to the U.S. attorney general and/or state and federal committees investigating "un-American" activities. In May of the following year, Holliday was subpoenaed to appear before McCarran's Senate Internal Security Subcommittee investigating subversion in show business and other matters related to U.S. immigration. She was terrified. The subpoena in itself was cause enough for Columbia Pictures to cancel her contract. Moreover, she would be blacklisted throughout Hollywood and possibly Broadway.

A Falling Star

In 1947, Hollywood's initial reaction to investigations by the U.S. House Committee on Un-American Activities into Communist infiltration of the film industry was one of derisive amusement until ten screenwriters and directors were sentenced to prison for contempt of Congress. At that moment, the snide remarks and derisive laughter stopped. The conservative press, goaded by the Hearst newspapers, denounced the film industry as "a hotbed of communist propaganda." These observations and headlines were now taken seriously by the movie-going public.

Columbia Pictures head Harry Cohn sent his brother, Jack Cohn, in charge of the New York office, to a meeting of studio heads at the Waldorf Astoria Hotel in November of 1947. The same day as the meeting, HUAC won contempt citations against the Hollywood Ten. Following heated debate, the studio heads issued the "Waldorf Statement" to cleanse themselves of uneasy investors, declining profits, and protests against salacious and immoral films. The two-page statement affirmed that the studios "will not knowingly employ a Communist or a member of the party or group which advocates the overthrow of the Government of the United States by force or by any illegal or unconstitutional means." The Hollywood blacklist had begun.[10]

Film producers were determined to restore Hollywood's image as an "American" institution, and a massive public relations campaign announced that "Movies Are Better Than Ever." Actor Robert Vaughn got to the heart of the matter: "Economic determinism, not democratic patriotism, created the blacklist that fell like a shroud over the entertainment world in the first years of the 1950s."[11]

Holliday's film career was in serious jeopardy. She was identified in *Red Channels* as "*Actress—Screen, Stage, Radio and TV,*" with nine "offenses" occurring between 1946 and 1950. They ranged from sending greetings to the Moscow Art Theatre on the occasion of its fiftieth anniversary to signing an advertisement in support of the Hollywood Ten, to assisting pro-Communist groups. She had also chaired a fundraising dinner for "Save the Voice of Freedom Committee," a group accused of promoting Communist propaganda on radio. She entertained at a fundraising event for the left-wing New York Council of the Arts, Sciences and Professions. Moreover, she recorded a speech for the Stop

Censorship Committee, joined a rally for the Council on African Affairs, and sponsored meetings and activities of such front groups as the World Federation of Democratic Youth and the Civil Rights Congress.

Holliday was further smeared in *Counterattack: The Newsletter of Facts to Combat Communism*, an anti-Communist newsletter compiled by Hartnett and three former FBI investigators to expose Communism in American business, including the film industry and the broadcast networks. She was tarred with the same brush that marked her celebrated collaborators on stage and in film who were also listed in *Red Channels*. Among them were Leonard Bernstein, Abe Burrows, José Ferrer, Ruth Gordon, and Garson Kanin.

Holliday did not take *Red Channels* seriously when it first appeared in bookstores. Nevertheless, during the filming of *Born Yesterday*, she was attacked for her left-wing politics by gossip columnists Hedda Hopper and Louella Parsons. Once the film opened, she became a prime target for the Red-baiters. Shortly after she was nominated for an Oscar in the best actress category, Jimmy Tarantino, a right-wing columnist for the trade paper *Hollywood Life*, wrote an exposé of celebrities, including Dashiell Hammett, Lena Horne, José Ferrer, John Garfield, Charlie Chaplin, and Howard Da Silva. His dossier on Holliday appeared to be little more than a jazzed-up version of the citations in *Red Channels*:

> JUDY HOLLIDAY, SINGER-ACTRESS . . . Holliday is up for an Academy Award "Oscar" for her work in Columbia's film, "Born Yesterday." . . . Judy only acts dumb. She's a smart cookie. . . . The Commies got her a long time ago. . . . She was a singer with the National Council of Arts and Sciences and Professions, a Commie red front, who supported the UN-Friendly Ten Hollywood Writers who went to jail. . . . Judy, in 1948, was a guest speaker during a rally in the N.Y. Hotel Astor, for the STOP CENSORSHIP COMMITTEE, a Communist front. . . . She was sponsor for the WORLD FEDERATION OF DEMOCRATIC YOUTH, a known Communist front. . . . In 1948, Holliday wired *greetings* of good luck and best wishes to the MOSCOW ART THEATRE. . . . She is a supporter of the CIVIL RIGHTS CONGRESS, a red outfit. . . . A few years ago, Judy performed free of charge at a dance and affair in the Hotel Capitol, N.Y.C., that was sponsored by the Commie *Daily Worker*. . . . Judy Holliday always knew what she was doing.[12]

Most riveting in Tarantino's litany was his assertion that in September "Senator Pat McCarran and a powerful 19 Senators' committee will heave-ho [the Communists] with rocking blows that will shock the nation."[13]

Two of the leading Oscar contenders in 1951 for best actor and best actress, José Ferrer and Judy Holliday, were listed in *Red Channels* and *Hollywood*

Life.[14] Moreover, rumors were circulating that they had received subpoenas to appear before congressional committees. The rumors were well founded. In a letter dated June 14, 1950, the Federal Bureau of Investigation instructed its Los Angeles office to determine whether Judy Holliday was a member of the Communist Party, and, if necessary, assign in her name a Security Index card, a list of persons to be rounded-up in the event of a national emergency. The FBI's New York office was also directed to make available any pertinent information in its files. The Bureau had received a confidential report prepared by the American Legion in response to many requests "for the records of various unsuitable individuals appearing on radio and television shows."[15] Appended to the list of "front organizations" with which the actress was presumably affiliated was a column from *Counterattack*:

> Please don't assume that Judy Holliday really pretends to know a great deal about Africa, Spain, the Russian theater, the world, progress, democracy, intellectualism, or peace. She has shown that she's ready to sign statements, lead a picket line, etc., when asked by party-liners.[16]

In August, an informant's report filed with the FBI's Los Angeles office purported to present details of Holliday's front activities between 1947 and 1950. In fact, the account was little more than an expansion of the citations found in *Red Channels*. A month later, a second report based on newspaper clippings was filed detailing Holliday's efforts on behalf of the Hollywood Ten with this conclusion: "The investigation of the subject did not reveal positive evidence of membership in the Communist party, and, therefore, no recommendation for a Security Index Card is being made at this time."[17]

Unaware of the FBI's surveillance, Holliday looked upon the rumors as unfounded and therefore harmless. Several of the listings under her name in *Red Channels* were the outgrowth of small cash contributions; other listings were associations with organizations whose goals and ideals she shared independent of any formal association; and still others had no basis in fact. As a voter, she was an independent who endorsed candidates not political parties. Nevertheless, in December 1950, when the celebrity spotlight shown on her with the release of the film version of *Born Yesterday*, the right-wing newspapers attacked both Holliday and playwright Garson Kanin as subversives.

The right-wing tentacles were long. Anti-Communist pressure groups reached through the advertising agencies to television sponsors to influence programming and casting. *Red Channels* became a de facto blacklist—Will Holtzman called it the "Madison Avenue Bible"—consulted by nearly every advertising executive before shows were cast.[18] As a result, Holliday's invitations for television appearances dwindled. When the sponsors for the panel shows "What's My Line" and "The Name's the Same" learned that she had a history of supporting Communist-front organizations, CBS and ABC dropped her as a panelist.[19] In turn, she was at risk with Columbia Pictures, who had not scheduled her next film. Then, McCarran's subpoena arrived on her doorstep and the anti-Communist siege began in earnest.

Not a Communist

On March 26, 1952, Judy Holliday appeared before Pat McCarran's subcommittee in the Senate Office Building in Washington, D.C. Dubbed "the Senate's answer to HUAC," McCarran's subcommittee had a wholly different agenda in its investigation of the entertainment industry.[20] McCarran's goal was to secure support for limiting the immigration of Eastern Europeans into the United States. One strategy was to document the susceptibility of entertainers of middle European background to Communist influence. Celebrity witnesses were key to the success of McCarran's anti-Communist agenda and to passage of his new legislation.

Between March and mid-May, four artists (three were Jewish) of Hollywood and Broadway fame appeared before the McCarran subcommittee: Burl Ives (actor and singer), Samuel Levenson (comedian), Philip Loeb (actor and former council member of Actor's Equity Association), and Judy Holliday (stage and film actress). On the morning Holliday testified in a private session, Senator Arthur V. Watkins, a Democrat from Utah and McCarran's close friend, was presiding. He was assisted by Homer Ferguson, a conservative Republican from Michigan, and staff director Richard Arens, who had previously drafted the Internal Security Act. McCarran was aggressively lobbying congressmen for support of his new legislation and did not attend the closed session.

Despite the fact that she had never been a member of the Communist Party, Holliday faced the now familiar dilemma of all witnesses. She could truthfully answer that she was not now and had never been a Communist. Nonetheless, if she did, she opened the door to answering questions about the political beliefs of her family and friends; if she refused, she would most likely be cited for contempt. Since the McCarran subcommittee was primarily interested in documenting the family history of the entertainers it was investigating, it seemed likely that her uncle Joseph Gollomb, who had been employed as a writer by the *Daily Worker* and even her socialist mother Helen Tuvim would come under scrutiny. The only way to protect her family and friends was to refuse to answer any questions and plead the Fifth, which was generally held by the public to be a confession of guilt. That route would result in blacklisting; her career in film, radio, and television would be over, and perhaps her stage career as well.

Support came from an unexpected quarter. Harry Cohn and Columbia Pictures came to her rescue. Angered by the witch-hunts that had embroiled such studio employees as Robert Rossen, writer and director of *All the King's Men*, and Larry Parks, star of *The Jolson Story*, Cohn was determined that Judy Holliday would not be the next victim. He was perhaps motivated more by commercial interests than by political conviction. Nevertheless, Cohn put Columbia's legal team to work preparing her case. One of Holliday's biographers said that this was one of the few instances and possibly the *only* instance where a Hollywood studio came to the support of a "red-suspected star or player."[21]

Columbia hired distinguished lawyer and former U.S. district judge of the Southern District of New York, Simon H. Rifkind, as Judy Holliday's legal counsel. Rifkind, in turn, hired Kenneth Bierly, a former FBI agent who had worked as an editor for *Counterattack* and had had a change of heart, to identify any damaging evidence that could be used against the actress. Bierly prepared the groundwork for Holliday's responses to the Senate committee.

Holliday was deeply troubled by the necessity to apologize for acts undertaken in good faith and sincere conviction. Rifkind convinced her that anything less than humble cooperation would amount to professional suicide. Public relations manager Robert L. Green advised her to play Billie Dawn ("How can they take you seriously as a political figure then?") and Holliday set about preparing the role for a final time.[22]

Her attorney informed the committee that Judy Holliday would appear as a cooperative witness, and, in return, requested two favors: first, that she not be asked to testify until after the opening of *The Marrying Kind*; and, second, that the transcript of her testimony not be made public until months after the opening of the film. The committee agreed to the first request but would not guarantee the timing of the release of Holliday's testimony to the public.

When *The Marrying Kind* opened in March 14, 1952, in New York City, the movie-house was picketed by members of the Catholic War Veterans, carrying placards that proclaimed JUDY HOLLIDAY IS THE DARLING OF THE DAILY WORKER, and, WHILE OUR BOYS ARE DYING IN KOREA, JUDY HOLLIDAY IS DEFAMING CONGRESS.

Twelve days later, Rachel Gollomb's granddaughter, accompanied by David Oppenheim, her husband of four years, and her attorney, entered room 457 of the Senate Office Building, raised her right hand, and swore to tell the truth. She was dressed in a provocative but tasteful outfit that Billie Dawn might have worn under similar circumstances. She wore a close-fitting black dress, white gloves, and a small veiled hat. Poised to give the performance of her life, she appeared composed but labored to contain her stage fright and concentrate on her lines.

In the closed hearing without cameras and press, staff director Richard Arens began the inquiry. He asked her name and address. She answered that she was "Judy Holliday" at 158 Waverly Place, New York City, but Arens wanted her to divulge for the record that she was Jewish. She replied that she was also Judy Tuvim and Mrs. David Oppenheim.[23]

With occasional questions raised by Senator Watkins, Richard Arens cross-examined the witness. The committee was interested in her employment activities, her memberships in unions, the political activities of the Revuers, and her associations with Communist-front organizations. Far from the last and certainly not the least were the political activities of her uncle Joseph Gollomb. As with all witnesses, the committee's overriding intent was to get the actress to name names.

Arens explored her union memberships in Actors' Equity Association, the Screen Actors Guild, and the American Federation of Television and Radio Artists, probing to learn if she had held offices in unions or been on the board of directors of Actors' Equity. Recalling that she had also been a member of American Variety Artists when she worked in nightclubs, Arens asked about her association with the Revuers: "And who were your associates in that unit?" She volunteered the well-publicized names of Betty Comden, Adolph Green, Alvin Hammer, and John Frank.

The Revuers lead to Arens's first substantive question: "Did the Revuers entertain at parties given under the auspices of the United American-Spanish Aid Committee?" Holliday explained that the troupe played parties and benefits to become recognized, but she really did not know or could not remember an American-Spanish Aid event.

> MR. ARENS: Well, now, I put it to you as a fact, and ask you to affirm or deny the fact, Miss Holliday, that in 1941 you were a part of the unit known as the Revuers, one of the entertainers in a party given by the United American-Spanish Aid Committee.[24]

Confronted with this fact, Judy Holliday indulged in a Billie Dawn–like response.

> MISS HOLLIDAY: You mean I should say "yes" or "no"?
> MR. ARENS: Yes, if you have a recollection.
> MISS HOLLIDAY: If I can't—you know, I can't place it.
> MR. ARENS: We just want the truth.
> MISS HOLLIDAY: If it doesn't sound familiar?
> MR. ARENS: Then you just state the facts.
> MISS HOLLIDAY: I don't know.
> MR. ARENS: You have no recollection?
> MISS HOLLIDAY: Yes.

Arens continued, "I put it to you as a fact and ask you to affirm or deny the fact that you were a sponsor for the Committee for the Negro in the Arts?"[25]

Settling comfortably into the familiar role, the actress answered: "That is something I looked into last summer. As you can understand, my employers, Columbia Pictures, were very much disturbed about all the things that have been happening and coming up and they *investigated* me."

Arens ignored this turn of events and turned to the "fact" that Holliday had marched in a picket line on November 30, 1946, in front of pier 53 in a strike sponsored by the waterfront section of the Communist Party. Holliday shot back: "I don't know anything that I ever did sponsored by the Communist Party." They debate the evidence of a publicity photo taken of Holliday in a bathing suit with striking workers in the background. Holliday insisted that she was not *in* a picket line but rather had a publicity photo taken on the pier. Watkins wanted to know if she did this of her own free will, and Holliday gave a response that she was to repeat several times during the hearing.

MISS HOLLIDAY: Undoubtedly I was asked to go. This is the way I found myself in everything. . . . The occasion should be something I would remember. The only way I can remember it, and it was a very slight thing, I didn't march. I would remember if I was protesting something. I went and had a picture taken and left. That is about what it was. The only reason I remember that was because I had been accused of picketing some place else, and I said I never picketed anywhere. Then I remembered, and I said, "Wait a minute, you once had a picture taken in a picket line," but I didn't remember where it was or why it was.

At one point in the discussion of the publicity photograph, Arens interrupted: "Do you have any difficulty with your memory?" Judy Holliday, who was noted for her gift of almost total recall, answered: "No. The only difficulty is that I met a tremendous lot of people and I get a lot of requests and phone calls. We get about 50 a day, and you just can't pay much attention to them unless you know them first."

At another time, Watkins reprimanded her for her inability to remember events in 1946: "It seems to me that a person in your profession has to have a trained memory." Holliday protested: "Now I'm getting one, but I didn't know then that I needed one."

Arens turned to a letter written to the *Nation* that she signed protesting the Peekskill riot on behalf of "the Communist singer" Paul Robeson. She was quick to say that she did not write or sign a letter to the *Nation* but admitted that she did send a telegram to either Governor Thomas Dewey or another New York state government official protesting the absence of police protection for unarmed people who were attacked in an effort to disrupt Robeson's outdoor concert in Peekskill, New York. She concluded, "This was to me a civic outrage, and I didn't have any personal ax to grind for anybody that was involved in it, but I thought it was a very frightening thing to happen that unarmed people should be stoned."

Arens asked if she had any "conversations with Mr. Paul Robeson." "I never met him," Holliday replied tersely.

Arens proceeded to ask about her birthday greetings to the Moscow Art Theatre cited in the *Daily Worker* for November 1948 and Holliday spoke from her heart:

> I would like to get it clear so that it won't be misinterpreted. I didn't send greetings to Moscow, I sent it to actors. To me the Moscow Theatre, like the Abbey Players or the Old Vic, have been a theatrical tradition that I have been brought up to respect highly. I admire the idea that these actors can play small parts one week and large parts another week, and it seemed to me that it was a wonderful way to show that artists could still respect each other no matter what their political backgrounds were. That is why I sent the telegram. It had nothing to do with upholding the Soviet Union because I don't uphold the Soviet Union.

Senator Watkins wanted to know if she is in the habit of sending telegrams to theatrical groups. "Only when I feel like it," she replied and referred to the appearance in New York of the Old Vic with Laurence Olivier and Ralph Richardson.

The sixty-five-year-old senator from Utah asked, "Old who?"

Holliday reiterated that she did not *send* personal greetings to the Moscow Art Theatre. Rather, she was asked in a telephone call if her name could be added to a list of names, and she had said "yes." "I must say I would never have known about the Moscow Art having a birthday or whatever they had," she insisted, but Watkins wanted the name of the caller. Holliday complained, "That is something that I have been through 150,000 times. I don't get any more, thank goodness, but I have gotten calls from secretaries."

Arens intervened and asked about her signature on an advertisement published in *Variety* on December 1, 1948, sponsored by the National Council of the Arts, Sciences and Professions, calling upon the film industry to revoke the blacklist. Holliday insisted that she had belonged to the organization when it was called the Independent Citizens Committee and worked to reelect Franklin Roosevelt.

> SENATOR WATKINS: If your purpose was to help elect Roosevelt why did you not do this for the Democratic Party directly?
> MISS HOLLIDAY: Because they never asked me.

Watkins then turned to the political activities of her friends: "Did you not have any friends that were Communists?" "Never," she replied.

Like almost all witnesses, Judy Holliday dreaded the questions about her friends and family. Biographer Gary Carey surmised that at this point in her testimony she might have perjured herself.[26]

Watkins opened the door to the important names and Arens seized the opportunity. He inquired about Alvin Hammer, Adolph Green, and Betty Comden. (Hammer had previously refused to testify before HUAC as to whether or not he was a Communist.) Arens asked if Comden and Green had Communist-front records?

MISS HOLLIDAY: No.

SENATOR WATKINS: Are you sure of that?

MISS HOLLIDAY: I am as sure of that as I can be of anybody that isn't me.

SENATOR WATKINS: You know them well?

MISS HOLLIDAY: I know them well, and I know them to be a completely unpolitical people. They are terrific hard workers, and that is their life.

When asked about Comden's and Green's activities with the Committee for the Reelection of Benjamin Davis and Comden's appearance at the Madison Square Garden rally for the Spanish Refugee Appeal, Holliday denied, doubted, or did not know.

Arens then asked about the "We Are for Wallace" advertisement signed by Holliday: "I put it to you as a fact that on October 28, 1948, you were a signer of an ad sponsored by the Communist-front organization of the Arts, Sciences and Professions?" Holliday rephrased his question: "I was a signer of an ad sponsored by the organization, which I did not know was a Communist front, but I was for Wallace."

She proceeded to explain how she came to sign a petition for the Scientific and Cultural Conference for World Peace. One day, a group of young people rang her doorbell and asked if she would sign a petition so that their "youth outfit" could be represented at the peace conference. "And it was put to me," she explained, "it was a question of peace, do you want peace, and I said, 'Yes, of course.'"

Arens and Watkins were incredulous.

MR. ARENS: Miss Holliday, you are not trying to tell us that the young people asked you whether you were for peace or war and you said peace? . . . Did you know that this peace 'conference' has been cited by HUAC as "actually a supermobilization of the inveterate wheel horses and supporters of the Communist Party and its auxiliary organizations"?

MISS HOLLIDAY: Yes; I have since learned that.

MR. ARENS: When?

MISS HOLLIDAY: I learned it when I picked up a copy of *Life* and read the article and saw all the pictures of the people who had been at the conference.

21

As though it was of vital interest to the committee, she hastened to explain how she read newspapers. "I go to the theater section and I read it. Sometimes I read the rest. Now, no, now it is not true, but at that time it was true. Now I read the papers. At that time I was interested in the theater news and auction notices and puzzles. . . . I am probably not a good citizen because I don't read the news or didn't."

Frustrated with the direction of the hearing, Arens turned to her listing in *Red Channels* as an "entertainer" at a carnival sponsored by the National Council of Arts, Sciences and Professions in March 1950. Holliday denied that she performed there. She complained that her name had been used without her knowledge by many organizations.

When asked about her affiliation with the People's Songs, described in *Red Channels* as an early Communist front that promoted folksy songs and music around hard-and-fast party propaganda, Holliday offered her opinion of folk songs: "I gave them a dollar after much nagging and pestering. I dislike folk songs intensely. I think the People's Songs are terrible." Arens insisted that her name appeared on the letterhead as a sponsor, but Holliday was quick to refute her collusion in the matter:

> That is what they told me. . . . That is probably because I gave them a dollar. But I would have no feeling for sponsoring them. I didn't even know that they were Communist. I just hated their stuff.

Watkins cautioned the actress that she should know the organizations to which she contributed money. "You watch it now; do you?" he asked, and she replied, "Ho, do I watch it now."

Inevitably, Watkins turned to the political activities of Holliday's family. His first question reverberated with infinite possibilities: "Did [your husband] ever call your attention to any of these matters?"

During their preparations, Rifkind had warned her about questions about her mail. "Usually I would sort out personal mail from mail in long envelopes," she explained to Watkins, "and throw the ones out that were not from friends . . . throw them right in the wastebasket without even reading it, most of the time before he [David Oppenheim] came home, so that he never even saw them and particularly lately."

> SENATOR WATKINS: He would see the papers. What I am trying to find out, did he not find out the fact that your name was being used in the newspapers?
>
> MISS HOLLIDAY: He didn't know about it either.

Later in the hearing, Watkins asked if she and her husband ever discussed politics. "Only lately," she replied. "And boy, we talk about nothing else now."

Watkins rephrased his question: "Did you not have some friends who were members of the Communist Party that were talking along the lines of the Communists?" Holliday took this opportunity to educate the senator on the ways of show business people without naming anyone.

> MISS HOLLIDAY: My husband's friends talked either music or records, and my friends talked show business and who was getting where and what you had to do to get a job and what kind of notices *Variety* gave this out of town. If you are among actors there is no limit to how much they can talk and gossip about that kind of thing. . . .

As expected, Richard Arens turned to the subject of the late Joseph Gollomb's activities as a former employee of the *Daily Worker* and a writer of books. (Her uncle died two years earlier.) Gollomb's activities had the potential for proving McCarran's case against Eastern European immigrants as tainting the American way of life with Communist propaganda. Nonetheless, Judy Holliday is prepared for this centerpiece of her testimony.

> MR. ARENS: Did your uncle, Joseph Gollomb, rear you?
> MISS HOLLIDAY: No.

Arens asked if she knew both then and now that her uncle was a Communist? "He was a very radical Communist," she fired back. "I don't know whether he was a member of the Communist Party."

> MR. ARENS: He was employed by the *Daily Worker*, was he not?
> MISS HOLLIDAY: Yes, he was. Then he had a change of heart and became a rabid anti-Communist. Holliday insisted that she and her domineering uncle did not have a close relationship because he wanted her to become a writer, not an actress. At age fourteen, she told her Uncle Joe, "You made my life unhappy, and I think our association should be on a casual basis, because from now on you can't live my life for me."
> MR. ARENS: When did he break with the Communist Party?
> MISS HOLLIDAY: I think it must have been, well, I know that he was terribly against them around 1941 or so, and from then on. He was an ardent Democrat, as a matter of fact.
> MR. ARENS: He had written a number of books in defense of Communist principles and was generally regarded as an ardent Communist philosopher was he not?
> MISS HOLLIDAY: No. His books were never in defense of Communist principles.
> MR. ARENS: He was employed by the *Daily Worker*, was he not?
> MISS HOLLIDAY: Yes.

MR. ARENS: The *Daily Worker* is a Communist publication, is it not?

MISS HOLLIDAY: That is right. The books were not. His books were novels about school life for young people, and also they were spy stories and detective stories.

The subject of Joseph Gollomb had not borne fruit, and the interrogators turned their attention to activists Jo Davidson and Stella Holt, who involved the actress in the Voice of Freedom Committee. Holliday's name appeared on the letterhead, and the stationery was entered into the record as Exhibit Number One, evidence that, by association with known Communists on the letterhead, she must also know some Communists. Holliday insisted that she did not know at the time that anyone was a Communist.

SENATOR WATKINS: That is the crux of this investigation. When were you told that these people were Communists?

MISS HOLLIDAY: I have been told every day for the past year practically. Not every day, but I have had my eyes opened like they have never been opened in the last year by Columbia, by lawyers, by people that I have hired to investigate me. I wanted to know what I had done.

Astounded, Arens inquired, "You hired people to investigate you? "I certainly did," she replied, "because I had gotten into a lot of trouble."

Concerned now, Arens asks if anyone had tried to *prosecute* her.

MISS HOLLIDAY: Yes.

MR. ARENS: Who?

MISS HOLLIDAY: Prosecute? No; I thought you meant *persecute*.

The farcical moment went to the comedienne who was also an expert crossword puzzler, and, according to one individual, could complete the *New York Times* crossword in the time it would take Richard Arens to tie his shoelaces.[27]

Holliday explained that her film contract had been threatened and her shows and films picketed by the Catholic War Veterans. She pointed out that the group also handed out leaflets describing her as a Communist.

"So when you want to know why I say I am in trouble," she concluded, "that is the kind of trouble I am in, because I didn't know the subversive character of any of these things." She underscored the lesson she had learned from the ordeal: "I don't say 'Yes' to anything now except cancer, polio, and cerebral palsy, and things like that."

Several times during Holliday's testimony, Watkins and Arens asked what she thought of the McCarran Act? Rifkind tried to divert this testimony by offering to "tell exactly what our investigation shows if that will help." Watkins admonished him, "If we need you, Judge, we may call you as a witness, but I want to know what Miss Holliday knows." Suspicious of his "friendly" witness, the senator wondered "whether she was really a dupe and just signed out of the goodness of her heart or whether she was associated in these movements."

Holliday insisted that she knew nothing about the McCarran Act nor had she contributed to the National Committee to Repeal the McCarran Act. Nevertheless, Watkins persevered:

SENATOR WATKINS: You knew what the general idea was, to register the Communists?

MISS HOLLIDAY: Now you told me. Frankly, I was wondering whether it was about *deporting* people. Is that part of it?

MR. RIFKIND: There is a McCarran immigration bill now pending.

Arens diverted the questions away from their pending legislation with, "Do you think that Communist organizations ought to be required to register?"

MISS HOLLIDAY: Yes, I do; that is all a part of knowing what they are about.

Arens turned next to the World Federation of Democratic Youth, another Communist-front organization, and her opposition to the efforts of the House Committee on Un-American Activities "to ferret out" Communists. Puzzled, Holliday said: "I don't know whether that was part of the Stop Censorship thing."

Earlier in the hearing she had described recording a one-minute anti-censorship speech upstairs at Sardi's Restaurant in 1948.

MISS HOLLIDAY: . . . I went to speak against censorship.

SENATOR WATKINS: When was this?

MISS HOLLIDAY: I made a one-minute tape recording. You see, I don't like to appear with large groups of people. I don't like to go to parties. I never go to Sardi's, which is a theatrical hang-out, or club. It is hard for me, I get very self-conscious, and, I don't like it. So that my participation when it was a participation of a physical nature was always very restricted.

In this case I went to Sardi's Restaurant upstairs, there were no people up there—you know, no diners—and talked against censorship.

SENATOR WATKINS: You made this recording?

MISS HOLLIDAY: Into this little recorder which was to be used for the Stop Censorship Committee; the book banning.

MR ARENS: Who is banning books in this country?

MISS HOLLIDAY: Books have been banned in Boston.

MR. ARENS: Those are licentious books, are they not?

MISS HOLLIDAY: Some of them have been proved not to be licentious.

Having reached another dead end and frustrated with Holliday's claims that she was contacted only by nameless "clerical workers and secretaries" who asked for her sponsorship or participation, Arens challenged her: "Do you know a lady by the name of Yetta Cohn, C-o-h-n?"

Holliday appeared delighted with the question, "Yes; she is my best friend." Asked to describe her association with Yetta Cohn, Holliday recalled that she met her friend of twelve years at a country house in Mount Tremper, New York. Asked about Cohn's occupation, Holliday informed Arens that her friend was a policewoman for New York City.

> MR. ARENS: Has she had anything to do in any respect with your signatures and affiliations with these Communist-front organizations.
> MISS HOLLIDAY: None at all.
> MR. ARENS: Has she ever counseled with you on this?
> MISS HOLLIDAY: No; she has no interest in that sort of thing. I was told that she was a Communist.

Caught off guard by this admission, Arens replied: "Who told you that?" Holliday had cleverly named her best friend, who might perhaps be of Eastern European extraction and of use to the committee, but Kenneth Bierly had earlier vetted Yetta Cohn's non-Communist status. Holliday continued,

> MISS HOLLIDAY: The only way that I can figure out that anybody could say that she was a Communist is because she knows me, and they say I am, because she is the most blameless creature, the most patriotic and honest creature that I know, and she is not only a member of the police force but she has been promoted to be the editor of the police magazine and I have full confidence that the police force of New York investigates their employees rather thoroughly, so that I think there is not only no basis for this but that it is a dreadful thing that she should be even mentioned simply because she is penalized by knowing me, and I am penalized by knowing her, and it just never ends anywhere.

When Bierly had submitted his findings to Columbia Pictures the previous summer, he assured the studio that there was no evidence that Judy Holliday belonged to the Communist Party. In effect, he "cleared" the actress. He also dispelled the rumor that Holliday's closest friend, Yetta Cohn of the New York Police Department, was "subversive or unpatriotic." He did recommend, however, that Judy Holliday be more careful in the future when she chose to support organizations.[28]

At the time of the hearing, Richard Arens probably had the same information as Bierly on the two women. Possibly not wanting to open up an investigation of the NYPD as an internal security risk, Arens changed the subject to

Holliday's earlier protests over the indictment of the Hollywood Ten and an advertisement paid for by the Stop Censorship Committee. Rifkind asked to see the advertisement. "We have not been able to find any such ad," Rifkind added. Arens ignored him and hammered away at the fact that Judy Holliday had signed a petition on behalf of people who had been indicted for contempt of Congress.

Holliday defended her actions on behalf of individuals whom she thought of as "underdogs": "The way it seemed to me, it was protesting the fact that the motion-picture companies could fire people and not defend them if they were even thought they were guilty. . . . I know that I at the time had a feeling about it, that it was wrong to do that."

> MR. ARENS: Do you not think that congressional committees, particularly Congressional committees charged with the responsibility of developing facts about the internal security of the Nation, have the right to inquire of witnesses with respect to Communist conspiracy in this country?
>
> MISS HOLLIDAY: Absolutely. As things have turned out and as I have learned more of what has been going on, my views have changed completely. At the time it was all shallow thinking. I admit I responded impulsively on an emotional basis many times and didn't realize the seriousness of the situation, which I do now.

Recalling Rifkind's warning to demonstrate some repentance no matter how distasteful, Holliday offered that her views had changed as she learned more about the Communist conspiracy. "When did you first have your eyes opened to the situation?" Watkins asked. Holliday gave a sober response:

> MISS HOLLIDAY: When I began to realize the possible imminence of a war, when I began to realize that there were such things as spies and people working against the country. I don't know when it was, but I know that the whole tenor of my thinking changed considerably in the last two years.

For the record, Arens asked if, during the course of the hearing, she had been treated courteously and fairly without "fear of coercion." She assured him, "The fact that I am nervous is not because of this, because I get nervous whenever I get a parking ticket." In a conciliatory gesture, Watkins opined that she had "conducted herself very calmly."

Sensing that things are winding down, Holliday volunteered that she had gone to a Wallace-for-President rally and had told a minute and a half of jokes. Watkins assured her that a legitimate political party supported Wallace's campaign. Nevertheless, she appeared puzzled by the fact that no "legitimate organizations" called to ask for her support. Rifkind intervened: "I think the witness misspoke herself. There have been a great many organizations, legitimate, to which she has responded." Holliday ignored the warning and persisted:

MISS HOLLIDAY: I mean political organizations. Sure, I responded to the Veterans of Foreign Wars and the Stage Door Canteens and USO and polio and church charities, and played benefits on battleships and things like that, but I mean political parties never asked me to respond to anything.

Watkins reminded her that since she had endorsed Communists, the Democrats and Republicans probably would not contact her for an endorsement. But, with impeccable timing, the comedienne administers the whammy: "No. Yet the American Legion and the Catholic Church have called me for contributions, which I have always responded to."

Flogging away at the way names of "respectable people" had been used to encourage others, like herself, to endorse causes, she referenced Albert Einstein, Eleanor Roosevelt, Thomas Mann, and Albert Schweitzer. Arens asked if she knew the Communist-front record of Thomas Mann?

MISS HOLLIDAY: No; how could I know?
SENATOR WATKINS: And Mr. Einstein as well? Do you know the Communist-front record he has?

Holliday was adamant: "Then I am sure that they got into it the way I did because I am sure that none of them are Communists. I mean, if you are a Communist, why go to a Communist front? Why not be a Communist? Whatever you are, be it."

Rifkind intervened to get Holliday's prepared statement into the record. Holliday advised Arens that she voluntarily prepared the statement for her employers, Columbia Pictures and NBC, to attest that she was a loyal citizen. "I volunteered this, that I was not a Communist, had never been, and had no interest in anything subversive." Then, she explained the facts of a celebrity's life in the climate of the witch-hunts.

MISS HOLLIDAY: All that has to happen to me is that I get publicity and I am through; that is true. But I am not simply turning tail because of that. I have been awakened to a realization that I have been irresponsible and slightly—more than slightly—stupid. When I was solicited, I always simply said, "Oh, isn't that too bad. Sure, use my name.

Despite the fact that she has an I.Q. of 172 and the committee had been warned that she was no dumb blond, they savored the admission of her stupidity.[29] Watkins gave permission for the actress to read her personal statement denying any sympathy for or affiliation with the Communist Party and ending with a testament to her patriotism. She closed with, "I love America. With all my heart I would defend it at any time, anywhere, against any enemy."

Not satisfied with her expression of patriotic fervor, Arens inquired: "Did you have all this hatred for communism at the time you joined in the protest of the trial of the Hollywood Ten?" Nevertheless, Holliday was prepared: "Yes, I did. I believe, and I know it sounds old hat, but, I believe in the right to be something without believing in what that something is." She explained her dislike of people who picketed her films, but she believed in *their right to picket.*

Not to be bested, Arens asked, "What is it that you abhor about Communism?"

Speaking with the heart and mind of her Russian émigré heritage that abhorred the loss of civil liberties, Holliday remarked,

> I hate the idea that you are dictated to in what should be the freedom of your own life; that you are told how to think and what to think and that you are policed in your thoughts. I hate the idea that they try to make everybody like everybody else and that the state comes first and that the individual doesn't matter for anything.

Arens inquired next into her thoughts on the "materialistic philosophy of communism."

MISS HOLLIDAY: I don't know what you mean.
MR. ARENS: Do you believe in God?
MISS HOLLIDAY: Yes; I do.
SENATOR WATKINS: Are you a member of a church?
MISS HOLLIDAY: No.

Despite her indignation over the anti-Semitic edge to the questions about God and church, Holliday refrained from pointing out to the senator, who was a Mormon elder, that people of her faith attended temple or synagogue. She remained silent.

Seeking a small revenge, Rifkind reminded the committee that they had not produced certain proofs. "We have searched for the kind of ad which Mr. Arens suggests that she supported for the indictment of the Hollywood Ten. We have not uncovered such an ad. Mr. Arens refers to it as an existing fact, and we do not want to challenge it, but I would like to see it."

Holliday insisted that since the committee said the advertisement existed, it must exist. "You are not suggesting that I made this up are you?" Arens retorted. Holliday used the opportunity to remind the committeemen that many of their allocutions were based on hearsay, unreliable sources, innuendo, and plain falsehoods.

Watkins cautioned the witness: "If we had had this hearing in public, you know what would have happened. . . . you would have had television and many other things."

"That would have been my last appearance," Holliday concluded.

Watkins reminded the witness that she was not on trial, although the committee tried "to preserve some of the procedures at least of a court or a legal inquiry in trying to get the facts." Moreover, he didn't know if her testimony would be made public but assured her that it would be released only if there was a compelling reasons. Within six months of the hearing, Judy Holliday's testimony was made public.

With the session winding down, Rifkind thanked Senator Watkins for his courtesy, and Arens moved to release the witness from the subpoena. When Rifkind asked for a copy of the transcript, he was told that, as Judy Holliday's counsel, he could study it in the committee's office, but he could not have a copy. Watkins then admonished the witness not to release details about what had transpired in executive session.

"Release anything? I would rather die," Holliday said. "I would be digging my own grave."

The hearing adjourned at 1:10 P.M. Judy Holliday had been grilled for two hours and forty minutes.

Repercussions immediately followed Holliday's appearance. Blacklisting by television networks continued; hate mail and anonymous telephone calls forced the removal of her name and address from the New York City telephone directory. Once the transcript of her testimony was released in September, the right-wing press vehemently denounced the actress all over again. Victor Riesel, a syndicated Hearst columnist, wrote with particular vehemence:

> This is to let Hollywood's Oscar-winning blonde, Judy Holliday, know that we weren't born yesterday. . . . Had she gone to Screen Actors Guild sessions in Hollywood she would have learned from Ronnie Reagan and other officers just what Communist infiltration meant . . . she says, in effect, she was played for a sucker. . . . Now she's free to resume her career. There will be no demonstration against her. She has denounced the Stalinist world. But what will [she] do for the world besmirched by those [like her] who lent their name as they would to casual endorsements of toothpaste? They owe the world of decency a debt. . . . Let them speak out. Now![30]

Holliday felt guilty about friends who had urged her to take a belligerent stand against the committee. She had not done so but she had not named names and had tried to protect everyone, especially the Revuers and her immediate family. Clifford Odets, José Ferrer, Lee J. Cobb, and Elia Kazan had not done as well. Many friends and columnists argued that she should take comfort in the fact that she bested McCarran's subcommittee. *Variety* gleefully pointed out that, by playing dumb, Judy Holliday had outsmarted Richard Arens, Arthur Watkins, and company.[31] Nevertheless, Holliday felt the need to defend her performance as a witness. She remarked to her friend Heywood Hale Broun, sportswriter and actor,

> Woodie, maybe you're ashamed of me, because I played Billie Dawn. Well, I'll tell you something. You think you're going to be brave and noble. Then you walk in there and there are the microphones, and all those senators looking at you—Woodie, it scares the shit out of you. But I'm not ashamed of myself because I didn't name names. That much I preserved.[32]

She had also shielded her mother from the congressional scrutiny. Will Holtzman has suggested that Judy Holliday withheld one bit of crucial information throughout the investigation. She knew that the deceased Joseph Gollomb would be targeted, but her mother was very much alive and potentially vulnerable. Holliday felt responsible. In an effort to give her mother something to do, she had permitted Helen Tuvim to act as her personal secretary. It is likely that her mother had talked with many of the telephone solicitors rather than Holliday herself. The fact was, according to Holtzman, "most of the documented donations to 'front' organizations had been made by Helen in her daughter's name." Furthermore, Holtzman conjectured, it is likely that Helen Tuvim had been an idealistic member of the Communist Party in the late thirties. As a consequence of Helen's political activities, Holliday had every right to be terrified that her mother would be investigated, called before HUAC, and suffer another emotional breakdown leading to a second suicide attempt.[33]

Garson Kanin best expressed Judy Holliday's true accomplishment on that day in March of 1952. "Of all of those who were harassed in the ugly days of *Red Channels* and blacklisting," he said, "no one was more steadfast or less craven than Judy. Her behavior under pressure was a poem of grace."[34]

Judy Holliday appeared before the McCarran committee with three other entertainers within a period of four weeks in 1952. In an effort to protect his television career, the Russian-born comedian Sam Levenson, described as a "bland, ingratiating raconteur," volunteered to testify and proceeded to name four entertainers who performed with him for Communist-front organizations.[35] Burl Ives, the rotund actor and folk singer, followed Levenson as a second voluntary witness. He admitted performing for Communist-sponsored gatherings, known then as "good causes," and now appeared willingly before the McCarran committee to set the record straight. "I am not a member of the Communist Party," the singer asserted. In the cleansing ritual honored by the committees, Ives named four individuals, including radio writer Norman Corwin and folk singer Richard Dyer-Bennett.[36]

Actor Philip Loeb was in the same leaky boat as Judy Holliday. When his name appeared in *Red Channels* and *Counterattack*, he was dismissed from television's *The Goldbergs*, where he played the gentle Jake Goldberg opposite Gertrude Berg. With a long list of "Communist-front" associations published beneath his name in *Red Channels* and a subpoena two years later, he was blacklisted and had no hope of further employment on television or radio.[37]

Even though Philip Loeb did not have Judy Holliday's celebrity status, he was an attractive candidate for McCarran's subcommittee. Visible weekly on a popular television show, his dismissal was evidence to some that he was a Communist. Moreover, he was undeniably Jewish, and in 1952, McCarran was playing upon the link in the popular mind between being a Jew and being a Communist traitor, now firmly established by the arrest of Julius and Ethel Rosenberg for espionage.[38]

Unlike Holliday's Billie Dawn persona, Loeb had no mask to conceal his vulnerability as he parried questions about his loyalty and patriotism. He did not name names and was cast into the outer darkness of unemployment and desperation peopled by unfriendly witnesses.

An Unfinished Woman

Judy Holliday survived harassment by the U.S. government but not by the Internal Revenue Service. She returned to Broadway in *Bells Are Ringing* and *Hot Spot* and made four more films for Columbia Pictures (*It Should Happen to You, Phff!, The Solid Gold Cadillac,* and *Bells Are Ringing*). Moreover, television opened up to her.

Following the McCarran hearing, she was told that she would never work again in radio or television. In early 1954, with her star status unchallenged with *It Should Happen to You* and her political voice silenced, NBC approached her for a half-hour drama telecast with Tony Randall, called *The Huntress.*

When there were no repercussions from sponsors and audiences, NBC approved a deal whereby Holliday would appear in three ninety-minute specials staged by Max Liebman, producer of the famous "Show of Shows" series starring Sid Caesar and Imogene Coca. Earlier, when the producer approached her, she told him that he would never be allowed to hire her, but Liebman persevered with the network. Although the Liebman series was little more than a motley group of entertainers saddled with second-rate material, the show was of historic significance. Judy Holliday had become one of the first *Red Channels* performers to override the blacklist. Nevertheless, her financial situation was precarious. The Internal Revenue Service was demanding payment of back taxes incurred through mismanagement of her finances by her accountants. Moreover, by 1960, she was seriously ill.

Even though Lillian Hellman appropriated the phrase "an unfinished woman" for the first volume of her memoirs, Judy Holliday's life and career were truly unfinished at the time of her death of cancer two weeks before her forty-fourth birthday. Others, stigmatized as Reds and accused of disloyalty to their country, also had their lives cut short by ill-health and clinical depression during the decade. The majority endured FBI investigations, subpoenas, blacklisting, headlines, and public hearings but survived to work another day. However, actress Mady Christians was not so fortunate.

Like Judy Holliday, Mady Christians was a leading Broadway actress and was best known for starring roles in *Watch on the Rhine* and *I Remember Mama*. Nevertheless, under surveillance by the FBI, her life was unexpectedly cut short before she reached the public arena of the congressional hearings. The Viennese-born actress was one of five distinguished stage and film actors who experienced early deaths attributed by those who knew them to the McCarthyites.

I believe that performers and writers are frequently more accurate seismographs of their era than politicians and statesmen.

—Stefan Kanfer, *A Journal of the Plague Years*

3 Death by Innuendo: Mady Christians

The fate of performers and writers that were subject to the Hollywood blacklists, the congressional committees, and the control of broadcast networks reveals the shocks and upheavals to the cultural landscape brought about by McCarthyism. Those seismic disturbances in many instances took away more than careers. Talented artists found their health compromised by FBI surveillance and the public hearings in which they were branded Reds, dupes, and fellow travelers. For those artists appearing on radio and television—and many careers combined film, theater, and television—the "controversiality" policies implemented by the networks became another ruthless variant of the Hollywood blacklist. Actors Mady Christians, Philip Loeb, and others were caught in a double bind. They were blacklisted by the film studios and fired by the networks. They were made *controversial*.

Controversy

Nineteen-fifty was a seismic year. The Hollywood blacklist was in effect, the Hollywood Ten were jailed for contempt of Congress after losing their appeals, and anti-Communist militancy was rampant among business groups and congressional committees. The blacklist of writers and entertainers had been ill-defined until June, when *Red Channels* appeared in bookstores. Four years earlier, Hartnett's group had launched the anti-Communist newsletter *Counterattack* and charged twenty-four dollars a year for a subscription. Advertising agencies and network executives subscribed to the publication in order to check the status of individuals they had hired or might hire in the future.

Not content with only publishing the newsletter, ABC (the acronym for American Business Consultants) offered research services to corporate clients who required clearances for their employees. Hartnett and his associates tarnished reputations in the columns of *Counterattack* and then offered to clear those named in their publication for a fee. Ted Morgan called this double-dealing practice "a dirty little business . . . private enterprise at its worst."[1]

Active with Hollywood's Anti-Nazi League (a group founded to propagandize against Hitler), actors Fredric March and Florence Eldridge (known in theater circles as "the Marches") came within ABC's purview as members of an organization that had been condemned as subversive by the California Committee on Un-American Activities. Their names subsequently appeared in *Counterattack*. In 1948, the Marches sued for slander and libel and the case was settled out of court, but it cost the actors their Hollywood careers and $56,000 in legal fees.

The publication of *Red Channels* consolidated Hartnett's files into a booklet that became a bestseller, and, according to Stefan Kanfer, the most effective blacklist in the history of show business.[2] The alphabetical index of names was the heart of the matter, along with the listings of pro-Communist activities and front organizations with which the listees were allegedly connected. Many of the entries were simply wrong. Others were cases of mistaken identity or the results of false reports by professional informants. Moreover, many of the "front" organizations that had been created in support of the Soviet Union and European refugees as part of the war effort were defunct by 1950.

Emboldened by his success with the clearance racket, Vincent Hartnett left ABC in 1952 to establish his own clearance service, called AWARE, Inc., and launch his own publication, *Aware*. He worked closely with Syracuse supermarket magnate Lawrence Johnson, who organized the Veterans Action Committee of Syracuse Supermarkets to impose economic sanctions against corporations that did not scrupulously apply the blacklist to the networks and the shows they sponsored.

Hartnett fed names to Johnson, who then called the networks to say his supermarket chain would boycott their sponsors' products if they employed subversive or "tainted" artists. Under Johnson's supervision, a "Monthly Box Score" was printed of untouchables; for example, Philip Loeb (Jake on *The Goldbergs*)—"Done for good"; José Ferrer—"Maybe we should not see his new motion picture," and so on.[3] The sponsors considered themselves vulnerable and brought pressure through their advertising agencies to dismiss or avoid controversial artists. The lists of untouchables grew long. Among the actresses were Mady Christians, Jean Muir, Madeleine Lee Gilford, Ireene Wicker, Lena Horne, Carol Atwater, Ann Shepherd, Anne Revere, and Kim Hunter. The list of controversial men was even longer.

Without explanation, contracts were withdrawn or not renewed, changes occurred in casting, or artists were simply no longer hired. Writing for the *New York Times*, Jack Gould exposed the practice of outlawing controversial artists. "In radio and television," he wrote, "there is a new type of displaced person—artists, writers, announcers, and directors who without hearing, without publicity and without much public interest, effectively are being deprived of their opportunity to make a living."[4] Before McCarran's subcommittee, Philip Loeb, with seventeen citations in *Red Channels*, put it another way: "I had a contract with her [Mrs. Gertrude Berg for *The Goldbergs*] which was broken on account of trouble, because my name was in *Red Channels*."[5]

The Untouchables

Mady Christians, Jean Muir, and Ireene Wicker became the poster-girls for radio and television's controversiality policy. Ireene Wicker, known in the business as "the Singing Lady," lost the sponsorship of the Kellogg Company (a subsidiary of General Foods Corporation) and her job. Although she had worked on radio for twenty-five years, she was not rehired because her name had appeared in *Red Channels*. She was listed as sponsoring the Committee for the Re-election of Benjamin Davis Jr., an African American elected in 1943 to the New York City Council on the Communist Party—USA ticket who also won the Democratic Party's endorsement as a candidate for re-election in 1945. The actress went to the offices of *Counterattack* at 55 West Forty-second Street to clear her name. She told Theodore Kirkpatrick that she never heard of Benjamin Davis. Nonetheless, she failed to convince Kirkpatrick of her veracity. Only when Wicker's lawyer obtained the nominating petitions for Benjamin Davis's re-election, examined thirty thousand names, and failed to find the actress's name, did Kirkpatrick relent. She was allowed to print an anti-Communist statement in *Counterattack* but she was not rehired. Ireene Wicker had created controversy.

Jean Muir also caused controversy. Shortly after *Red Channels* appeared, NBC (with its sponsor General Foods serviced by the advertising agency of Young and Rubicam) announced the television version of *The Aldrich Family*, based on the long-running radio comedy with Jean Muir as Mother Aldrich. In 1949, Muir had been named before the Martin Dies committee as attending left-wing meetings in California, and this information was repeated in *Red Channels*.[6]

Encouraged by American Business Consultants to protest NBC's hiring of Jean Muir, Hester McCullough, a Greenwich, Connecticut, housewife, telephoned NBC and Young and Rubicam, thereby creating a chain reaction against the casting of Muir. Despite the actress's protests, she was compensated for her eighteen-week contract but replaced on the show. General Foods delivered its dictum against controversial artists to its advertising agency and released a statement to the press:

> The use of controversial personalities or the discussion of controversial subjects in our advertising may provoke unfavorable criticism and even

antagonism among sizable groups of consumers. Such reaction injures both acceptance of our products and our public relations.

General Foods advertising, therefore, avoids the use of material and personalities which in its judgment are controversial.[7]

Actress Mady Christians proved a more problematic controversial artist than either Ireene Wicker or Jean Muir. She was foreign-born and, during the war years, actively supported agencies that helped European refugees and exiled writers. Her work in radio plays for ABC, CBS, and NBC made her a target of the crusaders, and she was dismissed a week before rehearsals began for the Somerset Maugham Theater program of *The Mother*, sponsored by Tintair. Moreover, she was listed in *Red Channels* with nine citations.

Although a significant number of artists were singled out in *Red Channels*, the case histories of a representative few stand for those who endured FBI investigations for a few years but failed to survive the atmosphere of suspicion, distrust, and betrayal that ended in lost jobs, smashed careers, broken marriages, and serious health issues. The case of Mady Christians focuses attention on the largely anonymous investigations waged by the Federal Bureau of Investigation against alleged subversives. It was most likely that her status as a naturalized citizen, her associations with the German émigré community in Hollywood, and her official capacity with the "Red" organization known as Actors' Equity brought her to the attention of the Bureau.

Acting upon directives issued by Director J. Edgar Hoover, FBI agents proceeded in 1950 to intensify their investigations of "subversives" in Los Angeles and New York. In August, two months after the publication of *Red Channels*, Mady Christians came under the scrutiny of the FBI's internal security division. The Bureau initiated file number 100–63757 (Subject: Mady Christians).[8]

Marguerita Maria Christians (called "Madi" by her parents) was born in Vienna, Austria, in 1900 and became a naturalized U.S. citizen in 1939.[9] Her father, Rudolf Christians, was a well-known German actor, who brought his wife and daughter to New York City in 1912, where he joined the Irving Place Theatre, located south of Gramercy Park, and became the theater's general manager on the cusp of the First World War. Amidst the anti-German fervor, the German-language theater was soon without a mandate. Before its close, however, Mady Christians made her acting debut there.

In order to further her acting career, she and her mother returned in 1917 to Berlin, where she enrolled in Max Reinhardt's acting school. Five foot, seven inches tall (taller than most leading men in Europe) with blond hair, gray-blue eyes, and a melodic soprano voice, she made her professional debut at the Deutsches Theater and rose to stardom on European stages and in film. In the early thirties, she was invited briefly to the United States to tour in a play called *Marching By* and was offered a contract to return to Broadway the next year. It was a fortuitous offer. Artists working in the Berlin theater in 1933 were aware of the rising tide of Nazi influence in the city and elsewhere in the country. Mady Christians joined a long line of ex-patriots, including Max Reinhardt, Elisabeth Bergner, Bertolt Brecht, and Hanns Eisler, seeking refuge in the United States. Once she relocated to New York City, she played in seven consecutive productions on Broadway within five years and appeared in five films in Hollywood. On Broadway, she appeared as Queen Gertrude in *Hamlet* and as Lady Percy in *Henry IV, Part I,* staged by Margaret Webster, and in Lillian Hellman's powerful new drama, *Watch on the Rhine.*

Watch on the Rhine was Hellman's message that fascism represented a mortal danger to even the most insular and privileged of Americans. As witness to the rise of fascism in Germany and to the Gestapo's intimidation tactics used against artists in the German theater who were political dissidents, anti-Nazi, or Jewish, Christians was well-suited to play Sara Mueller, the American-born wife of a German refugee who had been active in the anti-Nazi underground. Brooks Atkinson called *Watch on the Rhine* Hellman's finest play and described Christians's portrayal of Sara Mueller as "full of womanly affection and a crusader's resignation to realities."[10]

Moreover, in the Red-scare atmosphere of the forties, the creative work of artists in anti-fascist plays and films was frequently misunderstood. While she was appearing in *Watch on the Rhine,* FBI informants reported Christians's suspicious efforts on behalf of Russian war relief and Spanish aid committees.[11]

Early in 1941, Christians took a public stand against the House Committee on Un-American Activities and its investigations of Hollywood. In an interview with the *New York World Telegram,* she also deplored the Senate Internal Security Subcommittee's inquiries into war propaganda in American films. She viewed them as analogous to the "heckling" of film and radio artists by the Nazis in the thirties. Moreover, she found the SISS's work "un-American" and described it as endangering the very foundations of free expression. "I was there [in Germany], you know. I saw it all . . . They began with the movies and the radio making threats that were ridiculously unsubtle and calling for the firing of directors, script changes, and restrictions on radio broadcasts."[12]

Despite her outspoken opinions that made her unpopular with right-wing columnists, Mady Christians worked consistently between 1933 and 1950 in one or two films each year and on an average of one long-running or several shorter Broadway shows each season. She sailed to Broadway stardom in John Van Druten's *I Remember Mama,* about a Norwegian American family governed by a simple, wise mother, and garnered a chorus of approval from theater critics. She clearly viewed herself as an *American* actress. "My home's here, my feelings are here, my love is here, my loyalty is here," she told a reporter.[13]

Branding the Exile

During the war years, Mady Christians worked selflessly for liberal and humanitarian causes and for the welfare of American actors. Her record of good works would, in time, be used to brand her as subversive and un-American.

Engaged in political activities on behalf of refugees during the war years, she was a guest of honor for the United Nations in America dinner, sponsored by the American Committee for Protection of Foreign Born, and she entertained for the American Friends of the Chinese People. Along with other artists and writers, she signed an advertisement for "Russian War Relief" that appeared in the *New York Times*.[14] She also served as vice-chairman of the Women's Division of the National Citizens Political Action Committee and as honorary vice-chairman of the Connecticut State Division of the Independent Citizens Committee of the Arts, Sciences and Professions. In 1945, she was the subject of an article that appeared in the *Daily Worker* portraying her as a "Foe of Tyranny."[15] With the publication of *Red Channels* in June of 1950, her political and charitable activities acquired a Red hue, and she came to the attention of the FBI.

The FBI's file on Christians is retroactive to 1941, when Actors' Equity Association was split asunder by an election that hardened into accusations of subversion against a handful of Equity members. An election for new members of the governing council brought into focus the split in the union between liberals and conservatives, which hardened into a political divide.

That year the nominating committee for the council of Actors' Equity had rejected two names for new council members: Mady Christians and Alan Hewitt. Christians was rejected as being foreign-born, and Hewitt was rejected based on rumors that he was a Communist. Once the allegations were discovered, the inner circle of Actors' Equity erupted into a furor, and an independent ticket was formed to include the names of Christians and Hewitt. The independents then endorsed the three "regular" candidates—E. John Kennedy, Ethel Waters, and Margaret Webster. They, in turn, endorsed the independent candidates.

Describing the repercussions, Margaret Webster said, "Plenty of fur flew, plenty of mud was thrown and there was a 'stormy' annual meeting."[16] The candidates were elected, but there was now a schism in the ranks. Florence Reed, Winifred Lenihan, and Peggy Wood, along with seven other council members, resigned. Actress Winifred Lenihan declared to the press that the election "plus the professional bleeding hearts on the Council now gives the Communists seventeen votes."[17]

Looking back on this tempest in Equity's teapot, Webster said that the union continued on its charted course, "sensible, reasonable, a bit stodgy, rather to the right of the middle of the road, argumentative but seldom actively belligerent."[18] Nonetheless, the seeds were firmly planted for perceiving the actors' union and especially its governing council as made up of Communists and Communist sympathizers.

As an Equity council member, Mady Christians was firmly established in the public eye as a "pinko." While she was playing in Hellman's anti-fascist play, she received anonymous letters written on various pieces of hotel stationery addressed to her at the Martin Beck Theatre protesting her work on behalf of Russian war relief.

Concerned about the threatening contents of the letters, she wrote to FBI director J. Edgar Hoover to inquire if he had information about campaigns of intimidation against other public figures. She enclosed two items: a postal card calling upon her to stop making speeches "against your own Germany" and a letter written on hotel stationery accusing her of being a German traitor and spy. Her hand-written letter to Hoover became the first entry in her FBI file. She said,

> It is not a personal matter to me—I don't consider anybody in public life [immune] to criticism and I don't fear threats or intimidation and I don't think it is an insult to be called names by a crackpot if as an U.S.A. citizen one does one's best to serve in a very small way for War-Relief for our country and its allies. . . .

Hoover responded that the facts reported in her communication did not appear to constitute a violation of any federal statute coming within the jurisdiction of the Bureau. "Accordingly," he continued, "it is not possible to render you any assistance," then concluded, "however, your letter is being made a matter of official record in the files of this Bureau." The letter was placed in a newly constituted file.[19]

The FBI took no further interest in the actress until August of 1950. In the interim, the United States and the Soviet Union fought a world war as allies against Nazi Germany and Imperial Japan, but in America, lines were drawn between liberals and conservatives that engendered suspicion, distrust, and conspiracy theories. The election at Actors' Equity was just one instance of the larger political divide taking shape in the country.

During the war years, members of Actors' Equity and others in the entertainment industries on the home front directed their attentions to helping charitable causes: the United Service Organizations (USO); the Stage Door Canteen; Treasury Bond and Red Cross drives; British, Spanish, Russian, and Chinese war relief; and a multitude of war-engendered charities organized to assist refugees and exiles. Many artists worked not only to help the victims of war but planned for a time of cultural exchange in the postwar era. A number of theater people, including Mady Christians, Lillian Hellman, and Dorothy

Parker, supported five of these organizations, which were destined, as Margaret Webster said, "to cause as much grief to their supporters as aid to those they supported."[20] These five were the American Committee for Protection of Foreign Born, the National Council of American-Soviet Friendship, the American Committee to Save Refugees, the Joint Anti-Fascist Refugee Committee, and the Independent Citizens Committee of the Arts, Sciences and Professions.

The second explosion to rock Actors' Equity Association can be attributed to the Joint Anti-Fascist Refugee Committee (JAFRC), formed in 1942 by merging three groups dedicated to helping exiled writers and refugees. The JAFRC's original purpose was to help the anti-Franco Spanish refugees who had been interned under grim conditions in French refugee camps and largely forgotten among the more urgent demands of the war in Europe. On September 24, 1945, the JAFRC held a fundraising meeting in Madison Square Garden. Five members of Actors' Equity entertained early in the program and then departed to their respective theaters.

Actor Frank Fay, notable for his role as the eccentric Elwood P. Dowd, companion of the invisible rabbit in the long-running Broadway hit *Harvey*, was a volatile Irish-Catholic. He joined with publisher Howard Rushmore of the *Journal-American* to condemn the anti-Catholic rhetoric of Harold Laski, the British Labour Party economist who had spoken to the rally by radio hookup from London on the politics of the Roman Catholic Church in Spain. The *Journal-American* proclaimed that "the appearance of actors at a Red meeting which condemned religion is a far cry from the tradition and tolerance of the theater." Frank Fay was quoted as saying that this "inexcusable conduct" by the "participation of stars in a front meeting such as this deserves a full investigation."[21]

During an Equity membership meeting the following day, Fay stood up and declared the five actors—David Brooks, Luba Malina, Sono Osato, Jean Darling, and Margo (the professional name of dancer-actress María Castilla)—to have been "party to defamation of the Church, the Pope and the Vatican in the greatest insult to religion [he] had ever heard." The five members filed charges with Equity against Fay under the association's by-laws that covered "conduct prejudicial to the welfare of the Association or its members." They claimed that Frank Fay had "clearly damaged and injured them in their profession."[22]

As a council member, Mady Christians, who was playing in *I Remember Mama*, was present for the charges against Fay. The five actors testified that they had been "physically assaulted, insulted, threatened with violence to themselves and their families, picketed and informed that not only their plays but *any* plays, motion pictures or radio broadcasts in which they might appear from now on would be boycotted."

In the end, Equity's council passed a unanimous resolution sustaining the charges brought by the five members who "in no way participated in any attack on anyone's faith or religion." The resolution ordered the reprimand and censure of Frank Fay. The actor then took his case to the general membership, who backed the council's decision. Nonetheless, this event and its extensive newspaper coverage resulted in the branding of Actors' Equity as a "Red" organization and its councilors as "pinkos." Moreover, following his censure, Frank Fay declared Mady Christians an out-and-out Communist.[23]

The threats to picket and boycott the work of the five actors were prelude to the virulent activities of the secular blacklisters in the fifties. Margaret Webster assessed the situation correctly when she said, "The years of disgrace were upon us, of reckless accusations, of endless 'smear campaigns,' of innuendoes, of that most insidious of weapons, guilt by association."[24]

Even without knowledge of the existence of an FBI file in her name, Mady Christians considered herself vulnerable in the shifting political winds. Her liabilities were fourfold. She was born in Austria; she supported left-wing causes; she was on the governing board of a "Red" union; and she was listed in *Red Channels*. Within a short time, her associations with Lillian Hellman, Orson Welles, Hanns Eisler, Morris Carnovsky, Arthur Miller, Edward G. Robinson, Philip Loeb, Walter Slezak, Margaret Webster, and Paul Robeson would also prove political and professional liabilities.

An Anonymous Investigation

Mady Christians came under the scrutiny of the FBI's internal security division in 1950. She had been named by a confidential informant as a "concealed Communist," meaning, an individual who did not publicize herself as a Communist and who would, if asked, deny membership in the party. Most likely, the informant was the ex-Communist Louis F. Budenz, former managing editor of the *Daily Worker* and Communist Party functionary who broke with the party and listed Christians among four hundred concealed Communists that he reportedly knew. The Special Agent in Charge of the New York office reported: "For the information of the Bureau the subject [Mady Christians] is one of the 400 concealed Communists [name deleted] stated he knew. The names of those concealed Communists were sent to the Bureau in the case captioned 'Communist Party, USA, Internal Security—C.'"[25] The "C" was FBI coding for Communist.

Mady Christians was now an internal security matter. FBI procedures for investigating "concealed" Communists were biased from the start. Agents solicited confirmation from informants who were most likely to give a negative picture of the subject as subversive. The brush of anonymous informants tarred Mady Christians with unfounded rumor, malicious gossip, and damning information about her pro-Communist activities and alleged party membership.

In addition to informants' reports, Christians's name appeared in a variety of documents. She was on record in newspapers as supporting foreign-born

Americans and refugees of Russian and European origins.[26] As early as October 27, 1941, she was noted as one of the "prominent persons" who addressed a benefit for "Russian War Relief" held in Madison Square Garden. She was vice-chairman of the National Citizens Political Action Committee cited in 1947 by the California Committee on Un-American Activities as a Communist-front organization.[27] In reports submitted to the Bureau of organizational meetings for the Connecticut State Division of the Independent Citizens Committee of the Arts, Sciences and Professions —identified by an informant as the "swankiest of all the contemporary Communist front organizations"—Christians was listed with writer James Thurber and actor Paul Robeson as an honorary vice-chairman.[28]

In addition, the FBI also noted Christians's association with German exiles when she was in Hollywood in the forties, namely, Fritz Lang, Walter Slezak, Hanns Eisler, Lion Feuchtwanger, and Max Reinhardt. Informants suggested that she was "intimate with" the German film director Fritz Lang and "extremely friendly with" the alleged Nazi-sympathizer Walter Slezak.[29]

Christians and actor-singer Slezak, exiles from Nazi Germany, had been childhood friends in Vienna and appeared together in the 1928 German-language film of Franz Léhar's *Friederike*. Slezak had made an American career playing Nazi officers in Hollywood films to the confusion of FBI informants. The same memorandum that purported to confirm an affair between Christians and Slezak also reported that they were Nazi sympathizers.[30]

As part of her Hollywood dossier, Christians was noted as speaking ("although without political overtones") at the memorial service held for Max Reinhardt at the Actors' Laboratory in Los Angeles in 1943. In fact, her remarks were a personal tribute to her former teacher and director as her "guiding light."[31] Nonetheless, by 1948, any association with the Actors' Laboratory placed Christians in the middle of an alleged Communist cell.[32]

In addition, Christians's associations with composer Hanns Eisler further confirmed her status as an internal security risk. Identified as a member of the Communist Party in Germany in 1926, Hanns Eisler was the brother of Gerhard Eisler, considered by the FBI to be "the top Comintern representative in the United States."[33] Monitoring his activities in the 1940s, the FBI noted Gerhard Eisler's almost daily visits to the New York office of the "subversive and Communist" Joint Anti-Fascist Refugee Committee. Convinced that he was a top Soviet agent, the U.S. Justice Department proceeded to indict him.

In the backwash of these troubled waters, Mady Christians's associations with Gerhard Eisler's brother and other German émigrés brought her further scrutiny from the FBI and its cadre of informants. Her friends, the celebrated director Lion Feuchtwanger was thought to be a Russian espionage agent, and Hanns Eisler, the composer for the Bertolt Brecht–Charles Laughton production of *Galileo,* was subpoenaed as a Communist to testify before HUAC in 1947. Then, too, the "front groups"—the Joint Anti-Fascist Refugee Committee and the American Committee for Protection of Foreign Born—that Mady Christians fervently supported during wartime were directly linked to Gerhard Eisler's "subversive" activities on behalf of an international Communist conspiracy.[34]

Guilt-by-association looms large in the annals of the American anti-Communist movement and its ten thousand or more victims. In effect, Gerhard Eisler's front-page persecution as a "concealed Communist" by the U.S. government held very real fears for the actress. She feared an investigation that could result in any one of three dire scenarios under the 1940 Alien Registration Act (known as the Smith Act): denaturalization, deportation, or even imprisonment.[35] The Smith Act, passed by the U.S. Senate in 1940, required all aliens to be registered and fingerprinted and contained provisions for allowing the deportation of aliens for simply *talking* about overthrowing the U.S. government by "force and violence," or for *belonging* to an organization that advocated force and violence.

Perhaps the most damning allocution was the Budenz report. An individual of "known reliability," most likely Louis Budenz, duly reported that Jacob "Jack" Stachel, a member of the National Committee of the Communist Party—USA, and Sam Sillen, editor of the cultural pages of the *Daily Worker,* had revealed sometime in 1944 or 1945 that Mady Christians was a member of the Communist Party.[36]

By 1951, the actress's "Communist activities and connections," reported by informants of "known or unknown reliability," were entered in her FBI file. The following transgressions were duly noted:

- leadership in the left-wing faction of Actors' Equity Association;
- acting as sponsor or organizer for nine front organizations;
- sponsorship of U.S. visa applications for Communist sympathizers;
- correspondence with Germans interned in Canada;
- involvement in the mysterious departure of German agent Baronness Amalie von Reznicek for Japan;
- radio broadcasts for pro-Communist organizations and events;
- being guest of honor at the United Nations in America dinner;
- speaking at rallies and dinners to reelect Franklin D. Roosevelt;
- request to Hanns Eisler, a known Communist, to take part in an anniversary celebration for Austrian director Berthold Viertel;
- having been telephoned by Lion Feuchtwanger, a "Russian agent";
- having been branded by the American Legion as one of 128 "untouchables," whose "past activities make them unsuitable or inappropriate for Legion sponsorship";

- citation by a national Catholic magazine as a radio celebrity who was a "Red."[37]

As she was a documented internal security risk, the Subversive Activities Control division within the New York FBI office opened a second file number 100–99584, entitled "Mady Christians Security Matter-C." This second file in support of the Justice Department's Bureau file number 100–63757 held potential interest for Pat McCarran's Senate Internal Security Subcommittee.

Death by Innuendo

Beginning in 1947, the star of *I Remember Mama* found only sporadic work in the theater and in Hollywood. In the same Broadway season as Arthur Miller's *All My Sons* and George Kelly's *Craig's Wife* (both plays had appropriate roles for her), she played the title role in James Parish's *Message for Margaret,* which critics called "woeful" and "boring"—a "piece of arrant soddy," "old fashioned claptrap," "a piece of first-rate junk"—and bemoaned as material unworthy of an actress of Christians's caliber.[38]

In 1948, she appeared in two films—Arthur Miller's *All My Sons,* with Edward G. Robinson, Burt Lancaster, and Arlene Francis, and Max Ophuls's *Letter from an Unknown Woman,* with Joan Fontaine and Louis Jourdan. The following year, she was offered the role of the Captain's wife in a Broadway revival of *The Father* by August Strindberg, with Raymond Massey and Grace Kelly. As the wife in Strindberg's savage tragedy of a marriage in dissolution, Christians received glowing reviews.[39] *The Father* lasted for sixty-nine performances and closed in January 1950. It was Mady Christians's final Broadway appearance.

Throughout the months of diminishing work, she was frustrated by the fact that she had little direct evidence that she was being investigated. There was no subpoena, no press releases from congressional committees, no out-and-out accusations of pro-Communist activities by government officials to confront and refute. Meanwhile, FBI agents continued to collect information about her activities. In one instance, they recorded a query from a lawyer representing a Chicago theater company considering the services of theatrical stars, in particular Mady Christians. "He desired any information of a subversive nature concerning these individuals in as much as the theater did not desire to employ subversives." The Bureau advised that FBI files were confidential and available for official use only.[40]

Informants continued to advise the Bureau that the actress was a Communist, a Communist sympathizer, and a sponsor of front organizations. The telephone rang less often. Her earlier description to journalist Helen Ormsbee of the situation for artists in Germany in the thirties now applied to herself: "You can't put your finger on the reason. Directors don't happen to have parts."[41]

As the telephone grew silent, Christians began to suffer from high blood pressure, dismissed by doctors as a psychosomatic illness. Her health improved when the CBS Somerset Maugham Theater, sponsored by Tintair, offered her a role in a Saturday morning series of radio dramatizations of the novelist's stories. She was a featured guest artist on the broadcast of *Winter Cruise* in April of 1950.

CBS then offered her another role in the Maugham Theater series, also sponsored by Tintair. Nonetheless, the advertising agency Carl Byoir and Associates, who were responsible for approving employees for Tintair, disapproved her contract one week before rehearsals started.[42] When she asked why the offer was withdrawn, she was given to understand that it was because of the blacklist operating within the broadcast networks.[43]

Shortly after CBS cancelled her contract, the actress, suffering from acute hypertension, was taken to Flower Hospital in Manhattan. When she was allowed to return to her residence on East Seventy-second Street, she wrote to an old friend: "I cannot bear yet to think of the things which led to my breakdown. One day I shall put them down as a record of something unbelievable."[44]

Behind the scenes, the FBI accelerated their investigation. In January of 1951, the director advised the New York office to review Bureau files to determine if Mady Christians's name should be placed on the Security Index.[45] On April 4, the New York office prepared a twenty-one page memorandum in support of the recommendation to add her name to the index.[46]

In a reversal in early June, Hoover's office denied the recommendation, stating that it did not appear that an SI card was warranted at this time.

> A review of the file in this case reflects that the only information concerning Communist Party membership on the part of the subject was furnished by [name deleted] and that was prior to 1945. Also the last reported activities of the subject in alleged Communist organizations were in early 1949. In view of this it does not appear that a Security Index card is warranted at this time.[47]

This was not the end of the matter, however. The FBI director advised the Special Agent in Charge of the New York office that, unless there was information that would make an interview inadvisable, they should proceed to interview the subject to determine her "present sympathies and potential dangerousness." Only upon the completion of the interview and their finding, the director cautioned, should the subject's name be placed on the Security Index.

On the afternoon of September 15, two agents from the Bureau's New York office went to Mady Christians's apartment on East Seventy-second Street. She was expecting them, but a friend dropped by unannounced shortly before the agents arrived. She tried to hurry the visitor away, but the agents arrived, and she introduced the two as businessmen. Suddenly, a loud popping sound emanated from the kitchen, where Christians had left something cooking in the oven. The visitor reported that the two agents were visibly alarmed.[48]

Early in the interview, Christians denied being a member of the Communist Party, ever knowing a member of the Communist Party, or ever attending a Communist Party meeting. She acknowledged her support of Russian relief agencies and authorization of the use of her name in an advertisement published in the *New York Times* urging support of a national campaign in 1941 to raise funds for "Russian War Relief."[49] She advised that she was encouraged in her charitable efforts on behalf of the Russian people by President Roosevelt's request to Americans to help the Soviets in "their hour of need." The agents reported that she could not recall any particular instance of activity nor could she recall any of the individuals with whom she had worked in the relief agencies. She did not provide names.

Exhibiting copies of *Counterattack* and *Red Channels*, Christians stated that she had been active in two of the organizations cited in their pages: "Russian War Relief" (in 1941) and the Independent Citizens Committee of the Arts, Sciences and Professions (in 1944–45). She produced a copy of the *Daily Worker* and reminded the agents that she gave the interview when it became clear that the reporter was only interested in her performance in *I Remember Mama*. Despite the article's glaring title ("Christians: A Great Artist and a Veteran Foe of Tyranny"), she insisted that she talked only about her travels, not politics, during the interview.

The agents reported that the "subject" had been well prepared with her denials of Communist activities and fervent in her support of Roosevelt's ideals and policies. They concluded: "In view of the lack of reported Communist activity on the part of the subject since 1945, this case is being placed in a *closed status* unless advised to the contrary by the Bureau."[50]

Following the interview, Christians rejoined the tour of George Brandt's Broadway-bound production of *Black Chiffon*. However, she soon became ill and returned to New Canaan, where she collapsed in her Connecticut home. She died in Norwalk General Hospital on October 28, 1951. The attending physician wrote "cerebral hemorrhage" as the cause of death. Following a service in New York City, she was buried in Ferncliff Cemetery in Ardsley, New York. Mady Christians was fifty-one.

On October 30, 1951, the FBI's New York office reported her death to Hoover's office with a copy of the *New York Times* obituary published on the same day.[51] Nonetheless, the matter of Mady Christians versus the FBI was not quite at an end. On November 14, a memorandum from Assistant Director Louis Nichols to Hoover's number two man, Clyde Tolson, documented a telephone call from the liberal newspaper *Daily Compass* inquiring if the FBI had ever interviewed the "controversial radio personality" whose services were terminated when allegedly she was exposed as a Communist sympathizer. The office refused comment and a handwritten note in Christians's file asserted with unintended irony, "Right. The 'Compass' would intentionally distort the situation."[52] This is the last entry in Bureau file number 100–63757.

To honor their deceased council member, Actors' Equity appointed a committee to recommend an appropriate memorial for Mady Christians, who had been a devoted actress and fundraiser for the Equity Library Theatre. A five-member committee that included Margaret Webster set about studying how to counteract the "false light" cast upon Mady Christians by *Red Channels*. The committee recommended creating a theater in her name to house the Equity Library Theatre and also a publication to describe what "happened" to her.[53] In the political climate of the day, Margaret Webster resigned from the Equity council and neither project came to fruition.

Untimely Ends

Mady Christians was not alone in a breakdown of health that shortened the lives of many of those targeted by the anti-Communists, those performers that Victor Navasky said "seemed to die of the blacklist."[54] Actors Canada Lee, J. Edward Bromberg, John Garfield, and Philip Loeb were likewise visited by a cadre of investigators, found themselves unemployed, and subsequently died of health issues or by suicide.

Once witnesses discovered the legal protections of the Fifth Amendment, the threat of imprisonment was removed, but not the consequences of FBI investigations, unemployment, financial ruin, wrecked careers, and loss of friends and family. Mady Christians never reached Washington's hearing rooms to use the protections of the Fifth.

Despite her successful seventeen-year stage and film career in the United States and her anti-fascist convictions, Mady Christians failed to circumvent the forces of McCarthyism. Stefan Kanfer, writing of the "plague years," said that the "secular blacklisters . . . made her the classic figure of their century, *the exile*."[55] Six months prior to her death, Chairman John S. Wood commanded actress Anne Revere to testify before the House Committee on Un-American Activities. The actress's "un-Americanisms" were twofold. She had protested the government's censorship of the Hollywood Actors' Laboratory, and she was a member of the Communist Party—USA.

I consider any questioning regarding one's political views or religious views as a violation of the rights of a citizen under our Constitution.

—Anne Revere

4 Unfriendly Witness: Anne Revere

Between 1946 and 1951, Broadway had appeared too insignificant for the attention of the secular blacklisters and the congressional committees. Unlike film, radio, and television, the theater did not reach large numbers of people that translated into millions of dollars for sponsors, advertisers, broadcast networks, and film studios. Moreover, Broadway producers were *independent* in the sense that they created their funding, chose the plays to be produced, and approved their casts. No sponsors dictated their wares or controlled their markets. Nonetheless, in May 1951, the House Committee on Un-American Activities announced that it was preparing to switch its emphasis from Hollywood to Broadway.[1] In truth, most of Hollywood's luminaries had been exhaustively showcased in the earlier hearings, including Martin Dies's Committee on Un-American Activities, state senator Jack Tenney's California Joint Fact-Finding Committee on Un-American Activities, and J. Parnell Thomas's House Committee on Un-American Activities, which jailed the Hollywood Ten.

Once attention shifted to Broadway in 1951, the Committee subpoenaed over a period of three years such double headliners of stage and film as Lee J. Cobb, José Ferrer, Lillian Hellman, Elia Kazan, Clifford Odets, Larry Parks, Anne Revere, Edward G. Robinson, and Jerome Robbins. In addition, Joseph McCarthy was determined to root out Communism and its sympathizers from the U.S. State Department's teacher exchange programs and its overseas information centers and libraries. In the first category, he subpoenaed director Margaret Webster and composer Aaron Copland, and, in the second, authors Dashiell Hammett, Langston Hughes, Eslanda Robeson, and Arnaud d'Usseau and journalists Cedric Belfrage and James A. Wechsler. Pat McCarran, in turn, subpoenaed his own cadre of celebrities principally of Eastern European background to support his pending legislation to limit immigration. In effect, the trio of committees laid waste to the cultural landscape as they turned up a very small number of current Communist Party members, ex-Communists, or Cold War radicals.

As an unfriendly witness, Anne Revere, celebrated as a supporting actress for Elizabeth Taylor, Gregory Peck, John Garfield, and Montgomery Clift in *National Velvet, Gentleman's Agreement, Body and Soul,* and *A Place in the Sun,* stands out as a singular artist representing those who spoke up for their constitutional rights and were branded uncooperative and un-American as well. When Frank S. Tavenner, chief counsel for the House Un-American Activities Committee, asked actress Anne Revere about her associations with the Actors' Laboratory in Hollywood, she asserted her rights under the First and Fifth Amendments. By doing so, she effectively cast a shadow over her career for the next seven years.

A proud descendant of the revolutionary Paul Revere and constitutional signatory John Adams, she was at the peak of her film career when she was named in 1951 by actor Larry Parks as part of a Communist Party cell in Los Angeles. Subsequently, the award-winning actress was investigated by government agents, subpoenaed by HUAC, and blacklisted by Hollywood studios.

Refusing to cooperate with the Committee, the reserved New Yorker was effectively shut out of work in Hollywood. The previous year she was made "controversial" by her listing in *Red Channels* and denied work in radio and television. In the late fifties, Revere returned to New York, the scene of her Broadway triumph in Lillian Hellman's *The Children's Hour* and struggled for seven years to reclaim her stage career. She triumphed over the decade of adversity as Anna Berniers in Hellman's *Toys in the Attic.* Hellman's last original play vindicated Broadway's producers and audiences, who valued talent and serious artistry over mediocrity and political rectitude.

Finding a Career

Anne Revere was born in New York City in 1903, grew up in Westfield, New Jersey, received a Bachelor of Arts degree from Wellesley College, and enrolled in the American Laboratory Theatre, founded by Stanislavski-trained actors Richard Boleslavsky and Maria Ouspenskaya, who came to the United States on tour with the Moscow Art Theatre in 1923. The school (originally called the Theatre Arts Institute) was a significant first step in translating Stanislavski's ideas about truth in acting into an American idiom. Revere made a full-fledged Broadway debut in *The Great Barrington* with Otto Kruger in 1931, followed by *The Lady with a Lamp, Wild Waves,* and *Double Door.* Invited to Hollywood, she reprised her role as the romantic spinster Caroline Van Bret in the 1934 film of *Double Door.* Returning to New York, she appeared for three years as Martha Dobie in Lillian Hellman's first play *The Children's Hour,* called the "season's dramatic high-water mark."[2]

The names of Anne Revere and Lillian Hellman were first linked on Broadway by *The Children's Hour*. The women were linked again thirteen months apart in HUAC hearings and characterized as unfriendly witnesses. In the intervening eighteen years, Revere married and moved to Hollywood where she began a decade-long career before HUAC began investigation of Hollywood in 1947 and again in 1951.[3] In those years Revere felt the chill winds of national politics blowing over her career. In truth, she was among the early casualties of the requirement to name names, the ultimate test of a witness's cooperation in committee hearings.

Because of her uncooperative testimony and Paramount's reservations about blacklisted artists, her best scenes were cut from *A Place in the Sun* and her image removed from the final scene where, over a large close-up of Montgomery Clift, she is heard saying, "God bless you, my boy; God forgive me if I've failed you."[4]

On a Collision Course

During a day-long hearing in March of 1951, actor Larry Parks named Anne Revere, Morris Carnovsky, J. Edward Bromberg, Lee J. Cobb, Gale Sondergaard, Dorothy Tree, and Roman Bohnen as members of a Communist cell in Los Angeles. Screenwriter Budd Schulberg and actors Sterling Hayden and José Ferrer followed Larry Parks into the witness chair. They also testified as friendly witnesses. Revere and Morris Carnovsky were subpoenaed a month later.

Unaware that Larry Parks had capitulated under pressure and testified as a friendly witness, Revere thought that her left-wing connections in Hollywood and the six entries beneath her name in *Red Channels*—a small number when measured by the standard set by Dashiell Hammett, Lillian Hellman, and Dorothy Parker—were the ostensible reasons for the subpoena.

It is true that the FBI had dutifully noted Revere's activities with pro-Communist groups. She had signed an advertisement for the Committee for a Free Political Advocacy and a "We are for Wallace" advertisement placed in the *New York Times* by the National Council of the Arts, Sciences and Professions. As early as 1947, she spoke on a "Hollywood Fights Back" broadcast sponsored by the Committee for the First Amendment in support of the Hollywood Nineteen, and she signed a petition calling for the U.S. Supreme Court to set aside the convictions of John Howard Lawson and Dalton Trumbo—two of the Hollywood Ten. Moreover, she was on record that year as a sponsor of the Civil Rights Congress in the call for the abolition of the Thomas-Rankin Committee on Un-American Activities.[5] In 1948, her name was read into the record of the Un-American Activities Committee in California. In 1949, she signed an *amicus curiae* brief petitioning the U.S. Supreme Court to set aside the convictions of screenwriters Lawson and Trumbo. The only entry for 1950 was her membership in the Committee for Admission of World Peace Delegation.

As early as July 1943, Anne Revere was placed under surveillance as a national security matter. Bureau files recorded that she was a card-holding member of the Communist Party—USA in 1943 and 1944. In 1944, she was issued a card for the Los Angeles section of the Communist Political Association, where she worked as educational director.[6] On December 5, 1944, R. B. Hood, Special Agent in Charge of the Los Angeles office, recommended to Director Hoover that a Security Index card be prepared classifying Anne Revere, a.k.a. Mrs. Samuel Rosen, as a Security Matter—C.

A four-page office memorandum, prepared earlier in November, portrayed Revere as a card-carrying member of the Communist Party—USA, active in such "front" groups as the American Committee to Save Refugees, the Exiled Writers Committee, and the United American-Spanish Aid Committee. These committees were later combined to form the Joint Anti-Fascist Refugee Committee, central to the FBI files of Mady Christians, Lillian Hellman, Dorothy Parker, Margaret Webster, and others.

On March 6, 1945, the FBI director advised the Los Angeles office that the Bureau had prepared a Security Index card in the name of Mrs. Samuel Rosen, née Anne Revere. J. Edgar Hoover then instructed the regional office to enter the following caption on the 5" x 8" index card:

Rosen, Mrs. Samuel	Native Born	Communist
Née: Anne Revere		
139 South Camden Drive		
Beverly Hills, California (Res.)		
20th Century Fox Studios		
10201 West Pico Boulevard		
Los Angeles, California (Bus.)		

Anne Revere was subsequently assigned two file numbers: FBI Bureau file (the "Bufile") number 100–336762 and Los Angeles office file number 100–22606. In late July, without explanation, the Bureau changed its mind and ordered the Los Angeles office to cancel Revere's Security Index card.[7]

Two years following Hoover's directive, the Bureau submitted a seventeen-page memorandum to J. Parnell Thomas, then chairman of the House Committee on Un-American Activities. Despite the length of their document, the agency had reservations about their findings. In their view, they had not made "a good case of Communist Party membership against Anne Revere," although they had established proof of her affiliations with Communist-front organizations.[8]

The Bureau had noted that Anne Revere was a member of the board of directors of the Progressive Citizens of America, which held a conference on the subject "Thought Control in the United States" at the Beverly Hills Hotel in Hollywood. A membership flyer placed Revere in the company of John Garfield, Lena Horne, Edward G. Robinson, Gene Kelly, Betty Garrett, and Larry Parks. A facsimile of the conference program that featured papers and discussion groups on a variety of topics ranging from literature to medicine was duly entered into Revere's FBI file. The panel entitled "The Actor," chaired by Vincent Price, included a blue-ribbon group largely from the Hollywood Actors' Laboratory: Morris Carnovsky, Lee J. Cobb, Hume Cronyn, Paul Henreid, Alexander Knox, Selena Royle, Gale Sondergaard, and Anne Revere. Revere's speech "Actor's Search for a Stage" pointed to the struggles of the Federal Theatre Project and the hearings conducted by Martin Dies's Committee on Un-American Activities and by his successor J. Parnell Thomas. She remarked with some bitterness,

> We cannot tolerate Congressional Committees of this ilk in a democracy— Committees which may hold their hearings in public or private, as they see fit; may or may not hear witnesses, as they please; may cite for contempt witnesses who do not respond to their subpoena, but on the other hand may not be compelled to hear people who demand to testify. Operating as quasi-judicial bodies which are a law unto themselves, these Committees become dangerous—and the lesson of the Federal Theater has exposed their purposes and their methods. As actors and citizens, we must render impotent those who would control thought—so that the dreams and deeds of the Federal Theater did not end, but, as Hallie Flanagan says, "they were the beginnings of a people's theater in a country whose greatest plays are yet to come."[9]

Revere was also identified as one of the sponsors of the Los Angeles chapter of the Civil Rights Congress and signatory to an advertisement in the *Daily Peoples World,* noted as the "official newspaper for the Communist Political Association on the West coast," defending Gerhard Eisler as a "world renowned anti-fascist fighter."[10]

Given the FBI's reservations about their proof of Revere's Communist Party membership based on hearsay from a "highly confidential" source, the Bureau recommended that the Committee tread carefully:

> you may desire to suggest to Representative Thomas that he ask Anne Revere the following question: Are you now or have you ever been a member of the Northwest Section of the Los Angeles County Communist Party?

If Revere answered negatively to the question, Chairman Thomas was cautioned that the Bureau was not in a position "to refute her testimony at this time in connection with a perjury investigation."[11]

Then in September 1950, ex-Communist Louis Budenz gave the FBI the name of Anne Revere as one of four hundred concealed Communists. Protected as a confidential informant, Budenz expanded upon his recollection:

Although I had heard MISS REVERE's name mentioned as sympathetic to the Communist Party on a number of occasions by v. j. JEROME and ALEXANDER TRACHTENBERG, I was officially advised in connection with the discussions on the Independent Committee of the Arts and Sciences that she was an adherent of the Communist Party. This information was given to me first by ALEXANDER TRACHTENBERG and later on, in 1944, by JACK STACHEL. This estimate of MISS REVERE continued officially until I left the Party.[12]

A month later, Director Hoover wrote to the FBI's Los Angeles office requesting that the investigation into Anne Revere's Communist Party membership be reopened and another determination made to assign a Security Index card in the name of Anne Revere Rosen.[13] An eight-page summary report followed on January 29, 1951, but Revere's official Communist Party affiliation was still undetermined. "In as much as no information has been developed to show current membership or specific activity in the Communist Party on the part of ANNE REVERE, and since she is not connected with a critical industry, no recommendation is being made for a Security Index card to be issued regarding her."[14]

Despite the fate of the Hollywood Ten and the warnings contained in the Waldorf Statement, Revere did not temper her political activism. If anything, she accelerated her activities between 1948 and 1950. By January 1951, she was on a collision course with the House Committee on Un-American Activities.

The Bureau studiously recorded her activities but still made no recommendation to issue a Security Index card in her name. Taking notes and collecting flyers and brochures, agents and informants followed her everywhere. They noted that she sponsored a modern art exhibit under the auspices of the pro-Communist *New Masses*; signed a statement and a *New York Times* advertisement to abolish the House Committee on Un-American Activities; and publicly condemned the Mundt-Nixon bill, which would outlaw activities to establish, or look toward the establishment of, a totalitarian dictatorship in the United States under foreign control.

In July of 1950, the Bureau had a substantial lead on Revere's Communist Party membership. During the filming of *Deep Waters* in Maine for Twentieth Century Fox, actor Jerry Sheldon reportedly overheard Anne Revere admit that she was a Communist.[15] Sheldon gave the FBI a surreal account of a dinner sponsored by the governor of Maine in Rockland for the film company that included Dana Andrews, Anne Revere, Sam Rosen, and director Henry King. (Sheldon himself worked as a stand-in for Andrews.) Prevented from attending the dinner, the governor asked another state official to act as host for the evening. During his after-dinner speech, the governor's stand-in intimated that he knew more about the members of the film company than they realized. He looked around the table at the guests and remarked that "certain ones were or had been associated with Communist activity." Gazing directly at Anne Revere, he said that he knew for a fact that she was a Communist.[16]

Although others of the film company considered the remarks merely in poor taste, Revere and Rosen took issue with their host. When asked about the dust-up, Dana Andrews explained that Revere delivered a sarcastic retort ("Oh sure, all of us from Hollywood are Communists!") to a ridiculous question—"Why is everyone from Hollywood a Communist?"[17]

Furthermore, Andrews, who had made several films with the actress, deflected rumors of Revere's Communist affiliation onto her husband, whose radical politics were well known within the film community. Andrews thought Sam Rosen had likely exerted influence on his wife's politics and shaped her responses before HUAC, although there is no evidence to support this conjecture.[18]

Henry King, who had directed the actress in *Song of Bernadette* and *Remember the Day*, was also approached for his version of the Rockland fracas. He volunteered that he had no information as to the actress's connections, past or present, with the Communist Party.[19] And so the matter came to an end.

The Rosens were a closely knit couple whose work and politics were compatible—and all consuming. As an actress, Revere was more visible to the public than her producer-writer husband, and her many films and awards made her a more attractive candidate for congressional publicity-seekers. Following the Budenz report and the testimony of Larry Parks, both identifying her as a Communist Party member, the congressional gaze turned in Revere's direction.[20]

In March of 1951, the *Los Angeles Times* carried a news item that Anne Revere and two screenwriters had been subpoenaed by HUAC to testify on Communists in Hollywood.[21] The actress, along with Sam Moore, one-time president of the Radio Writers Guild and former writer for radio's *The Great Gildersleeve*, and screenwriter Harold Buchman were called to appear on the same day—April 17, 1951.

Dead in the Business

Dressed in a fashionable dark, long-sleeved silk dress with matching gloves, the tall, dark-haired Anne Revere, with a stern expression that belied her sense of humor, entered the great chamber of the U.S. House of Representatives where Chairman John Wood's committee held its hearings. The descendent of distinguished forebears had one of the shortest hearings in the history of the House Committee on Un-American Activities. Anne Revere testified for ten minutes.

Chief counsel Frank S. Tavenner Jr. began the questioning. After swearing to tell the truth, she gave her name, place of birth, current place of residence, profession, and educational background. When Tavenner asked where she was born, her reply injected some levity into the occasion. "Thank you for not asking me *when*," she replied. "I was born in New York City. Occasionally I play grandmothers, and it might jeopardize my professional standing."[22]

Tavenner was not amused. He wanted to know about her record of engagements as an actress. "Spotty, like all actresses," she answered. He turned next to her employment record. "Are you just interested in motion pictures," she asked, "or would you like my theater history?" Tavenner wanted her to begin with the theater for reasons that became quickly apparent.

MISS REVERE: I began in the theater many years ago. I presume that my most successful plays were *Double Door* and *The Children's Hour*, in which I had an extended engagement. I also established or helped to establish a theater, which I owned and operated, in Surrey, Maine. Subsequently, in 1934, I first came to Hollywood to do the picture version of *Double Door*, and then went back to New York. I have for approximately eleven years, I would say, been a resident of California, and during a great portion of that time employed in the studios.

The actress was prepared for questions about her actor-training (which she had omitted as part of her education) with her late Russian friends who had started the American Laboratory Theatre in New York City. Nonetheless, it was another studio altogether that was of interest to the Committee.

Tavenner asked if, while in Hollywood, had she been a member of the Actors' Laboratory, Inc., a non-profit theatrical school founded in 1941. Was she "affiliated with it in any way?" he wanted to know.

What was so important about this non-profit institution that constituted Tavenner's query? Founded by actor Roman Bohnen and other former members of the Group Theatre now working in Hollywood, the Actors' Laboratory was a loose association of some 250 members who volunteered as professional artists to pass along their training and experience to younger artists in an effort to elevate the standards of the craft and to serve the theater community. With the Japanese attack on Pearl Harbor, the Lab's mission had expanded to include sending troupes to entertain military servicemen. In the postwar years, the Lab added a workshop to re-train and showcase veteran-actors under the G.I. bill. Productions performed by casts of veteran-actors were *A Bell for Adano*, directed by John Garfield; *Volpone*, directed by Morris Carnovsky; and *Awake and Sing*, directed by J. Edward Bromberg.

In 1947, the Actors' Lab came under the scrutiny of state senator Jack B. Tenney, who headed California's Fact-Finding Committee on Un-American Activities (known as the Tenney committee), which was authorized by the legislature to investigate subversive activities. Tenney converted his committee into a HUAC clone and produced a committee report, bound in iconic red, containing hundreds of names of "subversives" in the film industry. At the time, the Lab's executive board was comprised of Roman Bohnen, J. Edward Bromberg, Morris Carnovsky, Rose Hobart, Sam Levene, Art Smith, Mary Tarcai, and John E. Vernon. The majority had been cornerstones of the Group Theatre and three were featured in *Red Channels*—J. Edward Bromberg, Morris Carnovsky, and Rose Hobart.

That year, Tenney's committee subpoenaed the entire board of this so-called "Communist-front organization." A fire storm erupted. Insisting that the Actors' Lab was a craft organization and not a political organization, the board sent a memorandum to the film industry notifying them of the subpoenas and saying, "We will not enter into a mud-slinging contest with Jack Tenney . . . However, we stand on our record as a free theater and an acting school approved for veterans. . . . For the record, Jack Tenney is out to stifle free theater and smear its proponents." The memo invited members of the industry to join as signatories in support of the Actors' Lab.

Sixty-five artists signed an advertisement supporting the Lab against the smear campaign and intimidation tactics of the Tenney committee. The ad appeared in Los Angeles newspapers and pointed with some irony to the fact that the committee's investigators had uncovered "evidence" that the Lab had produced two plays by a Russian named Anton Chekhov. (These two one-acts by the nineteenth-century playwright were *The Bear* and *The Evils of Tobacco*.) Anne Revere's name was among the sixty-five.

Sometime later, she remarked that "the Actors' Lab and I were at odds for years."[23] Nevertheless, she took the Fifth to avoid answering questions about the other sixty-four signatories or those artists associated with the Actors' Laboratory. Revere had worked in films with at least four—Roman Bohnen, Morris Carnovsky, Lee J. Cobb, and John Garfield.[24]

Like all witnesses appearing before the Committee, Anne Revere arrived with a prepared statement. Nine questions into the hearing, Tavenner queried her about the Actors' Laboratory and she delivered her statement:

ANNE REVERE: Mr. Tavenner and gentlemen, this would seem to me, based upon my observation in the course of the week in which I have listened to these testimonies, to be the first in a possible series of questions which would attempt in some manner to link me with subversive organizations; and as the Communist Party is a political party—legal political party—in this country today, and as I consider any questioning regarding one's political views or religious views as a violation of the rights of a citizen under our Constitution, and as I would consider myself, therefore, contributing to the overthrow of our form of government as I understand it if I were to assist you in violating this privilege of mine and other citizens of this country, I respectfully decline to answer this question on the basis of the fifth amendment, possible self-incrimination, and also the first amendment.[25]

Tavenner was not to be deterred. "Miss Revere," he said, "the committee is in possession of information to the effect that you were the holder of a Communist Party registration card for the year 1945, bearing the number 47346, and that you also held a card for the year 1944, which bore the number 46947. Is that correct?"

Anne Revere asked to see one of the cards. Handing a card to her, Tavenner queried, "Do you recognize that card?" She studied the card, conferred with her attorney, and returned the card without comment. Although she would have known that the card number did not belong to her and that the card was bogus, she remained silent to avoid self-incrimination.[26] Instead, she resorted to an unfriendly reply,

As this would in effect constitute an answer to a question which I have already declined to answer for the reasons given, namely, that it is an invasion of the privileges and rights of a citizen, I would respectfully decline to answer this question on the basis of possible self-incrimination. However, I do not—.

Chairman Wood interrupted, "Do you refuse to answer for that reason?" When Revere replied in the affirmative, her lawyer, R. Lawrence Siegel, asked to consult with her. After a pause in the proceedings, Tavenner once more addressed her membership in the Communist Party. "Miss Revere, the Committee also has information in the form of sworn testimony [Larry Parks's statement] that you were a member of the Communist Party in Hollywood. Do you desire to either affirm or deny that statement?" Again, she declined to answer. Wood intervened to assess the basis upon which she was refusing to answer. She reaffirmed that she was refusing to answer on the basis of possible self-incrimination and her Fifth Amendment rights. Tavenner was not to be deflected.

MR. TAVENNER: Have you at any time been a member of the Communist Party?

MISS REVERE: It would seem to me, Mr. Tavenner, that that is another—.

MR. WOOD: Just answer or decline to answer.

MISS REVERE: I decline again, on the grounds previously stated.

MR. TAVENNER: Are you a member of the Communist Party at this time?

MISS REVERE: That I also respectfully decline to answer, for the same reasons.

Tavenner tried another line of pursuit that added her husband's name to the record. "The name Ann [sic] Revere is your professional name, is it not?" Tavenner asked. "It is my professional name," she replied. "It is also the name which I was baptized with in the Presbyterian Church of Westfield, New Jersey," she added.

MR. TAVENNER: Have you been married?
MISS REVERE: I am at present married: yes.
MR. TAVENNER: What is your husband's name?
MISS REVERE: Samuel Rossen [sic].[27]
MR. TAVENNER: When were you married?
MISS REVERE: 1935; April 11.

Having documented that the couple was married during the years of her presumed membership in the Communist Party and also during the period of her likely association with the Actors' Laboratory, Tavenner ended the hearing. She tried to add to her testimony but Chairman Wood excused her in mid-sentence.

Newspaper headlines on April 18, 1951, effectively changed Revere's situation in Hollywood. "Ann Revere, 2 Writers Refuse Red Query Reply," blared the headline in the New York *Daily News*. The article continued, "Character actress Ann [sic] Revere and two Hollywood writers today refused to tell the House Un-American Activities Committee whether they have been Communists."[28]

Revere returned from Washington, D.C., to her residence in Beverly Hills and proceeded to resign from the board of directors of the Screen Actors Guild (SAG). The announcement, carried by the *New York Times*, attributed Revere's resignation to the fact that during her hearing she had refused on grounds of self-incrimination to answer questions regarding alleged membership in the Communist Party.[29] Moreover, her silence on Capitol Hill barred her from any future work in films because the studios had decreed that those who stood on the Fifth Amendment forfeited their rights to work in the industry. In effect, she reasoned that her continuing presence on the SAG board would only bring harm to the union.[30]

Hollywood Variety carried her explanation:

I resigned from the Board of the Screen Actors Guild because the (motion picture) producers have in effect decreed that those who stand upon the Fifth Amendment shall forfeit their rights to work in the industry. The Board was interested in knowing why I had signed a non-Communist Affidavit in 1948. My reply was as follows: "I am not now a member of the

Communist Party nor was I in 1948. I should have preferred to testify that I had never held a party card which they alleged to be mine and which had been so carelessly concocted as to carry an incorrect address.

However, a recent Supreme Court ruling imposes the risk of a contempt citation involving a possible fine and jail sentence upon those who choose to answer some questions and decline to answer others.[31]

With the stubborn tenacity of her revolutionary ancestors, she later excoriated the SAG board for sanctioning the blacklist. Within two years of her resignation, she wrote a letter attacking the board's ineffectual seven-year fight against the Communist conspiracy. "What have you accomplished?" she wrote. "You have sanctioned the blacklisting of your fellow members because they chose to defy an unconstitutional investigation into their thoughts and beliefs."[32]

Revere was not alone in her condemnation of the trade union. Actress Gale Sondergaard, wife of Herbert Biberman of the Hollywood Ten and famous as Hollywood's Spider Woman, wrote to the Screen Actors Guild on the eve of her first appearance before the HUAC, one month before Revere's hearing. She asked the board to denounce the Committee's attempt to intimidate witnesses and to say "that it will not tolerate any industry blacklist against any of its members who see fit to avail themselves of the privilege against self-incrimination" which the U.S. Supreme Court had established as a barrier to political and religious persecution. Even though the board had passed an anti-blacklist resolution, they acted with timidity and denied her request, with the codicil that its members "totally reject" the Communist Party line that HUAC was in the "witch-hunting" business.[33]

Gale Sondergaard (née Edith Holm Sondergaard) testified on March 21, 1951, with two other witnesses—Larry Parks and Howard Da Silva. She took the Fifth when asked about her knowledge of Communists among the SAG membership. When invited to answer the sixty-four dollar question, "Are you a member of the Communist Party at this time or have you ever been a member of the Communist Party?" she again refused comment. Even when chief counsel Tavenner confronted her with a Communist Party card in her name, she refused to blink.[34]

Anne Revere was on the SAG board at the time of Sondergaard's petition and realized that the union feared to tread in the face of Communism's "clear and present danger" to the American people. This knowledge informed her choice to resign from the board following her testimony.

In June of 1953, Revere's name surfaced in the testimony of one of her colleagues whom she had tried to protect two years earlier. Lee J. Cobb, most notable on stage and in film as Willy Loman in *Death of a Salesman*, testified in a private hearing in Hollywood's Roosevelt Hotel. As a cooperative witness, the actor testified that he had joined the Communist Party in 1940, or perhaps 1941, and named Morris Carnovsky and Phoebe Brand as recruiting him into the party when they were all working with the Group Theatre in New York. Cobb also volunteered twelve names of Communist Party members in Hollywood in 1943, including Anne Revere, Larry Parks, and Rose Hobart.[35]

Revere, the down-to-the-earth actress who wore her hair combed into a practical bun, complained to a reporter: "Nobody went to jail because they were Communists. They went to jail for contempt. But the awful thing about the whole bloody era was that whether you answered or didn't, cooperated or not, you were dead in the business."[36]

While her assertion was later contradicted by the post-HUAC careers of Elia Kazan, José Ferrer, Edward G. Robinson, Lee J. Cobb, Lillian Hellman, and Jerome Robbins, Anne Revere was not a director, playwright, or leading actor. She was a character actress employed in *supporting* roles—a useful actress but not irreplaceable. Moreover, she rarely appeared in the celebrity spotlight until awards were handed out. Unlike Judy Holliday and Lillian Hellman, she had not sustained both a film *and* stage career in the forties. When "everything fell apart in Hollywood" in her estimation, it took Revere seven years to reestablish herself on Broadway.[37]

Reminiscing about those lost years, she told columnist Rex Reed, "I don't know what my life would've been like without the blacklist. . . . Maybe, if I had stayed on in Hollywood, I would have fit into the new studioless structure, but it wouldn't have been the same as the golden years of Hollywood."[38]

Without film work, Revere struggled to remain a viable artist whose work addressed the times. She turned to the theater in Los Angeles and performed Arthur Miller's *The Crucible*, a modern parable of an earlier witch-hunt. She then toured with readings of the script for the controversial film *Salt of the Earth*, written by blacklisted screenwriters Paul Jarrico and Michael Wilson and directed by Herbert Biberman, one of the Hollywood Ten.

Salt of the Earth, a pro-union documentary depicting the strike of the Empire Zinc miners and the lives of Mexican American miners, was made between 1952 and 1955 with the miners and their wives and blacklisted artists. The film was unofficially censored and effectively suppressed by an anti-Communist network ranging from the International Alliance of Theatrical Stage Employers to the Immigration and Naturalization Service. Ellen Schrecker observed that few people ever got to see the independent film, which looked seriously at "racial issues, male chauvinism, and the problems of organized labor."[39]

Congressman Donald L. Jackson, a member of HUAC from California, condemned *Salt of the Earth* on the floor of the U.S. House of Representatives as Communist propaganda whose purpose was "to inflame racial hatreds" in the United States. The *Daily Worker* joined in the fray and praised it as "the trade union film that they couldn't stop."[40] Anne Revere made an effort to get attention for the film in the best way that she knew how—by performing the script. She toured as a blacklisted actress giving readings of the film script created by blacklisted artists.

The FBI was so incensed by Revere's public readings of *Salt of the Earth* during 1953 and 1954 that the Los Angeles office recommended for a third time that her name be placed on the Security Index.[41] With the approval of the FBI director, the Special Agent in Charge of the Los Angeles office followed up on September 10, 1954 and filed a Security Index card for "Anne Revere Rosen, née: Anne Revere, Mrs. Samuel Rosen." In support of this action, the agent cited her Communist Party membership during the first half of the 1940s, her refusal to discuss her activities before HUAC, and her active support of nine Communist-front organizations, including the Actors' Laboratory.[42]

The FBI continued to monitor the actress as a C-class security matter. Then, in 1957, the Los Angeles office expanded its rationale for retaining Revere's index card. They based their findings on her participation the previous year as a speaker at two meetings of the Citizens Committee to Preserve American Freedoms, a "Communist-front" group. Most persuasive, however, was her role as one of twenty-three plaintiffs who appealed to the U.S. Supreme Court for review of their case against the film studios for "alleged black-listing."[43]

Daily Variety carried the headline "Red Probe—Defiant 23 Appeal to High Court."[44] The twenty-three petitioners (film actors, writers, and other industry employees) lost their appeal in the California district court of appeals in June. The group had sued for punitive damages on the grounds that they had been blacklisted by the studios after refusing to testify before HUAC.[45] The Supreme Court's ruling determined that the plaintiffs did not have "specific contracts or expectations of contracts" with the companies named in the legal brief. In another part of the opinion, the Court opined that the film companies had made it a condition of employment that a person shall not have invoked his or her "constitutional privilege" before the congressional committees. In effect, the Court upheld the Waldorf Statement.

Exonerated

Embittered by the Hollywood scene, the Rosens relocated to New York City in 1957 and purchased a three-story brownstone at 315 West 104th Street. Continuing their surveillance, the FBI queried the building's staff, residents, and neighbors about the couple's activities. They conferred with the Department of Motor Vehicles to check the registration of a 1950 Chevrolet station wagon with California license plates parked in front of the brownstone.[46]

Using various pretexts, agents telephoned neighbors to obtain information about the couple.[47]

Nevertheless, the FBI did not formally interview Anne Revere. The New York office contemplated interviewing her but rejected the idea for the same reason they declined to interview Lillian Hellman. Why invite unfavorable publicity?" they reasoned.[48] Once Revere appeared in *Toys in the Attic* to spectacular reviews and an Antoinette Perry (Tony) award for best supporting actress, the Bureau determined to avoid her altogether:

> It is believed that due to her current appearance in *Toys in the Attic* she is in a position to command space in newspapers; it is felt that based on her uncooperative attitude with HCUA [sic] she would not be cooperative with the Bureau, and is in a position to possibly embarass [sic] the Bureau.[49]

By 1960, the FBI's confidential informants had run dry; they provided "no pertinent information concerning the subject."[50] Given the absence of information, the New York office concluded in April of 1960 that Anne Revere warranted no further surveillance or the retention of her name in the New York office's Security Index. (The Los Angeles office had transferred her SI card to the New York office in February of 1958.) "Her detention in the event of an emergency is not justified," the Bureau concluded.[51] On April 17, 1961, exactly ten years after her hearing, the New York office closed the 325-page file, number 100–33672.

Nevertheless, the tentacles of the blacklist were not so easily set aside. Four years later, when director Joseph A. Hardy invited Revere to join the cast of ABC's daytime television series *A Time for Us*, her agent told him that he might find it difficult to employ the actress because of her previous blacklisting. At her agent's prompting, she presented a sworn affidavit to ABC's legal department in an effort to counter objections about her casting.[52] The statement addressed her past and present political affiliations and beliefs, including her brief wartime membership in the Communist Party: "It was a rather loose association which I terminated voluntarily in 1945 or 1946, as soon as the war was over." Inviting understanding and restitution for herself as a viable and patriotic artist, Revere stopped short of an apology for having been a member of the Communist Party—USA, a legal organization at the time, and asserted that she had never been a card-carrying member of the Communist Party.

"I had always refused to accept a Party card," she wrote, "because of the reservations that abraded me when I joined. In fact . . . I considered myself a liberal reformer who had joined the Communist Party in order to bring about desirable social ends that would make this the best of all possible worlds."[53]

ABC's legal department approved her employment, and she worked for months on the series playing a doctor's mother. She told an interviewer who questioned her at the time about her blacklisting, "I've talked about it until I am tired of hearing myself, and I expect those listening are tired, too. I am very glad to be back working and hope to continue."[54] She lived another twenty-five years.

Postscript

Anne Revere learned to her deepest regret that 1951 was an aggressive year for the House Committee on Un-American Activities. She was not alone. Larry Parks, Sterling Hayden, Howard Da Silva, John Garfield, Gale Sondergaard, Morris Carnovsky, and José Ferrer were subpoenaed in the reopened war on Hollywood's "subversives." As friendly witnesses, Larry Parks named seven Hollywood artists, including Anne Revere and Gale Sondergaard, as members of a West coast Communist Party cell; Sterling Hayden named, among others, actors Howard Da Silva and Lloyd Gough; and, after waffling for two sessions, José Ferrer named his Broadway director of *Othello,* Margaret Webster, who had invited him to send a congratulatory telegram to the Moscow Art Theatre on the occasion of its fiftieth anniversary.[55]

The year 1952 was also an active one for the Committee, who brought stage and screen celebrities Abe Burrows, Elia Kazan, Jerome Robbins, Clifford Odets, Edward G. Robinson (for a third time), and Lillian Hellman into the witness chair in the Old House Office Building. Kazan's appearance in January and again in April was pivotal to the argument of the moral rectitude of the friendly versus the unfriendly witness and created a political divide between his detractors on the one hand and his supporters on the other, who felt he had made a difficult decision in the betrayal of the Group Theatre's Communist unit. Regardless of the arguments made and positions taken, Revere pronounced them all dead in the business.

Unlike her Hollywood cohorts, Hellman refused to cut her conscience to fit the day's political fashions and walked away assisted by her lawyer's quick-handed ploy to get her now-famous letter written to the Committee's chairman into the hands of the press. She returned to Broadway to restage *The Children's Hour* and write her last original play, *Toys in the Attic,* which gave Anne Revere her final Broadway role.

Hellman's dodging and weaving in the hearing room set a standard for congressional defiance and witness equivocations matched only by Dorothy Parker's vehement denunciations outside the halls of Congress. As unfriendly and contentious women, these two writers personified modern emblems of Scylla and Charybdis that, when closely encountered, held out certain dangers for the McCarthyites. Like the ancient signs, it was difficult to avoid the defiance of one woman without encountering the opposition of the other.

As national director of the Federal Theatre Project, Hallie Flanagan
Davis testifies before the Special House Committee on Un-American
Activities, known as the Dies committee for its chairman Martin Dies,
Texas Democrat, 1938. Courtesy of Bonnie Nelson Swartz, producer of "Who Killed the
Federal Theatre?" and Ira H. Klugerman of the Educational Film Center.

Judy Holliday as Billie
Dawn in the 1946 produc-
tion of Garson Kanin's
Born Yesterday. Photograph
Vandamm Studio. Used by
permission of the Billy Rose
Theatre Division, the New York
Public Library for the Performing
Arts, Astor, Lenox, and Tilden
Foundations.

Mady Christians as Sara Müller in Lillian Hellman's *Watch on the Rhine*, 1941. Photograph Vandamm Studio. Used by permission of the Billy Rose Theatre Division, the New York Public Library for the Performing Arts, Astor, Lenox, and Tilden Foundations.

Anne Revere in her "testifying dress" before the House Committee on Un-American Activities, 1951. Photograph by Marcus Blechman in the Museum of the City of New York, Theatre Collection. Used by permission of the Billy Rose Theatre Division, the New York Public Library for the Performing Arts, Astor, Lenox, and Tilden Foundations.

Playwright Lillian
Hellman speaking
at an artist's rally at
Carnegie Hall, New
York City, 1942. Photo-
graph by Herbert Gehr. Used
by permission of Time and
Life Pictures/Getty Images.

Writer Dorothy Parker
as shown in 1944. Photo-
graph used by permission of
AP/Wide World Photos.

Margaret Webster directing *Othello* with Paul Robeson and Uta Hagen, 1944. Photograph by Eileen Darby. Used by permission of the Billy Rose Theatre Division, the New York Public Library for the Performing Arts, Astor, Lenox, and Tilden Foundations.

Uta Hagen as Saint Joan in the 1951 Theatre Guild production directed by Margaret Webster. Used by permission of the Billy Rose Theatre Division, the New York Public Library for the Performing Arts, Astor, Lenox, and Tilden Foundations.

Kim Hunter as Stella Kowalski in the Warner Brothers Pictures film of *A Streetcar Named Desire* by Tennessee Williams, 1951. Used by permission of the Billy Rose Theatre Division, the New York Public Library for the Performing Arts, Astor, Lenox, and Tilden Foundations.

God forgives those who invent what they need.

—Lillian Hellman

I am not a traitor and I will not be involved in this obscene inquisition.

—Dorothy Parker

5 The Defiant Ones: Lillian Hellman and Dorothy Parker

Lillian Hellman called the political decade of the witch-hunting fifties *scoundrel time,* and Dorothy Parker likened the fear spread by the committees to the contagion of the Black Plague.[1] The two writers had been friends since the early thirties from the moment in a Hollywood bar when Parker knelt at the feet of novelist Dashiell Hammett, Hellman's lover, and declared her undying devotion to the writer of *The Thin Man.* Shortly thereafter, these accomplished, acerbic, hard-drinking, no-nonsense women shared their radical politics, their anti-fascist causes, their notoriety as alleged Communist Party members, and their defiance of government witch-hunts. Their politics in the thirties brought them a decade of discontents in the fifties. Parker named one of her pieces for the *New Yorker* "a terrible day tomorrow"—an apt description of their McCarthy years.

In 1952, Hellman, a southerner originally from New Orleans, appeared before the House Committee on Un-American Activities wearing a black and brown silk Pierre Balmain original (she called it her "testifying dress") purchased for the occasion. Despite the fact that she was a leading Broadway playwright, author of *The Children's Hour, The Little Foxes,* and *Watch on the Rhine,* Hellman was an unlikely heroine. She had reddish hair, heavy features, a protrusive nose, and a tough way of expressing herself. A blend of rebellious child and stylish southern lady, she stood before the Committee in the knowledge that she would not name names and would likely be sent to prison for contempt. She was one tough lady, and the Committee knew it. The literary world also knew that Dashiell Hammett, in writing *The Thin Man,* had modeled his independent-minded heroine Nora Charles after her.

65

On May 21, 1952, Hellman and her lawyer Joseph E. Rauh Jr. bested the Committee and walked away from the Old House Office Building pursued by a clamorous press. The next day's headlines in the *New York Times* read "LILLIAN HELLMAN BALKS HOUSE UNIT."[2]

Dorothy Rothschild Parker, born into a wealthy Upper West Side family in Manhattan, was twelve years older than the playwright. She was a small woman with dark hair pulled into a bun, with girlish bangs worn across her forehead. She had large, dark eyes and a soft, well-bred voice. She wore black skirts and sweaters with pearls but had a fondness for polka-dot dresses, feather boas, fancy hats, and expensive lingerie. Despite her disdainful attitude toward most people, her close friends knew that the façade masked a vulnerable woman, whose mood swings prompted Alexander Woollcott to call her a combination of Little Nell and Lady Macbeth.[3]

From an early age, Parker, who used her first husband's name throughout her career, mixed cynicism and idealism in her view of the world. Hellman described this wittiest member of the legendary Round Table in the Algonquin Hotel on Forty-fourth Street as "a tangled fishnet of contradictions."[4] By the time they met, Dorothy Parker, known to friends as Dottie and to others as Mrs. Parker, was an established short story writer and poet, whose turn into political activism can be traced to the notorious trial and execution of anarchists Nicola Sacco and Bartolomeo Vanzetti in Boston in 1927 and an unexpected encounter in 1932 with members of the Communist Party—USA among the third-class passengers aboard the luxury liner *Europa*. She was, naturally, traveling first class with her second husband, Alan Campbell, the Gerald Murphys, and Lillian Hellman.

When Parker and Hellman met in Hollywood, both were dyed-in-the-wool activists (some say radicals) who in the forties had devoted their political energies to supporting the Anti-Nazi League, created to marshal the energies (and money) of the Hollywood Left against European fascism and to the founding of a trade union to protect Hollywood writers from exploitation by the studios.

Unlike Hellman's calculated choices, Parker's crusades were freewheeling, on behalf of the poor, the disenfranchised, and the forgotten. In her zeal, she joined more than thirty organizations, contributed money to groups later described as Communist fronts, and permitted leftist groups to use her name on their letterheads in fundraising appeals. As she said in testimony before the New York state legislative committee in 1955, it never occurred to her to ask questions about the origins of the groups or how the contributions were actually spent.[5]

Even though Parker spoke out loud and often against government intrusion into American lives, she skated around the California Tenney committee, the House Committee on Un-American Activities, and McCarthy's investigative subcommittee. They did not subpoena the sharp-tongued, wise-cracking author of *Enough Rope* and *Death and Taxes*. In 1955, she was finally called to account by the New York State Joint Legislative Committee investigating corruption in philanthropies that had doubled as "front" organizations. Hellman offered to go with her to the hearing, but Parker expressed surprise at the offer. "Why, Lilly?" she asked, genuinely puzzled.[6]

Dressed in a smart woolen suit, Tyrolean-style hat, and mink jacket, Mrs. Parker acted before the committee, in Hellman's words, "as she acted so often with their more literate, upper-class cousins at dinner: as if to say, 'Yes dear, it's true that I'm here to observe you, but I do not like you and will, of course, say and write exactly that.'"[7]

A Time of Inquisitions

The year 1952 was a busy one for the House Committee on Un-American Activities. In mid-May, Chairman Wood subpoenaed Lillian Hellman along with other Hollywood screenwriters.

Lillian Florence Hellman had been approaching this moment before HUAC for over forty years. In Hollywood in the thirties and married to writer and press agent Arthur Kober, she began an affair with avowed Marxist Dashiell Hammett that lasted for thirty years. One of the conundrums of the Hellman-Hammett relationship is which one engaged the other in radical politics. An admirer of Marx and Engels and a supporter of the Popular Front—a label for various organizations allied against fascism and racism and favoring Franklin Roosevelt, the New Deal, and the Democratic Party—Hammett most likely set Hellman's political direction. Although the playwright had a more active political history, Hammett was her political tutor and her literary mentor.[8]

In 1933, Dorothy Parker joined with Hellman, Hammett, and others as chief organizers of the first trade union of Hollywood screenwriters, who at the time had no control over what was done with their work and what screen credit they received. Although the highly paid screenwriter of *Nothing Sacred* and *A Star is Born*, Parker found an outlet for her anger and idealism in social causes. Her socialism, rooted in her concerns for the plight of the poor and ignorant against the rich and powerful, appealed to the darker side of her personality.

Four years earlier (in 1934), Parker, responding to the promise of Communism to feed the hungry and clothe the poor, declared herself a Communist.[9] (There is no evidence that she was ever an official member of the Communist Party—USA, or possessed a membership card.) Her friends were baffled by her declaration. As a wealthy screenwriter, her radicalism appeared to many observers as playing revolutionary in a proletarian costume. Her enemies claimed that she was "preaching the pink gospel of Marxism."[10] Nevertheless, Parker's attraction to Communism as a means of opposing international fascism was genuine.

Less baffling were the rumors that Hellman (and Hammett) were Communist Party members. Some called the playwright a "parlor Radical" in an effort to define the dichotomy between her professed views in support of Stalinism and her life style of exquisite clothes, carefully coiffed hair, and expensive mink coats. United with Hammett in an acceptance of the Communist Party—USA, she was labeled a premature anti-fascist and a fellow traveler.

It is likely the duo joined the Communist Party in 1936. By June of that year, Hellman was confidentially urging Earl Browder, the head of the Communist Party—USA, to turn to Hollywood as a source of contributions.[11] Moreover, Hellman's associations with Browder and party theorist V. J. Jerome, her support of "front" organizations (the League of Women Shoppers and the American Council on Soviet Relations), and her signature on the Communist Party's "Open Letter to American Liberals" supporting the defense of Leon Trotsky convinced friends and associates that she was indeed a party member. The matter of her membership surfaced again in screenwriter Martin Berkeley's testimony before HUAC in 1951, when he placed Hellman, Hammett, Parker, and Campbell at a Communist Party meeting in his California home in June 1937. In this instance, Berkeley named all four as "concealed" members at large of the party, meaning they took an oath, paid dues, and took directives in secret from a single individual—either John Howard Lawson in California or V. J. Jerome in New York.[12]

Hellman, a woman of many contradictions that spilled over into her politics, was, nevertheless, a prickly activist. She neglected to sign party-inspired petitions, including the January 22, 1939, telegram to Secretary of State Cordell Hull from "Artists in Hollywood," urging the repeal of the embargo on Spain. She openly supported Stalin and the call by the League of American Writers for "full support of Great Britain and the Soviet Union in their struggle for the demolition of fascism."[13] Moreover, she was labeled a Stalinist when she added her signature to the statement in *New Masses*, published in 1938 and titled "The Moscow Trials: A Statement by American Progressives," defending the Soviet crackdown on dissidents.[14]

Unlike Dashiell Hammett, who never wavered from the party line, Hellman was inconsistent. She remained silent about the Hitler-Stalin anti-aggression pact, and, although concerned about the fate of European Jews, she opposed admitting Jewish refugees fleeing Hitler into Britain and the United States. Throughout her life, Hellman was conflicted about her Jewish heritage, often confirming and denying her Jewishness at different times.

Events in Europe in the late thirties tested the feisty political natures of both women. In Germany, Italy, and Spain, fascism was spreading rapidly and threatening to engulf the world. With President Roosevelt's policies of neutrality regarding the emerging civil war in Spain, the Communists offered, many believed, one of the few coherent programs to oppose fascism. Many in Hollywood joined the Communist Party as the hope for the future. They were soon disappointed as historical events revealed the brutality of Stalin's regime.

In the meantime, Hellman and Parker traveled to France and separately to Spain, which by 1937 had become a "flaming symbol" of the encroachment of fascism.[15] Their convictions about fascism (and Nazism) hardened as they experienced the air raids, destruction, and civilian casualties in Madrid, Barcelona, and Valencia. Acting as a war correspondent, Hellman made broadcasts and filed reports on the carnage, and Parker wrote articles for *New Masses* and the *New Yorker*, drained of her famous wit but not her mordant humor for life's absurdities.[16] In a short time, those sympathizers and contributors to Spain's Loyalist cause and Hollywood's Anti-Nazi League, organized by Dorothy Parker and Donald Ogden Stewart to raise money for victims of Nazism, were smeared with the "Red" label. Martin Dies was already marshalling forces to hold hearings on Communist activities in Hollywood. The congressman expressed his views in a coast-to-coast radio broadcast in August of 1938 that members of the Anti-Nazi League were perhaps themselves not Communists but rather dupes and the organization a creature of "loyal Communist *apparatchiks*."[17]

Hellman was back in New York in 1939 working on a new play with a provocative title suggested by Parker from the *Song of Solomon* about "foxes that spoil the vines." Their dissimilar temperaments were now taking the women down different paths. Hellman, the more disciplined writer, wrote three plays between 1939 and 1944—*The Little Foxes, Watch on the Rhine,* and *The Searching Wind* (dedicated to Dorothy Parker). Practical politics seemed not to interfere with her growing reputation as one of the most important playwrights of the American theater.[18] In contrast, Dorothy Parker, energized by her firsthand view of the plight of the Spanish people, appeared at rallies, gave speeches, and wrote less and less. In remarks at the home of Leon Henderson, New Deal economist, she effectively said farewell to her art. "A humorist in this world is whistling by the loneliest graveyard and whistling the saddest song," she said. "There is nothing funny in the world anymore."[19]

Nevertheless, inspired by Hellman's success, Parker and Campbell decided to write a play for Broadway. In the early twenties, during her flirtation with the stage as drama reviewer for *Vanity Fair, Ainslee's,* and *Life,* Parker had written sketches and lyrics for revues with Robert Benchley, Robert Sherwood, and Heywood Broun and collaborated with Elmer Rice (known for *The Adding Machine*) on *Close Harmony,* a play about suburban lives that closed after twenty-four performances. Stark Young said it was "full of grim gayety, domesticity and dull fates" and held no interest for audiences.[20]

The Happiest Man, adapted from a comedy by the Hungarian playwright Miklos Laszlo, was the story of a clerk at a plumbing supply house who is about to be fired just as he is to be married. Parker used the opportunity to inject Marxist doctrine about capitalist practices into the dialogue spoken by the young office worker, who receives a slip dismissing him at a time when jobs are scarce. Max Gordon agreed to produce the play and then without explanation dropped his option. Parker's radical politics were most likely the unspoken issue in the loss of Gordon's support. As early as 1941, Broadway producers were wary of authors whose left-wing politics surfaced in their plays.

During this period, Alan Campbell suspected that FBI agents were watching them.[21] He was correct. The FBI began compiling files on the couple's activities in September of 1947. Dashiell Hammett always assumed, and rightly so, that the FBI was scrutinizing his and Hellman's activities. The Bureau had created a file on Lillian Florence Hellman six years earlier.[22]

Key Figures

The FBI used the term "key figure" to designate those persons considered active in the Communist Party. The New York office of the FBI determined in 1943 that Hellman was a "key figure." In October, FBI director Hoover instructed the New York office to prepare a comprehensive report on Hellman's birth, citizenship, background, Communist activities and connections. Moreover, Hoover cautioned his agents that the writer was "trouble" and reminded them that the "subject has a national reputation through her writings in which she opposed Nazism and Fascism." He further cautioned that under no circumstances should it be known that the Bureau was investigating her.[23]

Their follow-up report, dated February 4, 1944, assigned file number 100–25858 to "LILLIAN FLORENCE HELLMAN, alias Mrs. Arthur Kober," and included a description of the playwright:

Name	Lillian Hellman
Race	White
Age	39 (born 6/20/05, New Orleans, La.)
Height	5' 3"
Weight	105 lbs.
Hair	Dark blond, sometimes reddish
Eyes	Greenish-grey
Nose	Aqualine
Citizenship	Native-born U.S. citizen
Religion	Jewish
Occupation	Playwright[24]

Within a month, the Special Agent in Charge of the New York office, with the approval of the Washington Bureau, placed Hellman's name on the Security

Index. The FBI created a second case file number, 100–28760, to indicate the reclassified Lillian Hellman as an Internal Security—C matter.[25]

In the mid-forties, Dorothy Parker was tagged as another key figure in the FBI's lexicon. The charitable causes that brought suspicion upon her were three-fold: American–Soviet relations, evacuation of European Jews, and clothing for Spanish refugees fleeing Franco's Spain. She spearheaded drives for books, clothing, and money for war relief agencies. As she took refuge in humanitarian causes, she concluded that her verse was "terribly dated."[26] Unlike Hellman, with her disciplined ability to give speeches *and* write plays on a world threatened by fascism, Parker responded to the world's affairs as a political activist, not as a major writer. When Viking published *The Portable Dorothy Parker* in 1944, critics pointed out that her clever, polished writing "had no very deep roots in human life."[27]

While Hellman was being assessed as a threat to national security, Dorothy Parker was in a quandary in Hollywood. It was rumored that she was blacklisted. ("Well, I was told so—how the hell do I know?" she fumed.[28])

Hollywood was on edge in 1947. As a result of the HUAC trials of the Hollywood Ten and the Waldorf Statement adopted by the studio heads, a chill descended over the film community. Sensitive to the mood of the public and fearful of boycotts, the studios compiled a list of more than three hundred names of writers, directors, and actors suspected of being Communists. Unless they cleared their names in some vague process of cleansing, they were unemployable. Dorothy Parker's name was among the three hundred.[29] She was, indeed, blacklisted.

Parker adopted an angry defiance as the only sane response to the growing hysteria.[30] She continued to speak at rallies and fundraisers. In 1947, she addressed a rally to raise money for the defense of composer Hanns Eisler. In her speech, she condemned the "shameful persecution" of the German anti-fascist refugee and vilified HUAC, saying that she was there to "damn the souls" of the Committee and its chairman J. Parnell Thomas.[31]

Newspapers reported her remarks the next day along with the information that HUAC planned to subpoena her.[32] No subpoena, or pink slip, arrived at her door. She joined the campaign to abolish HUAC, characterizing the Committee as "a bunch of fools." "For Heaven's sake, children, Fascism isn't coming—it's here," she shouted in defiance. "It's dreadful. Stop it!"[33]

Three seismic shocks rattled Parker's world between 1948 and 1951. First, her name was included in the fourth biennial report of the California State Senate Committee on Un-American Activities (better known as the Tenney committee). Then, her name emerged in the Tenney hearings held in Los Angeles to investigate Communist-front groups in California, including the Hollywood Anti-Nazi League, the Screen Writers Guild, the Actors' Laboratory Theatre, and the Congress of American Women.[34]

Parker was named during Florence Eldridge's hearing, in which the actress was queried about the Hollywood Anti-Nazi League, formerly the Anti-Nazi League. Chief counsel R. W. Combs wanted to know who was in charge of the organization. "Was it Mr. Herbert Biberman?" he asked. Eldridge replied,

> He was on the Board. Originally, I believe we started with Dorothy Parker, Donald Odgen Stewart, a group of people who met with a man [Otto Katz] who came from the German underground and who told us of the courageous work being done there under Hitler and of their efforts to save the victims of Hitler's oppression.[35]

Dorothy Parker was of no interest to Combs. Communist influence was the heart of the matter, but Eldridge was firm in her insistence that she and her husband (actor Fredric March) were committed anti-Nazis. March was more forthcoming in his testimony, but neither implicated Parker further. Nevertheless, accusations swirled around Parker. During the espionage trial of Judith Coplon, a political analyst for the Justice Department accused of stealing government secrets to aid the Soviet Union, a document that named Dorothy Parker and Edward G. Robinson as traitors was read aloud to the court.[36] Interviewed during the Coplon trial, Parker's response was straightforward. She was acquainted with no Russians—but wished she was—and had no plans to sell them secrets, for the simple reason that she knew none.[37]

In 1950, Parker was listed in *Red Channels* as a writer and versifier with nineteen pro-Communist citations. The same year, the FBI included her as one of four hundred concealed Communists based on information provided by informant Louis Budenz.

By 1951, Parker was clearly under FBI scrutiny. An FBI memorandum titled "Evidence of Communist Party Membership and Affiliation" detailed her activities reaching as far back as 1937 as a contributor to the Communist movement and as a Communist Party member. Agents collated materials from newspapers, magazines, and informants. For instance,

> *Time* magazine in it publication of January 6, 1941, in an article on "The Revolt of the Intellectuals," describes Dorothy Parker as an ally of the Communists in 1938 although not a Communist herself. She among others was described as a fellow traveler who wanted to help fight Fascism.

> The *Washington Times Herald* of September 8, 1941, carried an article saying that Congressman Martin Dies had accused Leon Henderson, director of the Office of Price Administration, of being a Communist. He

referred to Henderson's argument with a photographer at his home when the photographer tried to take a photograph of a nationally prominent Communist. The article said that Henderson identified the Communist as being Dorothy Parker.

[Name deleted] said that he had been advised by [name deleted] that Dorothy Parker had broken all her ties with the Communist Party.[38]

In April of 1951, the Bureau was investigating Parker to classify her as a concealed Communist eligible for a Security Index card. She received a visit from two agents conspicuous in dark hats and suits who arrived on her doorstep in West Los Angeles wanting to know about her ties with the Communist Party. She denied having been affiliated with, having donated to, or having been contacted by representatives of the party. When asked about her associations with Lillian Hellman, Dashiell Hammett, and Donald Ogden Stewart, she advised that she was personally acquainted with them but denied any knowledge that they were Communist Party members or that she had attended party meetings with them. She did confirm her associations with the Joint Anti-Fascist Refugee Committee, the Hollywood Anti-Nazi League, and other groups.

Throughout the interrogation, Parker's silver-colored poodle kept barking and jumping on the agents. When asked if she had conspired to overthrow the government of the United States, she was quick to inform them, "Listen, I can't even get my dog to stay down. Do I look to you like someone who could overthrow the government?"[39]

Following the interview, she expressed "only monumental scorn" for the Bureau.[40] At this time, the FBI made no recommendation to order a Security Index card in Parker's name.[41] Four years later agents would again visit her in an effort to document the writer's ongoing threat to national security.

A Troublesome Dilemma

FBI informants continued to provide information on Hellman's activities during the years leading up to her appearance before HUAC in 1952. In February, when the witch-hunting was most virulent, Hellman was handed a subpoena at her New York townhouse on East Eighty-second Street.[42] Over a period of five months, HUAC called five stage and film celebrities. With the exception of Hellman, the others proved, not without varying degrees of angst, friendly witnesses.

Hellman's behavior before and during the hearing has been thoroughly reprised by biographers and historians, in particular the circumstance surrounding her famous statement on fashion and conscience. What is important here is Hellman's reluctance to take the Fifth and her lawyer's strategy for her case.

When she received the subpoena, she called Abe Fortas (later a U.S. Supreme Court justice) of the Washington law firm of Arnold, Fortas, and

Porter. According to Hellman's account in *Scoundrel Time*, Fortas came to her townhouse and recommended that she take a moral position before the Committee and not depend upon the legalities of the Fifth, which were not playing well with Committee members or with the American public. He recommended that Hellman testify about herself, answer all questions about her life, but not give names or information about anyone else. Unable to represent her at the hearing (he was already representing Owen Lattimore, a China scholar accused by McCarthy of being a Russian agent), Fortas put her in touch with Joseph L. Rauh Jr. Although politically well to the left, Rauh had no use for Communism or the Communist Party. The choice of Rauh, a civil libertarian and founder of the Americans for Democratic Action, a group of New Deal democrats that excluded Communists, had the potential for sending a large signal to the Committee.[43]

Hellman presented Rauh with three conditions: She would not be a friendly witness and name names; she did not want to plead the Fifth and appear cowardly; and she wanted to avoid jail time. Faced with the perilous course proposed by his client, Rauh arranged a delay for Hellman's appearance. In the meantime, he met with Frank Tavenner Jr., chief counsel for the Committee, to explore what interested the Committee about his client only to learn that they had sworn testimony that Hellman had been a member of the Communist Party and they expected her to name names. Rauh failed to negotiate a middle ground. The meeting broke up on the note that "Miss Hellman was a maverick and they would be as nice as they could but there was no way of avoiding naming other people."[44]

Following the meeting, Rauh set his client the task of detailing her political history to be used as a formal statement during the hearing. In an early draft, Hellman admitted to being a party member between 1938 and 1940. Rauh was not troubled by this admission because he believed that Hellman had never been under the *discipline* of the Communist Party.[45] In the second draft, she rephrased her admission: "I joined the Communist Party in 1938 with little thought as to the serious step I was taking." "I am not a political person," she added, "and have no place in a political organization."[46]

Rauh was concerned about the language and tone of the letter. Not only had his client confessed to being a party member, but, in his view, she offered little criticism of the Communist Party—USA. She would likely come across in the hearing as endorsing the party. To resolve the dilemma, Rauh collaborated in the writing of the final draft. In truth, Joseph Rauh was the author of Hellman's famous statement, addressed to Chairman Wood and dated May 19, 1952, except for the one quotable sentence about conscience and fashion that was Hellman's: "I cannot and will not cut my conscience to fit this year's fashions even though I long ago came to the conclusion that I was not a political person and could have no comfortable place in any political group."[47]

Responding for the Committee the following day, Wood advised that HUAC would not enter into negotiations with witnesses to set forth the terms under which they would testify. The stage was now set for Hellman's appearance in Washington.

On May 21, accompanied by Joseph Rauh and his assistant Daniel Pollitt, Hellman walked into the hearing room as a celebrated artist—stylish, eloquent, defiant—and prepared to create a political drama with herself as the central figure.

Hellman answered the perfunctory questions about her place of birth, current residence, formal education, occupation, and employment.[48] Then Tavenner struck with the name of Martin Berkeley and proceeded to read into the record portions of his testimony that placed the "very excellent playwright" at a Communist Party meeting in his home. If Hellman admitted knowing Berkeley, it could be construed as an admission that she had been a party member. She would then be compelled to talk about others not already known to the Committee. Hellman counter-punched:

MISS HELLMAN: I would very much like to discuss this with you, Mr. Tavenner, and I would like at this point to refer you to my letter. . . .

For the first time Chairman Wood spoke. "In order to clarify the record, Mr. Counsel, at this point would it be wise to put into the record the correspondence that has been had between the witness and me as chairman of the committee, pertaining to her letter."

Tavenner produced Hellman's letter, dated May 19, 1952, and the chairman's reply of May 20 and made the documents exhibits one and two.

At this point Rauh leaped into action and became the hero of the hour. He directed Daniel Pollitt to hand out copies of Hellman's letter to the press. Noticing reporters passing copies among themselves, Tavenner wanted to know who was disseminating the papers. Rauh was quick to acknowledge that he had directed copies to be passed around the room. "I thought you had accepted them in the record and that was proper," he explained. "I am sorry if I had done anything that was not proper."

Realizing he has made a strategic error, John Wood tried to salvage the situation: "it is my view that in the function of this committee we cannot be placed in the attitude of trading with the witnesses as to what they will testify to, and that is the substance of my reply which is in the record and which should be read publicly now, in view of the fact that the witness has been circulating them among the press." Tavenner reluctantly read aloud Hellman's letter and the chairman's reply. Nevertheless, the damage was done. The reporters had in hand the witness's reasoned arguments.

I am most willing to answer all questions about myself. I have nothing to hide from your committee and there is nothing in my life of which I am ashamed. I have been advised by counsel that under the fifth amendment I have a constitutional privilege to decline to answer any questions about my political opinions, activities, and associations, on the grounds of self-incrimination. I do not wish to claim this privilege. I am ready and willing to testify before representatives of our Government as to my own opinions and my own actions, regardless of any risks or consequences to my self. . . .

I am prepared to waive the privilege against self-incrimination and to tell you everything you wish to know about my views or actions if your Committee will agree to refrain from asking me to name other people. If the Committee is unwilling to give me this assurance, I will be forced to plead the privilege of the Fifth Amendment. . . .[49]

Proceeding as though there has been no interruption in his earlier questions about Martin Berkeley's testimony, Tavenner asked if Hellman had attended the meeting in June of 1937 in the screenwriter's home. Hellman refused to answer "on the ground that it might incriminate me."

Hellman had taken the Fifth. Nevertheless, her moral victory was contained in her letter, which was now part of the congressional record and in the hands of the press. Throughout Tavenner's remaining questions, she continued to assert her Fifth Amendment rights.

The most troublesome part of Hellman's testimony was the splitting of hairs over the various years when she may have been a member of the Communist Party. She confirmed that she was not a Communist during the years 1950–1952 but asserted constitutional protection for earlier years.

The dilemma that Rauh had warned about was her unwillingness to name names and her unwillingness to go to jail. Under the law, admission of party membership followed by a refusal to name names assured a contempt citation and a likely jail sentence. Therefore, the better course of valor was to take the Fifth for those years where some proof might surface to contradict her denial and consequently deny her the protection of the Fifth Amendment. As she continued to refuse to answer questions, Tavenner decided to end the questioning that had produced no tainted fruit. The hearing lasted one hour and seven minutes with Hellman testifying for thirty-seven minutes.[50]

Hellman quickly left the hearing room with Daniel Pollitt guiding her.[51] She was hardly the first, or the last, witness to insist that she would talk freely about herself and not about others. Nevertheless, she had articulated her moral repugnance at forcing denunciations of friends and others with greater eloquence and restrained dignity than anyone previously, and certainly few with Hellman's stature. Most importantly, Joseph Rauh had taken quick advantage of Chairman Wood's lapse. Four years later, Rauh represented the equally celebrated playwright Arthur Miller and felt that Miller's refusal to cooperate based upon his rights under the First Amendment was the truly courageous position.[52]

Some commentators surmised that the Committee was wary of Hellman's reputation for speaking out. She had the air of the well-dressed southern lady about her and a reputation for "feisty troublemaking."[53] Indeed, Lillian Hellman brought "big trouble" to the Committee, which suffered its most long-remembered public relations defeat at her hands in the next day's headlines, which blared "LILLIAN HELLMAN BALKS HOUSE UNIT.[54]

Hellman returned to New York in the bitter knowledge that her life had changed. Whatever dignity and honor she had managed to preserve were tarnished by the fact that she had taken the Fifth. Moreover, she was blacklisted and could not work in Hollywood. Nevertheless, she was consumed by the need to generate much-needed income and restore her reputation. To circumvent the two years it would take to write a play, Hellman persuaded Kermit Bloomgarden to produce a revival of *The Children's Hour* and hire her to direct the show. She followed the revival with *The Lark,* the libretto for *Candide,* and *Toys in the Attic* before exiting the theater to write her semi-autobiographical books—*An Unfinished Woman, Pentimento: A Book of Portraits,* and *Scoundrel Time.*

In Hellman's HUAC year, three of her stage and screen cohorts testified as friendly witnesses with different outcomes. Playwright Clifford Odets, author of *Waiting for Lefty* and widely respected by critics on the right and left, refused to kowtow to the Committee's demands that he denounce the Communist Party. In rowdy testimony, he finally turned informer but remained blacklisted by the studios and shunned by colleagues. In contrast, screenwriter Isobel Lennart, actor Edward G. Robinson, and director Elia Kazan cooperated upfront with the Committee and continued to work in Hollywood. Nevertheless, Kazan was reviled by show business liberals in general not so much for his friendly, career-preserving testimony as for his "Statement," a paid advertisement that he wrote and placed in the *New York Times* justifying his testimony in global and historical terms. His biographer asserted that by this ill-considered action his name became in the public's mind synonymous with the celebrity informer who named names.[55]

As token females, Isobel Lennart's strategy stood in sharp contrast to Hellman's. Appearing as a friendly witness, the screenwriter, wife, and mother rationalized that she could testify as a friendly witness and not mention "new" names but give the Committee only names that had been mentioned eight or ten times previously. Moreover, MGM wanted their top screenwriter of such musicals as *East Side, West Side* and *Anchors Aweigh* to testify in order to prove that people could testify favorably (meaning give names) and continue to be employed by the studio. Robinson and Kazan had already proved their case, but a female screenwriter was also desirable.

Lennart became a rank-and-file Communist Party member in 1939 but soon met the anti-Communist John Harding, the *New Leader* columnist, actor, and writer who became her husband. She left the party soon thereafter, as she told the Committee, because of its new postwar militancy. She was subpoenaed in 1951, but she was pregnant and her obstetrician refused to certify that she could appear as a witness without serious danger to her health. Wanting to avoid unfavorable publicity by threatening the life of a pregnant woman, the Committee relented and a year later Isobel Lennart testified the day before Hellman. She named twenty-four people, including the deceased J. Edward Bromberg and several of the Hollywood Ten.[56]

A Fresh Hell

While Hellman was testifying in Washington, Dorothy Parker faced a dilemma in Hollywood. Once listed in *Red Channels* and named by Martin Berkeley before HUAC, she was unemployable as a screenwriter. She was never dismissed from a job, but, by her own admission, she was blacklisted.[57]

A year after Hellman's hearing, Parker read in the *New York Times* that Joseph McCarthy was convening hearings into the purchase of books written by Communists or leftist authors for the State Department's overseas libraries.[58] From the time Dashiell Hammett, Eslanda Robeson (wife of actor-singer Paul Robeson), and Arnaud d'Usseau were brought before McCarthy's investigative subcommittee, Parker expected to be subpoenaed as well.[59]

With the exception of one off-hand remark, she always disputed the charge that she was or had ever been a Communist Party member. Nevertheless, she was associated with the three writers. Parker and Hammett were allies in the Screen Actors Guild and the Civil Rights Congress, and she had spoken at dinners honoring the Robesons. Moreover, the same year that McCarthy launched his attack on overseas libraries and information centers, Parker and d'Usseau combined forces to write *The Ladies of the Corridor*, an unflinching portrait of lonely women living in a residential hotel, a piece that was both admired and rejected by critics. When George Jean Nathan named *The Ladies of the Corridor* the best play of the year, Parker told a journalist that the play was "the only thing I have ever done in which I had great pride."[60]

Anticipating a subpoena, Parker told friends that if McCarthy called her to testify, she would take the Fifth. She agreed with novelist E. M. Forster, who had written that if he were forced to choose between betraying a friend and betraying his country, he hoped he would have the courage to betray his country.[61] Nevertheless, Dorothy Parker was not called upon to betray either her friends or her country. No subpoena arrived, and McCarthy's censure by the Senate in 1954 granted her a reprieve, or so she concluded at the time.

During the early fifties, Parker was unrelenting in her politics and wholly dismissive of repercussions to herself. In 1953, she protested the deportation proceedings of Cedric Belfrage, editor of the *National Guardian*, and appeared at rallies to win amnesty for the Smith Act victims. Moreover, she was unwavering in her support of Paul and Eslanda Robeson and spoke once again at a dinner honoring the couple in October of 1954. During these years she solicited funds as national chairman of the Spanish Refugee Appeal of the Joint Anti-Fascist Refugee Committee.

When Parker's name emerged again that year during the HUAC investigation of radio and television actress Jean Muir, FBI agents appeared at the Volney, on New York's Madison Avenue, where Parker, now twice divorced from Allan Campbell, had taken up residence. The agents found that little had changed since their previous interview in Los Angeles. Surrounded by her two dogs in an apartment crowded with unread review copies of books, un-swept ashtrays, and other detritus of a neglected life, Parker gave the impression of a distracted, nervous woman who was no threat to national security. As she lobbed left-handed a rubber ball from her chair for the poodles to retrieve, she repeated a variation of her earlier defense: "My influence? Look at these two dogs of mine. I can't even influence them."[62]

Despite the many notations detailing her associations with "front" groups for sixteen years (1939–1955), the FBI's Special Agent in Charge of the New York office concluded there was no reliable evidence of Dorothy Parker's party membership, and the recommendation to enter her name in the Security Index was withdrawn.[63]

The subpoena that Dorothy Parker avoided for more than a decade finally arrived in 1955. In late February, the New York State Joint Legislative Committee, investigating the alleged diversion of charitable contributions to the Communist Party by front groups, turned its attention to the Joint Anti-Fascist Refugee Committee and the Civil Rights Congress. The committee had uncovered the fact that the JAFRC had spent "less than ten cents on the dollar" of the money collected on refugee aid.[64] As JAFRC's national chairman, Parker was called to testify on February 25 at the courthouse in lower Manhattan.

Dressed smartly for the hearing, she could not say what happened to the $1.5 million collected by the JAFRC, ostensibly to aid refugees from Franco's Spain. She conceded that she made speeches and signed appeals for funds but had not composed letters nor remembered who asked her to sign solicitations. As national chairman, she had signed checks that, as far as she knew, "were used to help people who were helpless." Moreover, she politely informed the committee that it had never occurred to her to ask if the Communist Party controlled the group or if funds were diverted for other purposes. Management of JAFRC finances was not her function. "My function was to try to help raise money," she explained, "and that was all it was."[65]

Bernard Tompkins, chief counsel for the committee, asked, "Didn't you know, Miss Parker, that the Joint Anti-Fascist Refugee Committee was thoroughly controlled by the Communist Party?"

PARKER: No.
TOMPKINS: You did not know that?
PARKER: No.
TOMPKINS: Did you ever ask?
PARKER: No.
TOMPKINS: It never occurred to you to ask?
PARKER: No.
TOMPKINS: Weren't there people of obvious Communist reputation concerned with the Committee?
PARKER: No.
TOMPKINS: It never occurred to you to ask. The same thing with the Civil Rights Congress?
PARKER: Yes.

When asked about the finances of the Civil Rights Congress (she was on record as a national sponsor), she again denied knowing anything about the group's finances.

TOMPKINS: Did you ever ask in that case whether the money that was raised was actually being used for the purpose that the public was informed it was being raised?
PARKER: No.

Ladylike and demure throughout the hearing, Parker balked at only one question. When asked if she was now or had ever been a member of the Communist Party, she refused to answer on the grounds of possible self-incrimination. E. M. Forster–like, she had protected her friends from the committee's probing questions.

Given Parker's cavalier attitude toward money, these were not uncommon responses. As JAFRC's national chairman, she was ultimately responsible for the use and misuse of the group's funds. Nonetheless, she saw herself as a fundraiser, not a bookkeeper. She had not concerned herself with financial details or with the board's dispersal of funds.[66] This lack of concern for money was characteristic of Parker. Sometimes she had little money; at other times her royalties and screenwriting fees brought her considerable wealth. Most often she claimed, particularly in later years, to be in a state of penury.

As chairman of the Civil Rights Congress, Dashiell Hammett was ensnared in the same legislative net. Two days before her hearing, Hammett testified that the Civil Rights Congress, as far as he knew, had no Communist members, and, even if they did, it would not matter to him. "Communism to me is not a dirty word," the novelist told the joint legislative committee. "When you are working for the advance of mankind it never occurs to you whether a guy is a Communist."[67]

In 1949, as president of the CRC, Hammett had gone to jail for five months rather than give information about the group's contributors, funds, or fugitive members. Six years later, he again took the Fifth.

Shortly after she testified during the JAFRC hearings, the Bureau closed its case file on Dorothy Rothschild Parker. A four-page memorandum concluded that she was not a security risk. "Although the foregoing information reflects CP front activity in the past three years, and the subject could technically qualify for inclusion in the Security Index, it is not felt that she is dangerous enough to warrant her inclusion in same. It is accordingly recommended that she *not* be placed on the Security Index."[68]

Dorothy Parker would not have liked this review. The closure of file number 100–56075 implied that her speechmaking and fundraising were just so much sound and fury—signifying nothing to the federal government.

Parker's last years were marked by failing eyesight, frail health, heavy drinking, and financial uncertainty. As her staunchest friend, Lillian Hellman came to her aid from time to time but stayed only long enough for the crisis to pass. Hellman was retooling her literary interests with *An Unfinished Woman* and found Parker's heavy drinking "dull and repetitive."[69] On one occasion, Hellman, in an act of charity, sold two gifts from Parker—a Utrillo landscape and later a Picasso gouache—and sent her friend the money from the sales but received no acknowledgement of the check for the Picasso in the amount of ten thousand dollars. After Parker's death, uncashed checks were found in a bureau drawer.[70]

On June 7, 1967, Dorothy Parker was found dead of a heart attack in her rooms at the Volney. She was seventy-three. The next morning, her obituary on the front page of the *New York Times* described her as "a disillusioned romantic, all the fiercer because the world spun against her sentimental nature."[71]

Lillian Hellman, whose friendship with Parker had survived for over three decades, spoke at the memorial service of her friend's individuality. "She was

part of nothing and nobody except herself... She was always brave in depriva-
tion, in the chivying she took during the McCarthy days, in the isolation of the
last, bad sick years. The remarkable quality of her wit was that it stayed in no
place, and was of no time."[72]

Despite the eulogies, Mrs. Parker had the last word. Her will, dated February 8, 1965, named Hellman as executrix and assigned her entire estate (about
twenty thousand dollars after expenses) together with copyrights and royalties to the Reverend Martin Luther King Jr., to be passed at his death to the
National Association for the Advancement of Colored People. She had never
met the civil rights leader, but her strong feelings for civil liberties and racial
injustice and for those struggling to secure them in the marches of the early
1960s shaped her last gesture.

Dorothy Parker had been marginalized by the fury of her politics. Moreover, for decades, she deflected her writing talent into political activism—into
speechmaking and fundraising—to hammer home her belief that artists could
make a difference in the struggle against fascism at home and abroad. Her
biographer Marion Meade summed up the dire effects of McCarthyism on the
writer in this way: "The decade-long shadow cast over the country's history by
McCarthyism poisoned Dorothy's personal and professional life and eventually
undermined her spirit."[73]

Other artists from stage and film shared Parker's and Hellman's anger and defiance and, like them, were not intimidated by the powerful conservative forces
opposing them. When faced by the gatekeeper of the U.S. Passport Division,
Lillian Hellman, Arthur Miller, and Paul Robeson were undaunted.

The passport office was a little known federal tool used to curtail the
travels of American citizens suspected of subversive activities. Hellman had
two encounters (1951 and 1953) with the head of the Passport Division, Ruth
B. Shipley, an anti-Communist who routinely denied passports to suspected
Communists. In both instances, Mrs. Shipley was not convinced that Hellman
was a Communist, and the playwright was awarded the required documents
to travel abroad on work-related projects. The actor-singer Paul Robeson and
playwright Arthur Miller were not so fortunate.

In June of 1956, a subcommittee of HUAC, now under the chairmanship
of Francis E. Walter of Pennsylvania, convened hearings on the unauthorized use of American passports as travel documents in furtherance of the
Communist conspiracy. Paul Robeson, an advocate for civil rights for black
Americans and a self-proclaimed Communist sympathizer with a record of
travel to the Soviet Union, was refused a passport in 1950 by the State Department. Thereafter, he challenged the violation of his constitutional rights on
behalf of all Americans.

On June 12, nine days before Arthur Miller's hearing, Robeson loudly protested his rights as an American citizen and invoked the Fifth Amendment thirty-one times, charging the committee toward the end with anti-Americanism: "you gentlemen belong with the Alien and Sedition Acts, and you are nonpatriots, and you are the un-Americans, and you ought to be ashamed of yourselves."[74] Chairman Walter finally dismissed him with a refusal to permit his statement even, without being read, to be entered into the record. Robeson waited eight years for the State Department to grant a new passport. He then lived abroad, mostly in Russia, until 1963. When he returned, he was in ill health and politically and artistically marginalized even by those African Americans whom he had struggled to help for so many years.

When Arthur Miller, author of *The Crucible*, a drama of the Salem trials as thinly-veiled metaphor for the "security trials" of modern Washington, found himself appearing before HUAC in 1956 on a charge of passport violations, he refused to name a writer who had attended a Communist Party meeting of writers a decade earlier. In response to chief counsel Richard Arens's questioning, Miller replied, "I will be perfectly frank with you on anything relating to my activities. I take responsibility for everything I have done, but I cannot take responsibility for another human being."[75] The playwright's risk with protections of the First Amendment was enormous. Over his lawyer's objections, he refused to claim the protections of the Fifth in the belief that he had done nothing against which he needed constitutional protection. For his defiance, he was cited for contempt. He appealed the contempt citation and was eventually fined five hundred dollars and given a thirty-day suspended sentence. In time, a court of appeals reversed the HUAC ruling.

Checkmate

In Hellman's post-HUAC years, her political activities were diminished by Hammett's illness and death (in 1961) and by a flurry of writing for Broadway that ended with *The Autumn Garden*, *Toys in the Attic*, and *My Mother, My Father and Me*. Nevertheless, Hellman's political chicanery revived when she turned to writing her memoirs: *An Unfinished Woman—A Memoir*, *Pentimento: A Book of Portraits*, *Scoundrel Time*, and *Maybe*. When literary critics first detected that Hellman was making prose dramas out of her life, she addressed the subject of creative truth: "What a word is truth. Slippery, tricky, unreliable. I tried in these books to tell the truth, I did not fool with facts."[76]

In time, many commentators (liberal and conservative) attacked Hellman's veracity, her manipulation of truth, her fabulations in the memoirs as they discovered a fabricated childhood friend (Julia) in *Pentimento*, questionable versions of her participation in events in wartime Madrid, Moscow, and Berlin, and mischaracterization of James Wechsler, the editor of the *New York Post*, as a "friendly" witness before HUAC. Nevertheless, it was Hellman's reexamination of the McCarthy period in her cautionary tale, *Scoundrel Time*, that unleashed an unprecedented barrage of outrage and refutation. In the slim volume (121 pages), she charged that American intellectuals had not done enough to combat McCarthyism and consequently were responsible, in part, for the Vietnam War and the presidency of Richard M. Nixon. By the fall of 1977, the hounds were running full-out chasing their wily fox. Irving Howe, Sidney Hook, Hilton Kramer, and Alfred Kazin inveighed against Hellman's hypocrisy, fraud, deliberate obfuscation, and literary meanness.[77]

Hellman responded to the furor with a dramatist's understanding of the power of *silence*. To the astonishment of her detractors, she maintained an impervious *silence*. When she finally appeared in print, it was in a full-page advertisement in national fashion magazines that served as an iconic checkmate to the sound and fury. Photographed wrapped in a Blackglama mink fur coat with cigarette in hand, Lillian Hellman was identified not by name but by the familiar caption, "What becomes a legend most?"

The publication and aftermath of *Scoundrel Time* brought an end to Hellman's encounter with the politics of the McCarthy period. Enduring failing eyesight and frail health, she lived to age seventy-eight in a perpetual state of distress and anger. At various times she threatened lawsuits for insults real and imagined. Four years before her death, she filed a two million dollar libel suit against another McCarthy. Responding to critic and novelist Mary McCarthy's denunciations of her as "terribly overrated, a bad writer and dishonest writer," she launched legal proceedings based upon the attempt by one writer to stifle another writer's freedom of thought and speech.[78] The suit was still in litigation at the time of Hellman's death of cardiac arrest on June 30, 1984, at her home on Martha's Vineyard.

Lillian Hellman had been a contentious presence in the political landscape for thirty-five years. She stood tall before HUAC in a statement of enduring eloquence about fashion and conscience. She dressed for the occasion, scripted her speech, and emerged from the political drama to live another three decades with wealth, celebrity, and literary repute. Her friend, novelist John Hersey, in a moving graveside eulogy at Abel's Hill Cemetery in Chilmark on the Vineyard spoke of her perplexing anger. "Anger was her essence," he said. "It was the rage of the mind against all kinds of injustice—against human injustice and against the unfairness of death."[79]

Unlike the post-HUAC ascendancy of Hellman's reputation, other stellar careers were sidelined by FBI investigations, associations with "Communist-front" organizations, rumors of blacklisting, and congressional subpoenas. Although Dorothy Parker failed to receive the subpoenas threatened by HUAC and Joseph McCarthy's subcommittee, stage director Margaret Webster received a pink slip from the senator in the spring of 1953.

The years of disgrace were upon us, of reckless accusations, of end-
less "smear campaigns," of innuendoes, of that most insidious of
weapons, guilt by association.

—Margaret Webster

6 Guilt by Association: Margaret Webster

Margaret Webster walked down the long corridor of the Old Senate Office Building noisy with reporters who had gathered in response to columnist Walter Winchell's tip that Senator McCarthy had called a well-known theater director and a famous composer as witnesses. Aaron Copland was scheduled to follow Webster as the second witness of the afternoon.

Unlike Lillian Hellman and Dorothy Parker, Margaret Webster was not "sartorially distinguished."[1] For the occasion she wore sensible shoes, a dark tailored suit with matching hat and gloves. As a stage director, she was a behind-the-scenes person interpreting the playwright's words and shaping the production with actors who themselves appeared in the limelight. This day in 1953 was different. Subpoenaed to take the witness chair in a *private* hearing before Joseph R. McCarthy's Senate Permanent Subcommittee on Investigations, she walked the length of the corridor on the arm of Sidney M. Davis, her counsel from the New York firm of Phillips, Nizer, Benjamin, and Krim. She took her place in the hearing room at 2:30 P.M. on the afternoon of May 25.

That spring, McCarthy was juggling two sets of hearings in Washington. Hearings on the State Department Information Service, in particular the Information Centers and Libraries located abroad, brought together such writers as Dashiell Hammett, Langston Hughes, Eslanda Robeson, and Arnaud d'Usseau. Moreover, the senator's inquiries into the State Department Teacher-Student Exchange Program ensnared Margaret Webster and Aaron Copland. In all, the FBI played a pivotal role in providing information to McCarthy on the activities of the witnesses.

Nineteen years later, Margaret Webster wrote about her decade of blacklisting, including inquiries by FBI agents, passport difficulties, joblessness, persecuted friends, and chilling subpoenas. She said that it all began with Actors' Equity, referring to the infamous union election of 1941. In fact, the support of activist causes that brought her to McCarthy's attention began in London where she grew up.

During the First World War, her mother, the actress Dame May Whitty, took up the "good causes," as she called charity work in support of the British war effort. She instilled in her American-born daughter an appreciation for charitable endeavors that supported the marginalized, the economically deprived, and those displaced by wartime events. Similar causes and organizations in the United States during the Second World War became postwar fodder for the anti-Communist campaigns of the Cold War.

The Good Causes

Margaret Webster was born in New York City on March 15, 1905, while her actor-father, accompanied by her mother, was engaged in a British touring production at the New Amsterdam Theatre on Forty-second Street. Their daughter's journey into the witness chair began in the Webster household on Bedford Street, a short walk from St. Paul's Church and Covent Garden.

Known to parents, friends, and colleagues as "Peggy," she began an acting career in London in the 1920s. In 1936, she received a telephone call from friend and actor Maurice Evans that brought her to the United States and a second career as a stage director, which placed her at the forefront of American stage history for more than two decades. Moreover, her newfound celebrity on Broadway as a director of Shakespeare's plays and a new set of wartime causes eventually thrust her into the eye of the hurricane of U.S. politics at mid-century.

At the time Webster launched *Othello* in 1943–44, with the first African American to perform the title role on Broadway, she was being drawn into the political maelstrom of the late forties by her arduous support of liberal causes and war relief agencies. She became the target of witch-hunts and smear campaigns along with her Broadway associates of *Hamlet, Othello*, and *The Tempest*; namely, Mady Christians, Paul Robeson, Uta Hagen, José Ferrer, and Canada Lee.

By 1950, the year the anti-Communist booklet with the red cover was published, Webster, with sixteen citations beneath her name, considered herself ripe for FBI investigation, industry blacklisting, and congressional subpoena. At the time, she was unaware that the FBI had begun compiling file number 100–370937 (Subject: Margaret Webster) two months following the publication of *Red Channels*.

Toil and Trouble

As was the case with many in the entertainment industry, innocent choices during the war years were transformed by congressional investigations in the forties and fifties into sinister, if not criminal, behavior alleged to undermine the sovereignty of the United States. During those years, Webster actively supported the United Service Organizations (USO), the Stage Door Canteen, treasury bond drives, Red Cross drives, British War Relief, and Russian War Relief. Two of the relief agencies and Actors' Equity Association were to cause their supporters a great deal of grief in the early fifties.

Webster attributed her "years of discontents" in the political arena to Actors' Equity.[2] In 1941, the Equity council had invited her to run on the regular ticket for council member. Both the regular and independent tickets were elected but not without resignations and charges that the "Reds" had taken over the actors' union.

Equity's internal quarrels, political factions, and name-calling erupted into headlines again in 1945. Actor-manager Frank Fay demanded an inquiry into the conduct of five Equity members and charged them with participating in a "Red-backed" rally for the Joint Anti-Fascist Refugee Committee in Madison Square Garden during which the Roman Catholic Church was reputedly attacked. There were charges and counter-charges, letters and telegrams that included Fay's allegation that council member Margaret Webster was affiliated with a number of Communist-front organizations.[3]

Webster remained on the Equity council for ten years and resigned when the national political climate suggested that her presence was detrimental to the work of the union.[4] As she described the dispute among Equity's members in response to the Red scare, she remarked, "if any of my fellow members were, in fact, Communists, I can only say that as actors they were brilliant, and as minions of the U.S.S.R. totally and utterly useless."[5]

In truth, the anti-Red tide was rising in the New York-based entertainment industry. The same week Actors' Equity censured Frank Fay, the House Committee on Un-American Activities began its probe into the broadcast networks, and blacklisting began on radio and television to offset the potential loss of advertisers.[6] Furthermore, Broadway was not immune from the fear and paranoia as picketing and boycotts of Broadway shows featuring "suspect" artists grew in number.

Webster captured the tenor of the times and the turbulent days to come when she wrote, "The years of disgrace were upon us, of reckless accusations, of endless 'smear campaigns,' or innuendoes, of that most insidious of weapons, guilt by association."[7]

Identified in *Red Channels* as "Author, Director, Producer," Margaret Webster's name was accompanied by sixteen committees, organizations, and meetings where she had served as sponsor, speaker, member, or contributor between 1941 and 1949.[8] Moreover, along with Lillian Hellman, Anne Revere, Mady Christians, Judy Holliday, Dorothy Parker, and others, she had signed an open letter to the members of the Eighty-first Congress urging the abolition of the House Committee on Un-American Activities. She sponsored leaflets on behalf of the Spanish Refugee Appeal and the Council on African Affairs; she participated in the "Artists, Writers and Professional Division" of the Citizens Committee for the Re-election of Benjamin Davis Jr., the Democratic candidate for the New York City council later convicted for violation of the Smith Act. She was also identified as a stockholder in the People's Radio Foundation, reputed to be a front organization. The compilers of *Red Channels* cited the *Daily Worker* and HUAC files as sources of information on Webster's un-American activities.

As a *Red Channels* listee, she was branded a "Pinko" and fellow traveler. She received letters and postal cards addressed to her at Actors' Equity excoriating her for affiliations with Communist-front organizations. Moreover, anonymous writers threatened to boycott any play in which her name appeared.[9]

Alarmed by the growing climate of hostility for members of Actors' Equity and for artists working in radio and television as members of the American Federation of Television and Radio Artists, Webster grew concerned that she would remain henceforth in a kind of "suspicious limbo" for the remainder of her career. In other words, she would be forever blacklisted from working in radio and television and potentially graylisted on Broadway.

Graylisting

It has long been held that blacklisting was not a factor on Broadway, although *graylisting*—defined as the "B" list of persons not officially blacklisted but existing in the shadows cast by their exposure in *Red Channels* and *Counterattack*—was an economic consideration.[10] The failure of the blacklist to capture Broadway is not disputed. Playwright Arthur Laurents, creator of the musical books for *West Side Story* and *Gypsy*, said unequivocally in his memoir, "there was no blacklist in the theatre." Actor Robert Vaughn agreed that the legit stage had "no organized blacklist." More recently, Actors' Equity project archivist K. Kevyne Baar, arguing that no blacklist was prevalent on Broadway, said, "try as they might, all of the different theys, the blacklist never appeared to rear its ugly head in the theatre community."[11]

Nevertheless, Kate Mostel and Madeleine Lee Gilford, married to black-listed actors Zero Mostel and Jack Gilford, experienced hard economic times up close and personal during the fifties. "The insidious thing about the blacklist," the women explained in *170 Years of Show Business*, "was that although we *could* sometimes work on Broadway—and more often off-Broadway—movies and television were closed to us and without that exposure it was hard to get the few well-paying jobs in the New York theater."[12]

The fact that there was no formal blacklist in the New York theater has been attributed chiefly to the independence of the producers along with their methods of financing shows. In those days, theater producers were not allied with corporate sponsors. Their funding came from moneyed backers and small investors. Brooks Atkinson explained the imperviousness of the commercial theater and its producers to political influence in this way: "Broadway is economic anarchy." He added,

> It is not financed or managed by corporate institutions as Hollywood and TV are. Broadway consists of individual producers. Every production is a new and separate adventure, financed by individual theater buffs or speculators. Occasionally, TV or Hollywood corporations invest in Broadway productions which they think they might make use of some day. But Broadway is not susceptible to domination by rational businessmen. Broadway showmanship is a local foible rather than a national exploit.

The critic concluded, "Hoodlums like McCarthy can never find who's in charge of Broadway or where the center of power lies."[13]

Nonetheless, in the early fifties, many were convinced that a graylist existed not only in Hollywood but within the Broadway theater. Nancy Da Silva, wife of blacklisted actor Howard Da Silva, surmised that even though Broadway had no *formal* blacklist, producers frequently avoided actors whose names would bring protests and picketers in front of the theater.[14] Moreover, there were many actors to choose from, and producers could selectively avoid the politicized playwright or the controversial performer. Atkinson put it this way: "Although no one was blacklisted, some were shunned."[15]

After the bruhaha at Actors' Equity, the headlines, and the publication of *Red Channels*, Mady Christians and Margaret Webster were convinced that they were on some informal list and were no longer marketable. Webster went so far as to write to her attorney Louis Nizer, "If the Un-American Committee gets to thinking the 'theatre,' apart from Radio and Hollywood, important enough to investigate, I shall surely be on their list. My guess . . . is that things will get worse, not better during the coming years."[16] She wrote to Nizer on April 23, 1951, two years before she was summoned to McCarthy's chambers.

Unknown to her at the time she wrote Nizer, the FBI had begun looking at her as a security matter (classification C) a month earlier.[17] She had been included among the four hundred "concealed Communists" of Louis Budenz's acquaintance. In August of 1950, he dictated the following information on the theater director:

> MISS WEBSTER was first called to my attention as an adherent of the Communist Party by V. J. Jerome around 1942. This was in connection with the activities of John Howard Lawson and other Communists on the Artists Front to Win the War. MISS WEBSTER was deeply impressed in her pro-Communist works by PAUL ROBESON, for whom she had a great respect,

according to repeated advices received by me from BENJAMIN J. DAVIS and ALEXANDER TRACHTENBERG.

Furthermore, he assured the Bureau, "Up until the time I left the Party in 1945, MISS WEBSTER was an adherent of the Communist Party, according to official advises received by me from both BENJAMIN J. DAVIS and JACK STACHEL."[18]

Margaret Webster was also unaware that her name had been read into the proceedings of the House Committee on Un-American Activities on five occasions between 1947 and 1951. First, Walter S. Steele, who published his own anti-Communist newsletter, had been indexing names for decades. He named her in 1947 as "active in Red Front circles for some years."[19] As chairman of the national security committee for the American Coalition of Patriotic, Civic, and Fraternal Societies, Steele requested to appear before the Committee. His goal was to encourage and support bills, pending before Congress, designed to curb or outlaw the Communist Party. He cited an American-Soviet cultural conference held in New York City in 1945 that featured such speakers as Helen Gahagan Douglas, Serge Koussevitsky, John Hersey, Lillian Hellman, Aaron Copland, and Margaret Webster.[20] In his effort to document "Red" organizations and their celebrity supporters, Steele named Webster a second time as a charter member of the "leftist" People's Radio Foundation, along with Charlie Chaplin, Langston Hughes, Rockwell Kent, and twenty-four others.

Walter Steele also cited as a suspect organization one of Webster's "good causes"—the National Council of American-Soviet Friendship—supposedly founded by openly Communist leaders to reach into the fields of science, medicine, education, religion, industry, and the arts. The names of Agnes de Mille, chairman of the dance committee, and Margaret Webster, chairman of the theater committee, were read into the congressional record.[21]

In order to avoid blacklisting in Hollywood, actors Edward G. Robinson and José Ferrer appeared voluntarily before the Committee to clear themselves of false accusations. With no Communist Party affiliations, they reached into "front" organizations for names to convince the Committee of their cooperation.[22]

When Webster read in the New York Times that HUAC had summoned José Ferrer, who played Iago in her production of Othello with Paul Robeson, she observed, "I knew it wouldn't be long now."[23]

Her words were prophetic. A little over a month before Ferrer named her, the FBI's New York office recommended that a Security Index card be prepared in her name as a Communist to be targeted for detention in a national emergency. The SI card was filed on June 5, 1951. The synopsis of the facts was brief but included four front groups and a Soviet-block country.

Subject on program of National Council of American Soviet Friendship in 1945. Sponsor of JAFRC [Joint Anti-Fascist Refugee Committee] in 1946.

Sponsor of World Youth Festival, Prague, Czechoslovakia, July and August 1947. Instrumental in organizing the Committee for the Negro in the Arts.[24]

The Bureau was likewise suspicious of Webster's citizenship: "She was born in New York City of British subjects," they reported. The New York office queried the local Immigration and Naturalization Service office on the possibility of deporting her as a resident alien. But the INS ruled that an individual, born in this country of foreign parents, is considered a U.S. citizen contingent upon their maintaining a permanent residence in the U.S.[25] Thereafter, the FBI monitored Webster's New York residences at 21 West Tenth Street and later at 50 West Twelfth Street.

In 1951, José Ferrer appeared before the House Committee on Un-American Activities, chaired by John S. Wood, on May 22, and again on May 25. He provided little information, but he did recall during the first of two sessions that "Margaret Webster" had asked him to send a congratulatory telegram on the fiftieth anniversary of the Moscow Art Theatre. "Who is she?" Representative Harold H. Velde of Illinois asked. Ferrer replied: "She was the director of *Othello*, for the Theatre Guild. She is an extremely prominent director in the theater."[26] After much sparing on Ferrer's part, he was sent away to recall other names and reconsider his cooperation.

Three days later he returned with four names. The first was, again, Webster's. Ferrer now recalled that she had spoken to him on behalf of a Spanish Refugee Appeal fundraiser, sponsored by the Joint Anti-Fascist Refugee Committee. She had invited him, along with her mother, Dame May Whitty, to speak at a luncheon to help refugees who had fled into France from Spain during the civil war.[27]

Ferrer then named theatrical manager Edward Choate, who, as secretary-treasurer of the Stop Censorship Committee, cited in *Counterattack* as a Communist-front group, had signed a letter inviting artists to an anti-censorship meeting at the Savoy-Plaza Hotel on March 23, 1948. Margaret Webster's name was on the letterhead as a sponsor. This meeting resulted in the signed petition to abolish the House Un-American Activities Committee. Webster, Lillian Hellman, Dorothy Parker, and Anne Revere were also signatories.

Ferrer mentioned two other women whose names were already emblazoned on letterhead stationery for their respective committees: Helen Bryan of the Joint Anti-Fascist Refugee Committee and Adele Jerome of the Independent Citizens' Committee of the Arts, Sciences and Professions. Nevertheless, these were not celebrity names and held little interest for the committeemen. Harold Velde pressed Ferrer on his knowledge of people in the theater who were Communists ("I do not know anyone to be a Communist in the theater," Ferrer insisted.); on his support for the re-election of Benjamin Davis; and on his friendship with the "Communist" Paul Robeson. Ferrer protested that at the time he had no knowledge of the politician's or the actor's affiliations with the Communist Party and that he himself was not now and had never been a party member. The Committee made little progress in this second hearing and adjourned at midday without thanking Ferrer for his cooperation.

At first, Webster had no idea why Ferrer named her and Edward Choate, former general manager of the Margaret Webster Shakespeare Company. She credited "Iago" with a perverse awareness that the naming of Choate was ridiculous since he had merely signed a letter protesting literary censorship and since Choate's signature, like her own on the Moscow Art Theatre anniversary letter, was of public record. She, on the other hand, was exposed. She had invited Ferrer and her mother to speak at the Spanish Refugee Appeal luncheon in an effort to raise funds for a group now labeled a Communist front.

Once Webster had an occasion to study Ferrer's testimony, she understood the actor's predicament and now her own. "We were in almost identically the same leaky old boat," she observed. "The things of which he was supposedly 'guilty' almost all applied to me too."[28] They shared such mutual offenses as

- good notices (and bad ones) in *The Daily Worker*;
- voting for Benjamin Davis, an African-American (and reputed Communist) running as the Democratic Party candidate for the New York City council; he had advocated a plan for creating new theaters for New York City;
- contributing to or supporting "Communist-front" organizations;
- signing protests against the Wood-Rankin committee and the Mundt-Nixon bill;
- employing and working with the known Communist sympathizer Paul Robeson;
- membership in Actors' Equity Association, reputed to have held a "Kangaroo Court" in judgment of actor Frank Fay.
- sending congratulations on the fiftieth anniversary of the Moscow Art Theatre.

Subversive activities were the heart of the matter, and Webster had been connected in the workplace with a number of questionable associates.

Shadow-Boxing

The lull before the storm of McCarthyism that swept over Margaret Webster's career lasted two years. Toward the end of 1951, the first of the reversals occurred. Mady Christians died unexpectedly of natural causes brought on by acute anxiety over her investigation by the FBI and dwindling offers of employment. In her grief over the death of her friend, Webster grew uneasy with the "shadowboxing," anonymous threats, innuendoes, and mysterious investigators. In the eulogy that she delivered at the memorial service for Mady Christians, she spoke from the heart of her own experiences. She described the shock, fear, and outrage experienced by individuals whose names appeared on a "list" and who were subsequently persecuted and denied employment.[29]

In late September when she was directing *Saint Joan* with the blacklisted actress Uta Hagen in the title role, she faced down the Theatre Guild's producer Lawrence Langner, who expressed alarm that several subscribers had objected to the Guild's employment of "controversial" artists." When he asked Webster to respond to the disaffected ticket-holders, she refused.

Instead, she wrote a letter to Langner in which she defended herself against unwarranted interference with her civil liberties. She argued,

> You are not buying from me my race (which happens to be Irish, Jewish and Anglo-Saxon), my religion (which happens to be a daily and active faith in God not attached to an organized Church), my voting affiliations (which have crossed the Republican and Democratic party lines in what used to be a system of "secret" ballot), my opinions of Hindemith, Saroyan or Picasso, nor my predilections as between the Giants and the Dodgers. You, and your subscribers, are buying my ability to direct *Saint Joan*. They have no right whatever to make further enquiry and you have no right to require any further answer of me.

She concluded with a stern admonition,

> You hired me to direct *Saint Joan*. This happens to be a play about God. I happen to believe in God. If I didn't I couldn't direct the play. I further believe in what Shaw states as the theme of the play: "the protest of the individual soul against the interference of anyone . . . between the private man and his God." If you don't believe in this, don't do the play. If you do, don't ask me to excuse myself to half a dozen Theatre Guild subscribers. You can't have it both ways.[30]

There were no political repercussions, no sign-waving picketers, no madding crowds as the Guild producers had feared. In effect, Brooks Atkinson described Uta Hagen's performance as "radiant simplicity" and called Webster's direction "brilliant." During the trial scene each night, Hagen was aware that the times had conspired to make the stage events seem true: "I felt it was McCarthy, not Cauchon [one of Shaw's inquisitors], who judged me and who threatened my beliefs."[31] Nonetheless, the controversy had taken the sparkle out of their accomplishment. Hagen thought the production not very good, and Webster said that it fell short of her hopes.[32]

In 1952, Webster had no employment on Broadway. In mid-May of 1953, she received a summons to appear on May 25 for a "private" hearing before McCarthy's Senate Permanent Subcommittee on Investigations in Washington, D.C.

The next day, Webster went to the law offices of Louis Nizer, where she reviewed the testimony of several witnesses, including José Ferrer's, previously released by the House Committee on Un-American Activities. She was also introduced to Sidney M. Davis, who would be the attorney accompanying her to the hearing.

Like most witnesses, she had few alternatives when under oath. She could refuse to answer questions and become liable for contempt of Congress. She could give names and be dismissed as a cooperative witness with faint hope of future employment. She could plead the Fifth, tantamount to an admission of guilt in the public's eye, and face severe economic and social consequences. Or, she could try Hellman's strategy—the "diminished Fifth"—where you answered all questions concerning yourself but not when they involved other people. Since names were the crux of the matter, she observed, this approach was "morally OK but legally dubious."[33]

Webster was in a quandary. She had no need to invoke the Fifth, for she had nothing to tell or refuse to tell. Paul Robeson was the only Communist sympathizer she knew, and she was certain to be questioned about her associations with the actor, which would undoubtedly lead to other names. Finally, she decided to use the circumlocutions of the diminished Fifth and "pray for the best."[34]

Sidney Davis warned her never to say "No." He encouraged her to use such phrases as "I cannot remember doing so"; "Not so far as I can recall"; or, "To the best of my recollection, no." Davis argued that it was important never to take an unequivocal stand on any issue since the tactic of the subcommittee's chief legal counsel, Roy M. Cohn, was to produce witnesses (or informers) to contradict unequivocal statements and subject the witness to a charge of perjury.[35]

"Say as little as you can," Davis counseled, "never elaborate. Never, *never* say 'No.'"[36]

At Nizer's suggestion, Webster drew up a two and a half page statement to deposit with the subcommittee. It contained a list of forty-six "blameless" charities and organizations to which she had subscribed or worked, including the United Jewish Appeal and the American Red Cross. She began her brief with an apology for underrating the extent and power of the Communist movement in the United States. "I viewed the American Communists as a small set of 'lunatic fringe' cranks," she wrote, "who were completely ineffectual and worthy of nothing but contempt." She reiterated her tireless support of the U.S. war effort, her work for relief efforts for children and refugees, her devotion to world peace, and her lifetime of service to the American theater and its charities. Although she would later feel degraded at having written the self-effacing statement, she, nevertheless, concluded with a heartfelt repudiation of Communism.

> In conclusion, I can only say that I am a person who can only exist in the climate of freedom; that I have a most profound faith in the workings of democracy, especially among American people, who, I do not for one moment think, can ever be seriously infected with any poisonous virus so alien to their whole way of life as Communism. I am quite sure that under any totalitarian regime I, personally, should be liquidated within a week. Regimentation, thought-control, physical cruelty, intimidation—every one of the processes of Communism are deeply and profoundly abhorrent to me and always have been. I would fight them with my life. Perhaps this must be apparent to everyone who has known me or worked with me; and that is why no-one has ever approached me with any attempt to convert me to the Communist faith. If there have been Communists among those with whom I have come in contact, they must always have been particularly careful to conceal the fact from me.

She ended with the declaration that she had "never been a Communist of any kind or adherence or knowing affiliation in any way, shape or form."[37]

Passport Difficulties

As Lillian Hellman, Arthur Miller, Paul Robeson, and others found out in the early fifties, the government used the U.S. Passport Division as a containment measure to curb the travels of citizens perceived as disloyal Americans. Margaret Webster's first encounter with the Passport Division occurred in 1951 when she was invited to represent the theatrical unions as part of an American delegation to a UNESCO conference in Paris. When William Green of the American Federation of Labor forwarded her name to the State Department, he received a guarded reply: the FBI would have to approve clearance before the Passport Division could issue a passport in her name, and the Bureau might not be able to provide that clearance in time for the conference. Rather than embarrass those involved, Webster withdrew her name.[38]

Her second encounter occurred in 1953. Two years earlier, Lawrence Langner had invited Webster and actress Eva Le Gallienne to create a benefit performance for the new American Shakespeare Theatre and Academy in Stratford, Connecticut. Webster arranged the script, called *An Evening with Will Shakespeare,* directed the scenes, and served as narrator and "general mortar between the bricks."[39] A stellar cast was recruited for the first performance on December 6, 1951, at the Parsons Theater in Hartford: Claude Rains, Arnold Moss, Wesley Addy, Faye Emerson, Nina Foch, Richard Dyer-Bennett, and

Eva Le Gallienne. As planned, the tour was to end in May (with several cast changes along the way) with a two-week performance at the National Theatre in Washington, D.C.

Following the tour, Webster planned to travel to the south of France, where she frequently vacationed. For the trip, she needed to renew her U.S. passport, which expired on March 15, 1953. She applied for a new one on March 10.

The day before she arrived in the nation's capitol to perform, Webster was notified that her passport application had been denied. The State Department had tentatively disapproved her application on April 23, citing as the basis for non-renewal the subject's consistent and prolonged adherence to the Communist Party line beginning in 1945, and connections with organizations cited by the U.S. attorney general as Communistic or subversive.[40]

Profoundly shocked, she opined, "it was so easily foreseeable."[41] In the general atmosphere of suspicion and caution, she had been denied radio and television jobs and had had no theater work for a year. In her opinion, her passport difficulties seemed a reasonable outcome of her newly acquired "un-American" status.

Webster telephoned Louis Nizer for counsel on dealing with the passport officials. He advised her to answer any questions that were put to her and "hope for the best."[42]

During the interview on May 5, Ruth Shipley asked her to write out a statement summarizing her "life story." She wrote and signed a statement, witnessed by Mrs. Shipley, which dealt principally with denial of Communist Party affiliations. "I have never been affiliated or attached to the Communist Party or an adherent of it," she wrote.[43]

Four days later, she amplified her original statement. In the later version, she addressed her "considerable ignorance of the background of some of the associations and persons which have now been mentioned to me as of a questionable nature. . . . But my very ignorance of this background made me, perhaps unduly trustful and inclined to accept at face value the avowed and innocent objectives presented to me by organizations which sought my help."[44] These two statements soon became the basis of a longer document that Webster prepared for McCarthy's subcommittee.

Treading carefully among the bureaucrats, she got her passport renewed on May 12, but not before the dour Mrs. Shipley chastised her for being a "joiner."[45] (Webster had submitted a list of thirty-eight charities and organizations that she contributed to or worked for.) Shipley gave her a loyalty oath to sign, and Webster signed without hesitation because, as she acknowledged, she was by nature a "truth-teller." She now had a new passport.

When she returned from Washington on May 21, the other shoe dropped. She was served with a subpoena at her New York apartment directing her to appear at a private hearing of the Senate Permanent Subcommittee on Investigations four days later. Had she known, she could have taken some comfort in the fact that the FBI had spent two days monitoring her apartment, calling various departments to check her permanent address, and attempting to serve a subpoena to the actress who was appearing onstage at the National Theatre in the nation's capital.

Tumult and Shouting

The year 1953 was a tumultuous one for McCarthy and his cohorts. As in previous years, the senator's investigations had a twofold purpose: to expose Communists and to garner publicity for his reputation as a no-holds-barred fighter against the Red menace. In February, McCarthy embarked on the investigation of the loyalty and security files held by the State Department and also gave attention to the department's information programs, including the Voice of America and overseas libraries. Powerful Republican leaders were convinced that the Voice of America was responsible for filling the airways with broadcasts by "Communists, left wingers, New Dealers, radicals, and pinkos."[46] In March, Roy Cohn and his assistant, G. David Schine, made a whirlwind tour of American Information Centers abroad and searched the libraries for materials written by Communists. When they returned, McCarthy began a round of subpoenas for pro-Communist writers whose books and articles were "found" on the shelves of the libraries and removed, replaced, and, in some instances, destroyed. McCarthy's goal in the hearings was to discover if Communists has written books and used their royalties to further the Communist conspiracy. Some on McCarthy's list were or had been Communists; others patently were not. But, as historian Robert Griffith attested, the appearances of well-known writers before the subcommittee created the desired tumult and shouting.[47]

The sweep of McCarthy's net brought Dashiell Hammett, Eslanda Robeson, and Arnaud d'Usseau to Washington. The authors were contemptuous of the manner in which the politicians impugned the integrity of their writing ("Did you write this book all yourself?" David Schine asked Eslanda Robeson) and were unwavering in their use of the protections of the Fifth Amendment. No friendly witnesses for McCarthy's hi-jinks were found among the literary crowd.[48]

The well-known writer of *Red Harvest*, *The Thin Man*, and *The Maltese Falcon*, Dashiell Hammett, had been convicted of contempt three years earlier for refusing to identify contributors to the bail fund of the Civil Rights Congress and served a short prison sentence. On March 24, 1953, Roy Cohn grilled Hammett for two sessions about his books that dealt with "social issues." Hammett recalled that a short story, "Night Shade," dealt with "Negro-White relations." When asked if he was a Communist Party member now or when he wrote his books and short stories, he took the Fifth. He also took the Fifth when asked if monies received from the sale of his books to the State Department had been contributed to the Communist Party. He was impatient with the predictable questions but practiced in avoiding incriminating statements. Shortly before he was excused from the public hearing, the novelist with a few choice words trumped McCarthy's grandstanding.

> THE CHAIRMAN: May I ask one further question: Mr. Hammett, if you were spending, as we are, over a hundred million dollars a year on an information program allegedly for the purpose of fighting communism, and if you were in charge of that program to fight communism, would you purchase the works of some 75 Communist authors and distribute their works throughout the world, placing our official stamp of approval on those works?
>
> MR. HAMMETT: Well, I think—of course, I don't know—if I were fighting communism, I don't think I would do it by giving people any books at all.[49]

In early July, McCarthy queried screenwriter and playwright Arnaud d'Usseau and author Eslanda Goode Robeson (Mrs. Paul Robeson) in executive and public sessions about their authorship of books purchased for the information libraries around the world. Senator McCarthy was especially hostile toward d'Usseau for his cantankerous behavior during the executive session. Under threat of a contempt citation, d'Usseau identified himself as coauthor with James Gow of the play *Deep Are the Roots* and proceeded to take the Fifth in answer to all subsequent questions from McCarthy regarding "whether he is a Communist today, whether he was a Communist at the time he wrote the book, whether his coauthor was a Communist."[50]

Seven questions into the hearing on Eslanda Robeson's authorship of *African Journey* and *Paul Robeson, Negro*, the senator asked if she was a member of the Communist Party. She asserted the protections afforded her under the Fifth and Fifteenth Amendments (an unusual measure since the Fifteenth guarantees protections of voting rights). McCarthy challenged her on the appropriateness of the Fifteenth Amendment, but she held firm: "I understand it has something to do with my being a Negro and I have always sought protection under it . . . I am a second-class citizen in this country and, therefore, feel the need of the Fifteenth." Mrs. Robeson was particularly hostile toward the "white" committee and refused to answer any questions about party membership and conspiracy theories.[51]

Not content with scouring the bookshelves of the State Department's foreign libraries for controversial authors, McCarthy turned to the State Department's Teacher-Student Exchange Program to expose the names of Communists being sent abroad at the expense of the American taxpayer. It was established practice for the theater committee of the exchange program to invite experts from the field to review applications and to advise on their merits. For four or five years, Margaret Webster had been one of those experts for the theater division. McCarthy subpoenaed her to establish evidentiary proof to be used against the State Department and the powerful chairman of the Senate Foreign Relations Committee. Webster had become a pawn in McCarthy's game.

No Recollection

Armed with her statement, the diminished Fifth, and a prayer from *Isaiah* ("Surely my labour is with the Lord and my work with my God"), Margaret Webster walked into the office of the secretary of state for her private hearing. En route she passed "a very battered-looking couple" emerging from an earlier hearing. She did not know, nor had she ever heard of, Dr. Naphtali Lewis and his wife Helen B. Lewis. She would learn later that he was a classical languages professor at Brooklyn College who had been awarded a Fulbright scholarship for study in Italy. He and his wife, both suspected Communists, had been summoned to McCarthy's chambers.

Webster walked into the lion's den innocent of the reason for her subpoena. She was unaware that the agenda for the McCarthy subcommittee on that day was the investigation of the State Department's teacher-student exchange programs for travel and study abroad under the Fulbright Act, named for Senator J. William Fulbright, Democrat from Arkansas and powerful member of the Senate Foreign Relations Committee. Webster's hearing was only peripherally related to the earlier testimonies of José Ferrer and Edward G. Robinson, during which she had been named. McCarthy's target was J. William Fulbright and the U.S. State Department.

McCarthy began the afternoon hearing with *pro forma* instructions to the witness about procedures, but he did not stay for the closed session. Roy Cohn took charge. Dispensing with preliminary questions (place of birth, education, career facts), he proceeded to address the subcommittee's agenda: "Miss Webster, do you have any connection with the exchange program of the State Department?"[52] And so the hearing began.

Democratic senators John L. McClellan of Arkansas, Henry M. ("Scoop") Jackson of Washington, Stuart Symington of Missouri, and Republican senator Karl E. Mundt of South Dakota were seated around the conference table. The senators were singularly interested in whether or not Margaret Webster made *final* decisions on theater applicants in the Fulbright Scholarship Division of the Institute of International Education, and, if she was asked to *approve* teachers. Foiling their effort to use her against the institute, she insisted, "I had nothing to do with the selection process of candidates."

Finding this line of questioning unproductive, Roy Cohn turned to her passport difficulties, her connections with "Communist-front" organizations, her support of the re-election of Benjamin Davis, her associations with the People's Radio Foundation, and her greetings to the "actors of Moscow."

The passport question came first and constituted a feint toward other State Department matters.

MR. COHN: Were you denied a passport for security reasons?

MISS WEBSTER: No, sir. It was questioned. I went to the passport office and answered all the questions they cared to ask me and I have a passport.

MR. COHN: When was it issued?

MISS WEBSTER: May 12th, or some approximate date of that sort.

SENATOR SYMINGTON: Are you a naturalized American citizen?

MISS WEBSTER: I was born in New York City.

MR. COHN: Miss Webster, have you belonged to a considerable number of Communist-front organizations?

MISS WEBSTER: I have never belonged to any organization which I knew to be influenced or dominated by Communists. . . .

As the questions continued, Webster took refuge in the language of the well-rehearsed witness. She either had "no recollection," could not "remember," or did not "recognize" the front group in question. She "had no recollection" that she sponsored Benjamin Davis's re-election. "The extent of her recollection" about the People's Radio Foundation was that she had agreed to take a share of stock in the radio station dedicated to public service programs. She could not recall actually receiving the share.

On the subject of her support of Communist-front groups, she equivocated among the jumble of titles used by the senators to identify the front organizations.

MR. COHN: Were you a member of the American Committee for the Protection of the Foreign Born?

MISS WEBSTER: I was never a member of that committee, sir. No.

MR. COHN: Has it ever been called to your attention that the *Daily Worker* published on February 10, 1944, a greeting to the women of the Soviet Union, which was signed by you and sponsored by the American Council of American-Soviet Friendship?

MISS WEBSTER: No, sir, I remember nothing like that.

MR. COHN: Were you ever a member of the Joint Anti-Fascist Refugee Committee?

MISS WEBSTER: I was never a member. I did make several fund-raising appeals for them for objectives which were entirely humanitarian and charitable. . . .

MR. COHN: Were you ever connected with the Spanish Refugee Relief Committee? Specifically, we have a letter on which you are listed as a national sponsor, which was February 26, 1946. That is the date which the letter containing your name appears.

MISS WEBSTER: If it was part of the Joint Anti-Fascist Refugee Committee, I have no recollection of that event or date. It is not inconceivable. What was I supposed to have done?

MR. COHN: National sponsor.

MISS WEBSTER: It is conceivable that I was solicited. I know that appreciably later—I wouldn't be certain of the year—two or three years later—I received a letter from the Spanish Refugee Appeal on which I saw that my name was then listed as a sponsor, the contents of which letter appeared to be political in character, something pertaining to Franco. I wrote to them at that time and stated that I had not given them permission to use my name and I had no sympathy, no political objective of that nature and would appreciate their withdrawing my name.

Cohn's tactic was to revisit topics in order to force contradictions and entrap the witness. Benjamin Davis's election was one of those recycled topics. Webster was perhaps disingenuous when she said that she had "no recollection" of being a sponsor for the committee to re-elect Davis. To avoid perjury, she fell back on circumlocutions, but the dyed-in-the-wool Democrat answered truthfully when she vowed that she would not have endorsed an *authorized* Communist Party candidate.

Recalling her lawyer's advice to give the committee something, Webster volunteered her connection with two organizations between 1943 and 1947: the National Council of American Soviet Friendship where she was on record as chairman of the theater division (orchestra conductor Serge Koussevitsky was on record as chairman of the music division) and the Joint Anti-Fascist Refugee Committee, for which she made public appeals for charitable purposes.

Weary of the litany of front organizations, Senator McClellan returned to the purpose of the proceeding: "As I gathered from your testimony, it was not part of your regular duties to pass on and approve applicants for this Exchange Student Service for the Fulbright Scholarship?"

MISS WEBSTER: No, sir. My understanding is that the relevant committee—the International Institute of Education—invites experts in different fields to pass on the qualifications of applicants in the different fields. . . .

SENATOR MCCLELLAN: Primarily, you were only called in the theatre field, is that right?

MISS WEBSTER: That is correct.

SENATOR MCCLELLAN: You have not had responsibility for or an assignment to pass upon student applicants other than in the area?

MISS WEBSTER: No, sir.

SENATOR MCCLELLAN: You would not be asked to pass on teachers?

MISS WEBSTER: No, sir.

Weary of McClellan's point of attack, Senator Jackson returned to her pro-Communist associations. Earlier in the hearing Senator Symington had asked the sixty-four dollar question: "Have you ever been a Communist?" Webster replied, "No, sir, at no time nor am I now."

SENATOR JACKSON: Did you ever join any of these groups knowing at the time that they were Communist fronts or dominated by the Communist Party?

MISS WEBSTER: At no time, sir.

SENATOR JACKSON: Have you ever expressed at any time Communist sympathy or sympathy with the Communist movement?

MISS WEBSTER: I have always been opposed to the Communist philosophy, its practices. It is a horror to me. In such a society I wouldn't last a week.

The witness had produced no evidence to use against the "subversive" activities of the State Department's teacher-student exchange programs. None-theless, Roy Cohn, not to be denied a final thrust, turned to the Civil Rights Congress. Without doubt, Webster was aware of the CRC's most notorious supporters—Dashiell Hammett, Dorothy Parker, and Paul Robeson. She stepped carefully around this minefield.

MR. COHN: Did I ask you about the Civil Rights Congress?

MISS WEBSTER: I refused to join the board. I did make one or two contributions. When they asked me to join, I refused.

MR. COHN: Did you sign a letter prepared by the Civil Rights Congress attacking the Subversive Control Act of 1948, which letter was published with your signature in the *Daily Worker*?

MISS WEBSTER: I would think that extremely doubtful.

Cohn had one final question: "Did you object to the Subversive Control Act?"

MISS WEBSTER: Which was the Subversive Control Act? There were so many of them.

"That is all, Miss Webster," Cohn concluded and adjourned the hearing.

Satisfied that Webster was a dupe of Communist-front organizations and had nothing to add in support of the committee's evidence-gathering hearings on the State Department, McCarthy recalled the battered-looking couple, the "teachers," as John McClellan called the Lewises.

McCarthy held a one-member subcommittee public hearing on June 19 for the purpose of learning whether Helen Lewis, the wife of Fulbright recipient Naphtali Lewis, was now or ever had been a member of the Communist Party. She refused to answer and invoked her rights under the Fifth Amendment. At the time Webster passed the couple in the corridor, Dr. Lewis, a professor of classical studies and former wartime translator for the War Department had been awarded a Fulbright scholarship to study ancient manuscripts at the University of Florence in Italy. He testified that he was not a member of the Communist Party; however, he refused to testify about his wife, who was to accompany him to Italy, on grounds of invasion of the privacy of marriage. McCarthy recalled the Lewises on June 10 and again on June 19. On June 20, McCarthy announced that the State Department had canceled Dr. Lewis's Fulbright award. "I think it [the cancellation] is an excellent idea," McCarthy said at the end of a thirty-seven minute hearing into the background of husband and wife. In a prepared statement handed out to the press, Dr. Lewis lashed out at McCarthy and his subcommittee:

> This inquisition, if it has its way established a novel and singularly un-American principle—namely, that before a man is permitted to pursue a career of research—even in ancient manuscripts—he must have the stamp of approval of a Congressional subcommittee on himself and family.[53]

A Miserable Business

Years later, Margaret Webster wrote a chapter in *Don't Put Your Daughter on the Stage*, entitled "Of Witch-Hunting," that captured the roiling clouds of McCarthyism over Broadway in the early fifties. She detailed the role of Actors' Equity in the Red-scare, the public humiliation of witnesses, the loss of employment, and the untimely deaths of artists. In effect, Webster described the runaway train of fear and paranoia that carried many Broadway artists away from vital careers and productive lives as "a miserable business from first to last."[54]

In May of 1953, Margaret Webster considered her career "undermined, if not ostensibly broken." Her friend and admirer Brooks Atkinson agreed that her Broadway career was "permanently tarnished."[55]

Within the year, Webster learned that she remained blacklisted in Hollywood, although she had not worked there for thirteen years and then for only six months. While traveling on her new passport in the south of France, she received a letter from her agent Charles Green. He advised that she had an offer from Twentieth Century Fox to direct the Shakespearean scenes in a film about Edwin Booth, called *Prince of Players*, starring Richard Burton. She cabled Green reminding him that she had been blacklisted and asked him to look into her status with the studios. Green made inquiries and learned that his client was still blacklisted. The studio had checked on Webster's *clearance* and was informed that she was "still active in associations that were on the Attorney General's subversives list."[56] Fox subsequently rescinded the offer.

By her own admission, Margaret Webster did not belong in a post-McCarthy world to any organized group. There were three exceptions: "Equity, the Blue Cross, and the Martha's Vineyard Community Services." Nonetheless, she was sanguine about the matter. "Once on the blacklist, you stayed there," she said.[57]

In addition to the harmful effects of the blacklist, the FBI's interest in Margaret Webster was ongoing. Following her appearance before McCarthy's subcommittee, the Bureau proposed that the New York office interview Webster under the following guidelines:

> she will be contacted at the most opportune time a secure distance from her residence or employment. . . . to ascertain her present sympathies and activities.[58]

Webster was subjected to two FBI interviews in Manhattan. The first took place on September 29, 1953, and the second on December 16 that same year. According to the memorandum written after the first session, Webster was interviewed in the basement of the Broadhurst Theatre on Forty-fourth Street between Broadway and Eighth Avenue.[59]

Webster's version in her memoir combined the two interviews into a single encounter. According to her account, two agents appeared at the theater on the afternoon of the opening of *The Strong Are Lonely*, a title that greatly appealed to her in the present circumstances. She and composer Lehman Engel were holding an orchestra rehearsal in the basement of the theater as "two of those heavily disguised, instantly recognizable types" came down the stairs. Webster described the scene:

> They stood silently. I went over and asked what they wanted. The badge-showing took place. They had to talk to me. Not just now, I said; after the opening night. Obligingly, they said I might come to their office on Broadway. We made a date.[60]

The FBI's accounts of their sessions with Webster were less colorful. The first interview, as she described, *was* held in the theater on the afternoon of the opening of *The Strong Are Lonely*, a play by Viennese playwright Fritz

Hochwalder. The play dealt with the actions of wrong-headed authority and the individual's plight in an unequal contest with the politically powerful. Given the circumstances, Webster was amused by the collision of life and art.

Webster took time-out from the rehearsal to explain her participation in front organizations as charitable endeavors for humanitarian purposes and swore that she ended any affiliation once she became aware of "Communist domination." Moreover, she reminded the agents that she had submitted statements to the Passport Division of the State Department and to McCarthy's subcommittee in which she denied any affiliation with the Communist Party.[61] Convinced of the sincerity of her allocutions, the agents recommended that her name be deleted from the Security Index. Nevertheless, the Bureau wanted a *second* interview before authorizing the removal of Webster's name. Agents were urged to question her about the identities of other individuals associated with her in front organizations.[62]

Webster went to the FBI's New York office on December 16, a month after *The Strong Are Lonely* closed. Satisfied that she had no affiliations with "any portion of the Communist movement since 1947," the Bureau removed her name from the Security Index in February of 1954.[63] Nevertheless, the FBI maintained an active file on their subject until 1966.[64]

When Webster took up her loss of employment in Hollywood and her ongoing scrutiny by the FBI with Nizer's firm, Paul Martinson told her that the investigations by the FBI and the Senate subcommittee were "closed." Moreover, the attorney urged her not to write to the local FBI office in New York because, he argued, a "general inquiry would produce no results and be of no help." He advised that the sole purpose of the FBI was investigative and it must refrain from "appraising, evaluating or basing conclusions upon the evidence obtained by it."[65]

Endings and Beginnings

Censored by the U.S. Senate in 1954, Joseph McCarthy died three years later. Margaret Webster lived another eighteen years in England and the United States. She and J. Edgar Hoover died within six months of one another in 1972. Writing several months before her death of cancer, Webster reflected upon the politics of that long-ago era of Edmund Burke–like *discontents*. "There is plenty of justification for despising the 'liberals' of twenty years ago," she wrote. "But we are tougher than we look. We shall still be around when a lot of the shouting and the shooting and the burning to the right and left of us has gone with the wind."[66]

Actress Kim Hunter and radio talk-show host John Henry Faulk were two of those tough-minded liberals that Webster envisioned as enduring beyond the sound and fury of the McCarthy era. The testimony of the actress in *Faulk v. AWARE, Inc., Laurence Johnson, and Vincent Hartnett* brings to a close this saga of unfriendly witnesses. For McCarthy's celebrity women, 1962 was a pivotal year for endings—and for beginnings.

For a long while, I wouldn't talk about it [the blacklist] at all. I do now, because there's a whole new generation that doesn't remember...

—Kim Hunter

7 The Blacklist Is On Fire: Kim Hunter

Best known as the original Stella Kowalski in *A Streetcar Named Desire*, Kim Hunter stepped forward in 1956 to confront the blacklisters and dismantle AWARE, Inc. The diminutive actress with light brown hair and large hazel eyes joined with radio and television artist John Henry Faulk, attorney Louis Nizer, and others to challenge the power of Vincent W. Hartnett and Laurence A. Johnson to influence the networks. As she approached the witness chair in the New York Supreme Court, she appeared nervous, but the presiding judge offered sympathetic advice: "Miss Hunter, even though you are in a courtroom you can relax. Just assume that we are all in the living room."[1]

Hunter made her Broadway debut as Stella in Tennessee Williams's *A Streetcar Named Desire* in 1947. The production with Marlon Brando and Jessica Tandy, directed by Elia Kazan, ran for two and a half years. Kazan then cast her in the screen version with Vivien Leigh as Blanche DuBois and Brando reprising his role as Stanley Kowalski. The scenes of an anguished Stanley in the yard of their seedy New Orleans French Quarter home calling up to his wife ("Stella!"), followed by Hunter's sexually charged descent down a spiral staircase into his arms, comprise two iconic moments in modern cinema.

Shortly after the film was released in 1951, Hunter became the object of a second-round of investigations into Communist activities in Hollywood. A self-described liberal, she joined the Americans for Democratic Action, which started in the forties as a liberal organization committed to social reforms. She also signed petitions for organizations later designated as front groups and sponsored the World Peace Conference in New York City. Subsequently, she became a target of the anti-Communist hunters.

Hunter's political activities were a hodge-podge of unremarkable choices. Americans for Democratic Action was made up of Cold War liberals who had turned against the Communist Party long before McCarthyism heated up.

Nevertheless, the necessity to defend against the conservative right induced such groups as the National Association for the Advancement of Colored People, the American Civil Liberties Union, the American Association of University Professors, and Americans for Democratic Action to pull their political punches. Consequently, according to Ellen Schrecker, these liberal groups put up little opposition to the firing of Communist teachers, the Smith Act's erosions of the First Amendment, or "any of the other big and little violations of civil liberties and political freedoms" during the Cold War.[2]

Unlike Lillian Hellman, Dorothy Parker, and Anne Revere in the forties, Kim Hunter did not position herself at the barricades of the radical left. As a liberal Democrat in her twenties, she acknowledged being pro–civil rights and signing petitions. By her own admission, she was "never a Communist, or even a pro-Communist."[3] She was a gentle, well-meaning person, not an ideologue, who wanted to protect her career and safeguard the rights of individuals at the same time. While she was playing in *Streetcar* on Broadway, she agreed to sponsor the 1949 Scientific and Cultural Conference for World Peace. *Life* magazine published a photo spread of celebrity sponsors that documented Hunter's participation as a cohort of the radical left.[4] This issue of *Life* became a trophy in the files of Vincent Hartnett, a professional clearance consultant for AWARE, Inc. and the author of the anti-Communist bulletin *Aware*.

Despite the success of the *Streetcar* film and her Golden Globe Award and Academy Award (the Oscar) for best supporting actress, she received few offers of employment in film or television for four years and took refuge in the Broadway theater. For more than two years, she appeared in Sidney Kingsley's *Darkness at Noon*, Horton Foote's *The Chase,* and Lillian Hellman's *The Children's Hour.* Nonetheless, television work eluded her. When Hartnett offered his clearance services to her manager for a fee of two hundred dollars, the actress baulked at paying: "I said that I would not, that my life is absolutely an open book."[5]

Hunter's struggle against blacklisting took her in 1962 before the New York Supreme Court, where she voluntarily testified for John Henry Faulk against the forces that denied employment to politically inconvenient artists. She had lost four crucial years to McCarthyism and was determined to engage the blacklisters, who had brought so much harm to so many.

All-American Girl

Born on November 12, 1922, in Detroit to Donald Cole and Grace Lind Cole, Hunter grew up in Miami Beach. Starting out as an un-produced adolescent playwright and failed contestant on radio's *Amateur Hour,* she soon discovered her true creative outlet—acting. "That youthful, rather daring urge to make some sense of my private world public," she wrote in her memoir, "was a shy girl's need for a creative outlet."[6]

Bedazzled by films, she studied acting, refused parental suggestions of college, and entered the world of stock companies, which took her to the Pasadena Playhouse in California. One of David O. Selznick's talent scouts saw her in *Arsenic and Old Lace* at the playhouse. Shortly thereafter, Selznick signed her to a seven-year contract with Vanguard Films, renamed her Kim Hunter, and gave her a Hollywood makeover. Then, he loaned her to RKO for two films, B-horror film *The Seventh Victim* with Tom Conway and *Tender Comrade* with Ginger Rogers and Mady Christians, directed by Edward Dmytryk. Within a few years, the film about women living communally while their men were fighting in the war was labeled Communist propaganda. Moreover, director Edward Dmytryk and screenwriter Dalton Trumbo were soon to be included among the unfriendly Hollywood Ten, and Mady Christians was blacklisted.

Hunter's film career was sidelined by a wartime marriage to Captain William A. Baldwin of the U.S. Marine Corps and the birth of a daughter, named Kathryn. Within a two-year span, Hunter married, gave birth, divorced, and was dismissed by Selznick's office with "the gentlest of boots."[7] Nevertheless, another Selznick—Irene Mayer Selznick—soon appeared with the supporting role of a lifetime.

Stella for Star!

"Loud and clear," agent William Leibling told his client as she went to read for the part of Stella Kowalski.[8] After the audition, Irene Selznick and Elia Kazan mutually agreed that they had found the actress for Stella. "The minute I saw her I was attracted to her," Kazan recalled, "which is the best possible reaction for a director when casting young women."[9]

Rehearsals were not easy for the newcomer. Terrified of a Broadway show, she went to the first rehearsal in "a state of rigid panic." At the end of the third rehearsal day, Kazan walked with her to the Algonquin Hotel, where she was staying, bought her a drink in the bar, and let loose a barrage of four-letter words: "What the f—— did I think I was doing? If they hadn't thought I could play the f—— part, they wouldn't have cast me!"[10]

Through the fog of an actor's insecurities, she heard Kazan's reminder that he and Irene Selznick *wanted* her for the part but she must *become* Stella Kowalski or be fired. Theater gossip also related that Kazan, known for involvement with actresses during the span of a production, took Kim Hunter to bed that evening. During the next day's rehearsal and those to follow, she progressed and played Blanche's younger sister to critical acclaim. Ward Morehouse called her a "first-rate young actress," and Brooks Atkinson praised her for acting "with freshness and definition.[11] She won the Donaldson Award and the New York Drama Critics Poll for best supporting actress.

Thereafter, Hunter worked consistently on Broadway and in Hollywood for five years. She played in *Streetcar* for over two years and worked with Uta Hagen as Blanche when Jessica Tandy left the show. When *Streetcar* closed, she played in Sidney Kingsley's *Darkness at Noon* with Claude Rains and followed with Horton Foote's *The Chase*, directed by José Ferrer. In Hollywood she made the film version of *Streetcar* and *Deadline U.S.A.* with Humphrey Bogart and *Anything Can Happen* with José Ferrer, both released in 1952. Then, the film contracts abruptly ended and her film career vanished for a period of four years.

Hunter found refuge from the blacklisters on Broadway and in a second marriage. She married actor and writer Robert Emmett in 1951; the couple adopted Kathryn and three years later Sean Robert Emmett was born. She returned to Broadway in the revival of Lillian Hellman's *The Children's Hour* as Karen Wright opposite Patricia Neal as Martha Dobie, the role Anne Revere originated in 1934. Critics extolled, as the playwright predicted, the newfound political relevance of Hellman's play as an allegory of the Red scare.[12]

Vincent Hartnett, Ace Investigator

Stefan Kanfer called 1954 a "vintage" year for the blacklisters.[13] Having compiled material for *Red Channels* and exposed supporters of "front" groups in *Counterattack*, Vincent Hartnett, a graduate of Notre Dame who had served in naval intelligence, left American Business Consultants in 1952 for a new enterprise. Joining with Fordham University's constitutional law professor and anti-Communist crusader Godfrey P. Schmidt, they started a new business, AWARE, Inc., publisher of a new anti-Communist publication *Aware*, and announced their services to investigate "Communist influences in all the varied aspects of entertainment-communications and the fine arts." They also promised to distribute facts on organizations and individuals employing Communists and fellow travelers.[14] With Schmidt as president, the board of professional blacklisters included Vincent Hartnett, conservative radio writer Paul Milton, and other conservative members of the American Federation of Television and Radio Artists.

As an official of AWARE, Inc. and editor of the newsletter, Hartnett worked closely with supermarket magnate Laurence Johnson, who owned several stores in upstate New York, was head of the Veterans Action Committee, and retained influence with American Legion Post 41 in Syracuse.[15] Hartnett fed names to Johnson, who then shared them with advertising agencies and sponsors and called the networks to say his supermarkets intended to boycott their products if they hired controversial artists.[16]

Hartnett had a clever business. He studied old photographs of May Day parades and peace marches to identify "Red sympathizers." Once identified, the culprit received a letter asking, "Have you changed your views?" If the answer was "yes," Hartnett offered to clear that person for a fee. If not, the individual's name appeared in *Aware* as engaged in Red-related activities.

Ted Morgan pointed out that Hartnett's treatment of Kim Hunter was typical of his methods.[17] The actress came to his attention through public opposition to blacklisting. Hartnett found that a group of actors paid for the reprinting and distribution of a pamphlet entitled "Blacklisting," taken from a *New York Post* series. Kim Hunter's film celebrity in *A Streetcar Named Desire* offered a business opportunity to the professional blacklister. For a fee, he offered to review her entire record but she refused. This transaction became part of her testimony about the clearance racket in 1962.

Long a professional clearance consultant to the networks, Hartnett took up the actress's challenge. Hartnett wrote his client, the American Broadcasting Company, targeting writer James Thurber and actress Kim Hunter. "In my opinion you would run a serious risk of adverse public opinion by featuring on your network James Thurber and Kim Hunter," he warned.[18] To support his allegations, he identified the "front" records of writer and actress. The effect was almost immediate. Hunter had starred in NBC's *Robert Montgomery Presents: Rise Up and Walk*, sponsored by Johnson's wax and Lucky Strike cigarettes. In February of 1952, she was featured in *Counterattack* as taking part in a 1948 meeting of the Freedom from Fear Committee, named a front group by the Tenney committee in California. Moreover, she raised money for the defense of the Hollywood Ten described as "front-line shock troops in the battle for individual freedoms," sponsored the "notorious" Waldorf Peace Conference, and signed an appeal urging President Truman to intervene in the case of Willie McGee, a condemned black man in Mississippi.[19]

Hunter made six television appearances on major networks (ABC, CBS, and NBC) in 1949 and filmed *Streetcar* in 1950. Between 1951 and 1953, she appeared in four shows for ABC and NBC. In 1954, there was no television work for the actress. Within two years, according to Kanfer, "the master blacklisters had made her almost unemployable" on the major networks.[20]

To offset the networks' diminishing interest and guided by her press agent Arthur P. Jacobs, she turned for advice to conservative Hollywood labor leader Roy Brewer of the Motion Picture Alliance for the Preservation of American Ideals. Engaged in vetting politically tainted liberals for the studios, Brewer recommended that she work with him on an affidavit; he would consult with Vincent Hartnett, and then advise her on what she needed to say in succeeding statements to meet Hartnett's requirements for removal from the industry blacklist. Her satisfactory affidavits would then be submitted to clearance offices set up by the networks to administer loyalty oaths to employees and assure sponsors and viewers that "Communist infiltration was impossible."[21]

Hunter wrote a remorseful statement, dated May 6, 1955, in which she attested to her patriotism and loathing of Communism. "It was only after I had made several errors in judgment," she said, "that I was finally alerted to a clearer and more intelligent understanding of the insidious workings of the Communist conspiracy."[22] Within two weeks of submitting the statement, Hunter received a telephone call from Vincent Hartnett offering his clearance services.

Hunter's autobiography, three-parts memoir and one-part cookbook called *Loose in the Kitchen*, has a three-year gap in the narrative (1953–1956). Even though she worked on Broadway in 1952–53 in the revival of *The Children's Hour*, in *The Tender Trap* in 1954–55, and was elected to the Actors' Equity council (1953–59), she remained blacklisted with the networks. In the atmosphere of guilt by association perpetrated by *Counterattack* and *Aware*, Hunter's work in Hollywood and Broadway allied her with persons of interest to HUAC, namely, Elia Kazan, José Ferrer, Edward Dmytryk, Uta Hagen, and Lillian Hellman. Moreover, Hunter was identified with two front groups—the Freedom from Fear Committee and the National Council of Arts, Sciences and Professions world peace conference.

Although her activities were those of a civil rights activist, she had been cited in *Counterattack*, customarily published weekly as four legal-sized pages full of capitalized or underlined names of "subversives" with brief paragraphs warning of new conspiracies. Found repeatedly within the pages of *Counterattack*, published between 1947 and 1952, were the names of Florence Eldridge, Judy Holliday, Dorothy Parker, Lillian Hellman, Uta Hagen, Gale Sondergaard, and Lee Grant. In contrast, Hunter went unnoticed by the anti-Communist crusaders until 1952. That year, she came to the attention of Hartnett, and her name appeared in *Counterattack* as one among four women with reputedly "long Communist front records."[23] By publicizing suspected Communists and front supporters in their pages, *Counterattack* and *Aware* became semi-official guides to an industry-wide blacklist.

Even theater critic Brooks Atkinson was taken to task by *Counterattack* for writing that the "hoodlums are in control here as well as in Russia. We cannot expect to have vital art in our theater if we . . . yield the control of cultural life to the Yahoos and hoodlums."[24] Moreover, opera impresario Rudolf Bing did not escape Hartnett's scrutiny. Bing was rebuked for hiring artists with records "supporting Communists" at the Metropolitan Opera Company, namely, actor Jack Gilford and directors Garson Kanin and Margaret Webster.[25]

Blacklist Burning

The American Federation of Television and Radio Artists is a national union of performers and writers in radio and television. The AFTRA annual election for board members in 1954 was prelude to the trial of John Henry Faulk and the uprising of radio and television artists against blacklisting and clearances.[26]

AFTRA was controlled by a board of thirty-five elected from the membership. In the early fifties, the union's anti-Communist faction, supported by AWARE, Inc., was elected year after year. Matters changed in 1954 when a slate of candidates, called the "Middle of the Roaders," challenged the status quo. Although the insurgents were defeated, AWARE, Inc. retaliated by attacking the opposition's patriotism and calling for a full-fledged investigation of the entertainment industry in New York.[27]

A year later at a general membership meeting in March, a resolution was offered to condemn AWARE, Inc. for unwarranted interference in the union's affairs. Following fiery speeches, the membership voted to condemn the conservative group and proceeded to elect the Middle of the Road slate opposed to Communism *and* to blacklisting. The "Middlers," as they were called, won twenty-seven of the thirty-five seats on the AFTRA board and named CBS news commentator Charles Collingwood as president, actor-comedian Orson Bean as first vice-president, and radio talk show host John Henry Faulk as second vice-president.

By July of 1955, Francis E. Walter had gained the chairmanship of the House Committee on Un-American Activities. Despite his promise to end the era of probes into specific professions, the lure of show business proved irresistible to the representative from Pennsylvania. Walter launched the last investigation into Communist activities in theater, radio, television, and their unions. In the process, the Committee ensnared folk singer Pete Seeger, impresario Joseph Papp, and comedian Zero Mostel.

The stage name "Zero" was given to Mostel by Ivan Black, the Café Society's press agent, to suggest a man who has made something of nothing," or, in the comedian's view, a reflection of his bank account.[28] Later celebrated on Broadway for the peripatetic fool in A *Funny Thing Happened on the Way to the Forum* and the good-natured Tevya in *Fiddler on the Roof,* the actor was in California playing in *Lunatics and Lovers* when he was questioned in a special hearing in Hollywood by a subcommittee of HUAC during the fall of 1955. When pressed to confirm that a business associate was a member of the Communist Party, Mostel took the Fifth and continued throughout the interview to assert his constitutional rights. He said, "I will be glad to answer any questions of that sort where I don't have to talk about other individuals." Moreover, he astounded the Committee with his imitation of a butterfly at rest as a hypothetical example of a harmless, apolitical performance given during an alleged Communist Party fundraiser. "There is no crime in making anybody laugh," he told the Committee. "I don't care if you laugh at me."[29]

The HUAC hearings in New York during the week of August 14, 1955, did not proceed as Chairman Walter expected. The Committee convened in the federal building on Foley Square in lower Manhattan and ended a four-day hearing of twenty-two show business witnesses on August 18. Eighteen witnesses, largely from radio and television, included the loquaciously unfriendly Madeleine Lee Gilford, who invoked the protections of the First, Fourth, Fifth, and Eighth Amendments when asked about Communist infiltration in AFTRA and Communist Party membership. Four others defied the Committee on the grounds that it had no right to question them on their political beliefs or associations and faced contempt charges for their defiance.[30]

A disgruntled Francis Walter told reporters, "I was under the impression that some of our witnesses would testify openly and frankly."[31]

In the climate of reprisals, *Aware* announced that the AFTRA vote to condemn AWARE, Inc. was a Communist plot.[32] When the new board took office in January 1956, Vincent Hartnett struck back with a "News Supplement to the Membership Bulletin," *Aware 16*.[33] Citing back issues of the *Daily Worker*, Hartnett accused radio celebrity John Henry Faulk of Communist activities.

Faulk, whom writer Studs Terkel called a "maverick" Texan, worked for WCBS radio, an affiliate of the Columbia Broadcasting Company, as a talk show host and sometimes television performer.[34] "I spun a few yarns," Faulk said of his popular one-hour daily show, "reminisced about my childhood in Texas and commented on the news of the day and the foibles of the world."[35]

After the new AFTRA board took office, Faulk soon learned that Laurence Johnson was falsely linking him to Communism and lobbying his sponsors (Libby's Frozen Foods and Vegetables) to withdraw from his show. Network officials suggested that he answer AWARE's allegations with an affidavit addressing his loyalty and patriotism to share with concerned sponsors. Faulk's affidavit stressed his years with WCBS, his army record, his overseas Red Cross service, his appearances before hundreds of patriotic charitable groups, and his many years of service to the American public. His reasons for taking office in AFTRA were "solely to help eradicate blacklisting."[36]

On the day Faulk signed and notarized the affidavit and took it to CBS, he had a luncheon appointment with Sidney Davis, the attorney from Louis Nizer's office who had accompanied Margaret Webster to her hearing before McCarthy's subcommittee three years earlier. Faulk made the luncheon date to talk with the lawyer about representing the union as legal counsel, but circumstances prevented the performer from extending the invitation. Instead, Faulk found himself talking about the looming threat to his livelihood at CBS. "I asked him if he thought Nizer would be interested in taking the case should it come to a lawsuit," Faulk recalled.[37] Davis said he would discuss it with Nizer.

With a subsequent loss of employment at CBS in the summer of 1957 (poor ratings and program changes were given as reasons for the cancellation of his contract with WCBS) and faced with reluctant employers at other stations, Faulk turned to the celebrated civil rights attorney. On June 26, 1956, Louis Nizer filed *Faulk v. AWARE Inc., Laurence Johnson, and Vincent Hartnett* in the New York Supreme Court. The legal complaint charged that AWARE had entered into a conspiracy with the advertising agencies and networks to defame John Henry Faulk's reputation and professional integrity, to destroy his livelihood, and to "eliminate him as a foe of the defendant's extortion of monies and use of racketeering practices to intimidate and terrorize through blacklisting."[38] The curtain was going up on the final act of the blacklist.

Supporting Player

When the case went to trial six years later, Kim Hunter stepped forward to assist in the fight to end the blacklist. Echoing Dorothy Parker and others in the industry, she knew, although there was never any proof, that she had been blacklisted. "No one ever came to me directly and said, 'You are blacklisted.' . . . There were only signals, such as the fact there were no film offers after I won the Oscar, not even from Warner Brothers, which simply never picked up on the contract they had with me."[39] The same occurred with the networks. "No one ever announced that she was on a blacklist," Hunter remarked. "It gradually became clear when there were simply no calls first from CBS, then ABC, and finally NBC."[40]

A theater colleague described Kim Hunter as a sweet, generous woman who could be stubborn and feisty.[41] Even though the actress was needed as a witness on behalf of the plaintiff because of her grim associations with Vincent Hartnett's clearance racket, she had reestablished her stage career by 1962. Faulk thought she might be reluctant to risk her career a second time. Nevertheless, he asked the actress for help and described their encounter.

> From the expression on Kim's face, I was sure she was going to apologize, wish me well and say that she thought it best to stay out of the case. Instead, she placed her arms around my neck and kissed me, and said quite solemnly, "I have decided I'm going to testify. I want to be part of this trial. I'm going to do it for your sake, Johnny, because I admire you. But most of all I'm going to do it for my own sake and in behalf of my children and my profession and my country.[42]

With Blanche DuBois's advice to her sister perhaps uppermost in her mind ("Don't—don't hang back with the brutes!"[43]), Kim Hunter followed television producer David Susskind, actor Tony Randall, and advertising account executive Tom Murray into the witness chair on May 16, 1962.[44]

Photographers waited on the sidewalks and in the hallways for the actress to arrive at the courthouse on Foley Square. Louis Nizer refused their requests to pose for photographs. Hunter was taken into the courtroom, where she listened to the testimony of Tom Murray, account executive at the Grey advertising agency, who established the link between Laurence Johnson and the blacklisting of Faulk by CBS.[45]

NIZER: Now in March 1956 did you receive a communication from one Laurence Johnson?

MURRAY: Yes, I did.

NIZER: Tell us about it.

MURRAY: First, Mr. Johnson identified himself as Larry Johnson of Syracuse. He said that he owned several supermarkets and had influence over a number of others in central New York state. He gave me an indication of the total gross volume of food business that was done in the area and it was most impressive. It ran into the millions. I believe the figure was $18 to $20 million.

. . . Mr. Johnson then said that he felt that it was a disgrace that our company was using a Communist, John Henry Faulk, to advertise products. I replied that I had no such knowledge about Mr. Faulk. And he said, "Well you had better get in line because a lot of people along Madison Avenue are getting in line and the display space which the Pabst Brewing Company [Murray's client] has in the stores that I either own or control is what he called 'hard-won' space. . . ." In other words, it had been difficult to achieve [the] status that Pabst Brewing Company had, in a display sense, within his stores. That happens to be a very accurate statement, by the way.

Uninterested in advertising space, Louis Nizer brought Murray back to his conversation with Laurence Johnson.

MURRAY: . . . I said that I could not accept a telephone implication of this kind. I felt that there were legal ways of establishing whether or not Mr. Faulk—Mr. Faulk or for that matter, anyone else—was a Communist, and that I had no intention of firing or recommending the firing of a man who was a first-rate salesman for our product. Then he [Johnson] said, "How would you like it if your client were to receive a letter from an American Legion post up here?"

And I said that I was a veteran myself and that I could not believe that the American Legion would lend itself to what I considered to be an obvious blackmail attempt, and he said, "Well, you will find out."

At the conclusion of his testimony, Tom Murray had established the connections among Laurence Johnson, the American Legion, and Hartnett's *Aware* publication.

By mid-morning, a nervous Kim Hunter took the stand and was sworn in. She testified to her appearances in Broadway plays, television shows, and films. Nizer asked if she had found that she was unable to obtain television appearances. "It was a gradual awareness," she remarked. "It started in 1950."[46]

Thomas A. Bolan, representing the defendants, objected to Hunter's testimony. Justice Abraham N. Geller overruled his objection subject to the connection of the actress's testimony to the defendants. Testimony continued:

> MISS HUNTER: There was, as I recall, a firm bit of awareness during 1952 when I was on a television program. I think it was the Celanese Theatre. I know the name of the play. It was [Robert Sherwood's] *Petrified Forest*. There were objections. From what? Where? How? I don't know. I was never told. All I know is that my agent came to me and said—
> BOLAN: I object, your Honor.

The judge sustained Bolan's objection, and Nizer rephrased his question.

> NIZER: Did your former employers report to you why they did not employ you during this period?

Kim Hunter was reluctant to name, or even discuss, her employer, but the defense counsel wanted the name. Justice Geller ruled that Nizer could not pursue the line of questioning unless the witness stated her employer's name. Nizer turned to other questions, and during the evening Hunter consulted others about her dilemma. The next day, she gave the name of William Dolger, at the time an executive of CBS, and Justice Geller allowed her to repeat the earlier conversation.

> MISS HUNTER: I went to Mr. Dolger's office at CBS and talked to him. I can't remember the exact conversation but the substance of it was this, I am having difficulty getting employed, are you aware of that? And he said, "Yes, I am." And I said, because I didn't know who to go to—I wanted to know whether it was possible in any way for him to help me or advise me what I might do to clear away the fog.
> THE COURT: What was his position at WCBS?
> MISS HUNTER: At CBS he was an executive producer. I cannot remember the exact position.
> NIZER: Producer of television shows?
> MISS HUNTER: Yes.
> NIZER: Go ahead, finish your answer.

MISS HUNTER: He said, "I am not sure there is anything I can do, but if I possibly can do something, I will."

The actress recalled that some months later she got a role in NBC's *Gulf Playhouse: A Present from Cotton Mather*, the only television work she had in 1953. She had no work in 1954.

Nizer then asked about the letter her press agent wrote to Vincent Hartnett on May 12, 1953, and Hartnett's subsequent offer to investigate the actress for a fee of two hundred dollars. Nizer directed her to tell the court how she responded to Hartnett's request.

MISS HUNTER: May I explain that Mr. Jacobs [her press agent] called me on the telephone . . . and asked if I were willing to pay the $200 for information from Mr. Hartnett. I said that I would not, that my life is absolutely an open book, and I did not feel I needed Mr. Hartnett's information or investigation and I certainly wasn't going to pay $200 for it.

NIZER: And you did not?

MISS HUNTER: And I did not. However, Mr. Jacobs said "Please"—

Nizer asked permission to read Hartnett's letter, written on October 7, 1953, to Geraldine B. Zorbaugh, general counsel for the American Broadcasting Company, which revealed the cozy workings of the blacklisters with the network clearance offices.

NIZER [reading]: "Dear Gerry, On October 2 (1953), I received from you the enclosed list of names for the purpose of evaluation. . . . I note that on the list appeared the following names . . . and one of these names is Kim Hunter. . . . In my opinion, finally, you would run a serious risk of adverse public opinion by featuring on your network Kim Hunter."

Nizer turned to his witness: "Miss Hunter, had you known that Mr. Hartnett had written to the American Broadcasting Company to this effect? That they would have a serious risk if they ran you on their show?" Hunter replied that she did not know about the letter.

Hunter later testified to a late-night telephone conversation with Hartnett shortly before the resolution to condemn AWARE came before the union membership for a vote. As a television performer, Kim Hunter had joined AFTRA in 1948.

NIZER: Will you give us the substance as well as you can recall and take it easy, Miss Hunter. Give us the substance of the conversation.

MISS HUNTER: The substance of it was that he said to show—kind of show my good faith, that I was truly a loyal American and not pro-Communist, that affidavits were not sufficient, that I should by all rights do something actively anti-Communist and did I object to doing any such thing, and I said, "No, certainly not."

He asked me then if I knew about the AWARE resolution, the resolution to condemn AWARE that was pending within our television union at AFTRA, and I said yes, I know about it.

And he said, well one way that I could show a strong anti-Communist stand would be to go to that meeting and speak up in support of AWARE, publicly, in front of everybody.

I said, "Mr. Hartnett, it would be very difficult for me to speak in support of AWARE because I am not in support of AWARE, Incorporated."

He said, "Well, it wouldn't be necessary to support AWARE, Incorporated, as such, and, in fact it wouldn't even really be necessary for you to go to the meeting, if you would be willing to send a telegram that could be read before the meeting publicly, speaking, saying in so many words that you are against this resolution to condemn AWARE."

I said, "Mr. Hartnett, I will do my best to form a telegram. . . ."

Nizer turned to Hartnett's statement during pre-trial depositions in June 1958.

NIZER: I read from Mr. Hartnett's deposition . . . this question to Mr. Hartnett on the examination before trial. [Reading] "Q: Did you ever ask an actor who was trying to clear himself from an accusation of pro-Communist affiliation and you were guiding him, did you ever ask him to demonstrate . . . his patriotism by voting a certain way in AFTRA, in other words for an AWARE group in AFTRA?'

Bolan stated his objection, but Nizer continued to read.

NIZER [reading]: "Q: Did you ever ask him to vote in a certain way in AFTRA, in other words, voting for an AWARE group in AFTRA? A: Yes I did. Q: Did you ever ask him to make certain speeches for the AWARE group in AFTRA? A: On at least one occasion I did. Q: Who was that one occasion? A: Kim Hunter. Q: Did you do so as making that one of the tests of their clearing themselves, in other words, seeing the light of anti-Communism? A: I did."

Nizer turned to his witness, "Now, Miss Hunter, did you thereafter send a telegram to the union?"

MISS HUNTER: Yes, sir.

NIZER: Was there annexed, did you annex to a copy of that telegram a note to Mr. Hartnett?

Again, Bolan objected, but Nizer was allowed to enter into the record a copy of the telegram that Hunter sent to the AFTRA membership. For the jury's benefit, Nizer read from the text:

> NIZER [reading]: " . . . I'm neither a member of AWARE, Inc. nor a friend, nor am I in sympathy with any of its methods, but I urge you all to think very carefully indeed before voting for this resolution. The individuals hurt by Bulletin No. 2 have recourse to right any wrong that may have been committed, but AFTRA will have no recourse whatsoever if it places itself on record as protesting and aiding the Communist conspiracy, even if this action is taken in the noble desire to aid and protect the innocent. Signed, Kim Hunter."
>
> And annexed to it, this is from Mr. Hartnett's files, May 25, 1955: "Dear Mr. Hartnett. Enclosed is a copy of the wire I sent to the AFTRA membership meeting last night. I was unable to attend the meeting so I have no idea whether it was read or not. Signed, Kim Hunter."

NIZER: After this date, did you get television appearances?

BOLAN: I object, your Honor

THE COURT: Overruled.

MISS HUNTER: Yes, Mr. Nizer, I worked.

THE COURT: I didn't hear that. Did you finish your answer?

MISS HUNTER: I worked quite frequently after that and to the present date.

Kim Hunter miraculously appeared in eight network shows in 1955 and four in 1956, including the award-winning *Requiem for a Heavyweight*. Her television career continued for another forty-three years.

Nizer was not yet finished with his witness. He proceeded to read a letter from Vincent Hartnett to Laurence Johnson, dated May 23, 1955.

> NIZER [reading]: "Dear Larry, Confidentially, I had a good telephone conversation this morning with Kim Hunter who just returned to New York from Bucks County Playhouse. I stressed to Kim Hunter that she had [underlined] to take a public stand against Communism. She assured me that she would do so and if she comes through tomorrow night at the AFTRA meeting as she promised she would do, you will hear the comrades shrieking all the way from New York to Syracuse. . . . Keep up the fight, Larry. You and your associates have done wonders. Sincerely, Hartnett."

Bolan began his cross-examination of Kim Hunter with the telegram that Hartnett asked her to send to the union.

BOLAN: Did Mr. Hartnett ask you to do anything you did not wish to do?

MISS HUNTER: Yes.

BOLAN: What was that?

MISS HUNTER: I did not really wish to go on record in my union as opposing the resolution.

Bolan then introduced an affidavit that the actress gave to Hartnett in 1955, but Nizer objected unless all of Hunter's affidavits, written between 1952 and 1955 under the guidance of Roy Brewer and Vincent Hartnett, were also introduced into evidence. Nizer argued, "They have tried to present the last one that they accepted from her. I say that it is incomplete under the context of the circumstances, and that either they offer all of them to show how she was squeezed, otherwise I object to the whole thing."

At this point, Hunter testified that she worked on affidavits with Roy Brewer to meet Hartnett's specifications for removing her from the blacklist. Nizer's redirect went to the heart of the matter: The series of statements that Hunter had written under pressure from the clearance consultants, beginning in 1953, were evidence of her punitive treatment at the hands of the blacklisters.

Kim Hunter was excused as a witness late in the afternoon of May 16. As she walked by the counsel table, she embraced John Henry Faulk.[47] She had been an admirable witness. As a blacklisted actress caught up in the clearance game, her testimony irreparably harmed the defendants' case.

There was widespread interest in Faulk's case, and witnesses came forward with offers to testify, but Nizer stayed with his original list. Character-actor Everett Sloan testified that his unemployment began when he was confused with *Red Channels* listee radio writer Alan Sloane. Mark Goodson, a distinguished television producer of quiz and panel shows, described his difficulties hiring actress Judy Holliday and writer Abe Burrows for the celebrity panel show *The Name's the Same*. Goodson testified that Laurence Johnson protested the appearances of Holliday and Burrows as guest celebrities. Rebuked by the show's advertising agency for hiring the controversial actress, Goodson testified that he did not hire Judy Holliday a second time and dropped Burrows as a panelist as well.[48]

Nizer asked Goodson, as he had asked television producer David Susskind earlier in the trial, to describe the system of clearances that required producers to submit lists of names for each show to either the network or the advertising agency. If there were objections, Goodson told the court, they were made by telephone or a list would be returned with notations by unacceptable names. Then, producers repeated the procedure, submitting other names, until a cast was cleared for use. No reasons were offered. However, Goodson's point was clear: "nonclearability meant unemployability."[49] It was also transparent that sponsors, agencies, and networks colluded in the practice of blacklisting.

After a parade of witnesses, Louis Nizer rested his case on May 25, a month after the trial began.

Thomas Bolan's witnesses, Paul Milton and Vincent Hartnett, did little to counter the evidence of malicious libel and conspiracy to deprive John Henry Faulk of his livelihood and exercise control over the networks. On the afternoon of Louis Nizer's summation, the seventy-three-year-old Laurence Johnson died of natural causes in a motel room in the Bronx.[50] The trial proceeded, and Nizer returned to the heart of the matter: "The issue is not Communist at all. It is *private vigilantism* for profit."

NIZER: This is dangerous, ladies and gentlemen. It is far more dangerous, dangerous as Communists are. This is far more dangerous to permit the culture, the entertainment medium to be controlled by a few people for profit. That is the real issue; that is the framework.

At the trial's conclusion, Justice Geller instructed the jury on compensatory and punitive damages, if they decided for the plaintiff. The jury awarded John Henry Faulk $3.5 million, a record verdict in libel cases in the United States. The defendants appealed the decision, the verdict was upheld, but the amount of damages was reduced to $500,000 by an appellate court, which decided this amount was in line with Faulk's estimated earnings. Nevertheless, the verdict brought against AWARE, Inc., Hartnett, and the estate of Laurence Johnson ended the practice of blacklisting. As Stefan Kanfer said, "In 1962, the blacklist had at last proved unprofitable."[51]

A year later, John Henry Faulk published a book that featured the trial's issues and principal players: the dapper Louis Nizer, the Ivy League–looking Thomas Bolan, the blue-suited, cigar-smoking Vincent Hartnett, and the many witnesses speaking about their personal experiences with blacklisting. *Fear on Trial* recapped the punishing aspects of the blacklist: "not the economic hardships that it worked on its victims, but the painful inability to use one's creative resources. It shuts one off from contact with the public at the most important level of existence, the creative level."[52]

Kim Hunter's hiatus from film and television highlights the importance of Broadway and its independent producers for artists with *theater* credentials. Although her career was stymied in Hollywood and on television she, unlike radio-television artist John Henry Faulk, could turn to the stage as a creative outlet. She worked on Broadway, in stock companies and regional theaters, and in the national tour of *And Miss Reardon Drinks a Little*. John Henry Faulk, on the other hand, never recovered his fame as a performer. "Like many performers who were blacklisted and later 'cleared,'" his biographer Michael Burton wrote, "he could not regain the momentum he had lost in a highly competitive medium."[53]

"Wage Peace Not War"

Kim Hunter's absence from the screen ended long before her hiatus from television. In 1956, she appeared opposite Bette Davis in *Storm Center*, a film about a librarian's refusal to remove a subversive book from library shelves, that is, a form of book burning. "I thought, un-oh, here we go again," Hunter said. Nevertheless, her problems with the studios failed to resurface.[54]

Six years after the Faulk case, Hunter made the first of the sci-fi classics *Planet of the Apes*, in which she had another iconic moment. Encased in the ape-like costume as the psychiatrist Dr. Zira, she held up a sign that read "Wage Peace Not War." This snapshot image registered the civil disobedience of the Vietnam era. The barely recognizable actress (only her eyes were visible) stood before the public again as an emblem of quiet defiance.

Nevertheless, with no elaborate costume masking her identity, Hunter had taken a courageous stand on behalf of John Henry Faulk and all artists whose creative pursuits had been stymied by the blacklisters. She took another public stand in 1999, when many in Hollywood rebelled against presenting the Motion Picture Academy award for lifetime achievement to Elia Kazan. Many considered his naming of names in 1952 grounds for disqualification and denounced the presentation of the award to the friendly witness who, when he first appeared in executive session before HUAC in January 1952, refused to name names. Pressured by the president of Twentieth Century Fox and the producer of his recent film *Viva Zapata*, Kazan testified again after writing the Committee a letter that said: "I have come to the conclusion that secrecy serves the Communists.... The American people need the facts and all the facts.... It is my obligation as a citizen to tell everything I know."[55] He proceeded to name eight members of a Communist Party unit in the Group Theatre that included J. Edward Bromberg, Phoebe Brand, Morris Carnovsky, Clifford Odets, Tony Kraber, Lewis Leverett, Paula Miller Strasberg, and Art Smith along with others without connections to the Group Theatre.

For a half century, Elia Kazan remained a figure of controversy. When he was finally awarded an honorary Oscar at the age of eighty-nine, many still condemned him, but others praised his testimony before HUAC as an act of patriotism. Karl Malden, the original Mitch in *Streetcar*, proposed the honorary Oscar for Kazan's lifelong *artistic* achievements, and Kim Hunter offered her support. "Artistic achievement," she said at the time, "and the mistake someone made years ago don't belong together."[56]

This sensible, generous artist held a long view of her experience with blacklisting. Following the interruption of her career at the highpoint of the Oscar award in 1951, she experienced depression during the intervals when she was not working. Her daughter, Kathryn Emmett, who became a civil rights attorney, recalled that her mother was happiest when she was working. The denial of work by "invisible" conservative forces had a "terrible impact" on her career and reduced the family's income and, in time, contributed to the actress's forceful representation at the trial of John Henry Faulk.

In high school in the early sixties, Kathryn Emmett witnessed firsthand the injustices perpetrated by the powerful on the powerless in the political arena of the day. "All that my mother wanted was to be an actress and to work," Emmett volunteered. "She was in the category of a 'mother for peace' in her politics and dedicated, not to political activism, but to her family and to her creative work."

At the memorial service in 2002, Emmett spoke of the courage her mother exhibited during the Faulk trial largely because she was not a "public person" in the sense of standing at the "barricades" to protest injustice. Nevertheless, in her testimony on behalf of John Henry Faulk, she spoke out because she thought the entire business of blacklisting was simply "wrong."[57]

In an interview in the mid-eighties, Kim Hunter expressed her belief that the dismal period must not be forgotten in order to guard against a recurrence of those years of political repression. "For a long while, I wouldn't talk about it at all," she remarked. "I do now, because there's a whole new generation that doesn't remember. And the more one knows, the more one can see, and not allow history to repeat itself."[58]

No one on either side who was touched by the hunters escaped
undamaged.

—Arthur Laurents, *Original Story By*

Postscript

Fifty-two years after screenwriter Leo Townsend named the actress in testimony before the House Committee on Un-American Activities, the diminutive Phoebe Brand sat in her New York apartment among memorabilia marking her and her late husband Morris Carnovsky's theatrical careers.[1] A former member of the Group Theatre and teacher at the Hollywood Actors' Laboratory, Brand expressed herself in the same resonant voice captured in Louis Malle's film *Vanya on 42nd Street*. In her view, the period of the Red-baiting had been a "horrific thing."

With her gray and white cat, Feste, wandering about the apartment, Brand talked about the loss of work in Hollywood and the closing of the Hollywood Actors' Laboratory in those long-ago years. At age ninety-five, Phoebe Brand still found it difficult to reflect upon that "killingly frightening" time, as she called it, that compelled artists before investigative committees, resulted in loss of employment and tarnished careers, and, in the case of Brand and Carnovsky, motivated their return to the East coast and their efforts to reclaim their livelihoods in teaching and the theater. The couple became part of the daring production of *The World of Sholem Aleichem*, produced, directed, and performed by blacklisted artists in 1953, which defied McCarthyites in the belief that talent trumped political agendas with New York audiences and critics. They were proved correct.

Just as Phoebe Brand vividly remembered that frightful time, so, too, other actors, directors, designers, playwrights, composers, and choreographers cast light on the abridgements of civil liberties in the fifties and the powerful effects of the congressional committees on citizens and the cultural landscape. For over fifty years, historians and cultural and literary critics largely ignored the unique personal histories of the professional women of film and stage who were witnesses before the committees. With the exception of the playwright Lillian

Hellman, the leading actresses of *Watch on the Rhine, Born Yesterday, Toys in the Attic,* and *Saint Joan* have been neglected in the writings on the period largely because these women were silenced by the opprobrium they experienced and the embarrassment they felt as unfriendly witnesses under McCarthyism. Their case histories share the political, social, and moral issues that were lived and debated by congressional witnesses, including the concealed Communist Party memberships, the associations with groups that were created in the forties to help victims of war and later viewed in Cold War terms as subversive, and the personal and professional penalties levied against them for refusing to bring harm to others by naming names.

Moreover, the case histories examined here clearly mirror the forensic structure of the hearings: indictment, trial, verdict. The personal experiences of the witnesses incorporated the forensic pattern of subpoena, legal counsel, the hearing before a committee acting as judge and jury, the defendant's testimony (friendly and unfriendly), and the verdict that returned the defendant to her career or cast her into the outer darkness of the unemployed. Brenda Murphy in her engaging book *Congressional Theatre* pointed out that HUAC's major weapon was the committee hearing, "which was in reality a trial without a defense, a jury, or even, in many cases, evidence against the accused."[2] Revere was handed a bogus Communist Party card by HUAC's committeemen to encourage incriminating comments; Hellman's lawyer rained down copies of her famous letter onto reporters; Margaret Webster and Uta Hagen reintroduced Joan of Arc, the archetypal scapegoat, as the natural historical analogy for modern witnesses who followed the dictates of conscience and were pilloried by those in authority.

With the exception of Mady Christians, the modern women emerge as *survivors*, but their careers in film and television were damaged for years. To paraphrase Anne Revere, the majority were "dead in the business" for almost a decade. Like Lillian Hellman, Anne Revere, and Kim Hunter, the women, even the lesser playwright Dorothy Parker, turned to Broadway as a means of restoring their reputations, careers, and incomes.

In general, Broadway was considered untouched by the antics of the Mc-Carthyites. In particular, New York's commercial theater district was looked upon as an artistic and economic refuge for those blacklisted by Hollywood and the networks. The practice of blacklisting, which enthralled Hollywood and the networks, never reached into the theater "not so much because theatre folk were liberal," playwright Arthur Laurents wrote, "but because the producers were self-employed individuals, not companies, and weren't beholden to corporations or banks."[3] Controlled by the creative decisions and pocketbooks of such independent producers as Kermit Bloomgarden, Cheryl Crawford, Roger L. Stevens, and Robert Whitehead, the anti-Communist crusade could not take hold in America's central theater district. Talent and availability overrode all other considerations within the forty blocks of New York City real estate called Broadway.

Even though Broadway held out the means to recover stage careers, although not the higher salaries of Hollywood and television, a general haze, some called it a *graylist*, hung over many theater careers in the late forties and early fifties.

An Atmosphere of Caution

When measured against the larger scheme of things, Broadway's grayness diminished a relatively small number of careers. Nevertheless, those affected found their careers and financial losses, however minimal, impossible to ignore. After appearing to acclaim in *Watch on the Rhine* and *I Remember Mama*, Mady Christians found stage work elusive. Agents, producers, and casting directors stopped calling with offers of employment. As she expressed to a reporter, there were no explanations offered for the lack of employment. This was likewise true of Anne Revere, whose career vanished in Hollywood after she took the Fifth and was subsequently branded an uncooperative witness by the committeemen and the studios. Revere relocated to New York and took minor roles for nine years before appearing to critical acclaim in Hellman's *Toys in the Attic*. In 1951, the same year as Mady Christians's death and Anne Revere's congressional hearing, the celebrated stage actress of *Othello*, *The Country Girl*, and *Saint Joan*, Uta Hagen, who was a naturalized citizen, found herself stigmatized by her listing in *Red Channels* and subpoenaed to appear before HUAC. During this period, her agent dropped her as a client and she was trailed by FBI agents down grocery store aisles and across theater lobbies. In order to keep working, Hagen accepted roles in undistinguished touring productions, which in her biographer's estimation may have affected her stage career more so than the blacklisting.[4]

In a sense, Uta Hagen's experience with blacklisting from film and television and the difficulties of getting cast on Broadway mirror the experiences of other artists in this period. Divorced from José Ferrer and with a daughter to care for, she was in a touring production of *Tovarich* when she read in the *New York Times* that she was to be summoned before the Committee to "explain her political beliefs" and "connections" with Communist-front organizations.[5] She was subpoenaed for the same set of Washington hearings as actor J. Edward Bromberg and her former husband, actor-director José Ferrer. Newspaper columns described her as a "mystery witness" called to provide additional information to fill in the gaps in Ferrer's testimony that had irritated the Committee. Although she waited in the halls of Congress for three days, she was never invited into the hearing room. As it so happened in his second session before the Committee that Ferrer denied any leftist leanings, named names, and returned to Hollywood to continue work in film. Hagen, on the other hand, sat in the outer corridor, was never called, and remained blacklisted. She returned to New York, joined actor-director Herbert Berghof in founding a school for acting (the HB Studio) and took refuge in off-Broadway's Phoenix Theatre to sustain her craft until 1962, when she appeared to Broadway acclaim as Martha in Edward Albee's *Who's Afraid of Virginia Woolf?*

Of the hiatus in her stage career, the actress told Edward R. Murrow that great writers, philosophers, artists, and musicians "helped me drown out the frenetic racket made by the compromisers who try to bend ideals to fit their practical needs and personal appetites, and to deprive us of our spiritual salvation."[6]

Although Uta Hagen experienced a hiatus from Broadway for almost a decade, no formal *agenda* afflicted the theater district even though the politically inconvenient were oftentimes deprived of work. Lillian Hellman's assessment was stoically unadorned. "Life had changed," she remarked following her return to New York after her appearance before HUAC.[7]

In the ascendant days of the House Committee on Un-American Activities, survival was difficult for most, but impossible for the timid. Playwrights were the strongest (and most outspoken) of the discredited. Hellman improvised in her designer clothes before HUAC and restored her career with a revival of *The Children's Hour* followed by her adaptation of Jean Anouilh's version of the Joan of Arc story called *The Lark*. Furthermore, she hired the blacklisted Kim Hunter for *The Children's Hour* and later Anne Revere for *Toys in the Attic*. Moreover, playwright Elmer Rice refused to be intimidated by conservative forces. Upon learning that John Garfield had been barred from appearing in ABC's television revival of Rice's *Counsellor-at-Law*, the playwright called the advertising agency for the Celanese Company to express his outrage: "I have repeatedly denounced the men who sit in the Kremlin for judging artists by political standards," he told them. "I do not intend to acquiesce when the same procedure is followed by political commissars who sit in the offices of advertising agencies or business corporations."[8]

Grief-stricken by the untimely death of his friend Mady Christians, Rice raged in a letter to the drama editor of the *New York Times*: "She was slandered, falsely accused, hounded by investigators, deprived of employment, faced with destitution."[9] John Van Druten, who wrote *I Remember Mama*, also deplored the "persecution" to which the actress had been subjected and which "greatly speeded her death."[10] Many were not so bold, including the usually outspoken Margaret Webster, who declined the use of her name on a questionnaire.

When asked to respond to a survey about the effects of *Red Channels* on the entertainment industry, Webster gave a timid response: "*Red Channels* had certainly affected my professional life, but not, so far as I can judge, my personal one—except for the general atmosphere of caution that surrounds almost all free discussion of public problems these days." She noted that she had definitely been debarred from important radio and television jobs, but she had no direct evidence that she had been excluded from work in the theater. She ended with a word of caution:

> It is my personal view that . . . the dangers of having public opinion act in the place of law to circumscribe a man's life and deprive him of his livelihood are only too apparent and have historically been proved, over and over again, perverted, disastrous and usually foolish in the long perspective.[11]

Cautious of the times, she gave the reporter permission to quote her opinions but not to name his source. Nevertheless, Webster could not hide from the gathering forces of the committees armed with FBI files, copies of *Red Channels* and *Counterattack*, and congressional subpoenas.

Shadow-Boxing

As the testimonies of these artists suggest (and the same was true of blue-collar workers, teachers, lawyers, scientists, and government officials), McCarthyism bequeathed to the cultural landscape a record of blighted lives, relationships, marriages, families, careers, and social programs.[12] Webster called the experience "shadow-boxing," to describe the futile efforts to recognize accusers and their libels among shadowy lists, unsubstantiated rumors, anonymous reports, and sealed testimonies.[13]

In terms of the overall experience, some people flourished; others were marginalized; and still others had their careers and lives destroyed. Nevertheless, without perhaps the same exuberance as in previous years, most managed to survive to work another day. The majority experienced FBI investigations and face-to-face interviews with Hoover's agents. All touched by the political blight experienced paranoia, fear, emotional and economic distress as telephones sounded tapped, mail appeared rifled, bank records were scrutinized, and livelihoods eroded. Hundreds received subpoenas and appeared in congressional courtrooms; though few were actually jailed, contempt citations were issued to some, including playwright Arthur Miller as late as 1956.

Viewed collectively, the women of film and stage featured here crossed the many divides of legal and extra-legal investigations in an era where the entertainment industry was held in the glare of anti-Communist headlights. Moreover, the undocumented case histories of the Hollywood and Broadway women featured here spanned the arc of the national experience with congressional and state committees. As liberals active in social and political causes, they were concerned in the thirties and forties with the defeat of fascism and the establishment of world peace. Mady Christians, Dorothy Parker, and Margaret Webster were activists in search of a way to oppose fascism in Europe. Judy Holliday and Kim Hunter were innocents abroad in the forums of peace marches and civil rights protests. Anne Revere and Lillian Hellman were most likely members of the Communist Party—USA at a time when the party was a legal entity and when Communism appeared to offer a viable solution to fascism. As witnesses, Revere and Hellman took the Fifth to avoid admitting their party membership and answering follow-up questions that would subsequently tarnish friends and colleagues and crush all of their careers.

Like most witnesses, these women were not proud of their unfriendly performances before McCarthy or McCarran or HUAC but looked upon their choice to take the Fifth as the lesser of two evils. Whether they took the Fifth or called upon the protections of other amendments, they entered the hearing rooms as stylish, confidant women prepared to mask their uncooperative demeanor in stage-worthy performances or dramatically flaunt their noncompliant attitudes. Notably, they did not name names during the course of the hearings. Consequently, they were stigmatized—portrayed during the Cold War as members of a national conspiracy that threatened America's security—and their names were entered into the FBI's database as security risks to be detained in a national emergency. Once named a Communist or a Communist sympathizer by informants, friendly witnesses, or right-wing columnists, the means of establishing innocence was unclear, although many opportunists were willing to accept fees to investigate and provide clearances. Moreover, the sanctions for Communists, sympathizers, and dissenters were broad: economic, psychological, cultural, and political.

Financial problems were uppermost in the minds of those embroiled in blacklisting and the congressional hearings. The women and men who refused to cooperate with investigators, or who were identified as Communists or labeled as supporters of front groups, routinely lost their jobs in Hollywood and with the broadcast networks. Under the Waldorf Statement agreed upon by the studio heads, the film studios fired uncooperative witnesses who took the Fifth without naming names, and the broadcast networks refused to employ those who became controversial unless they were cleared by professional clearance agencies. They adhered to the old saying "Where there's smoke, there's fire!" Employers also paid attention to letters from associates or telephone calls from supermarket executive Laurence Johnson and other purveyors of products advertised by the networks. There was no restitution from the blacklist other than by the clearance consultants, with their questionable business practices.

Loss of employment often reduced artists and their families to dire financial straits. Hellman's loss of a screenwriting career reduced her annual income from $150,000 to $10,000; the IRS further exacerbated her predicament by reappraising her taxes and adding $175,000 to her tax bill.[14] John Henry

Faulk's income during his six years at WCBS was in the neighborhood of one million dollars. His earnings dropped to zero when the network fired him. To offset expenses, many sold their homes or rented cheaper ones. Others found alternative employment.

In the early fifties, Phoebe Brand and Ann Shepherd turned to teaching and clerical work. A performer on popular daytime radio serials *Jack Armstrong All American Boy* and *Big Sister*, Ann Shepherd (née Shaindel Kalish) learned to type when she was blacklisted and dismissed from CBS. She found work with the New York Federation of Jewish Philanthropies and later taught for many years at the University of North Carolina at Chapel Hill.[15] Phoebe Brand, who taught acting with the Hollywood Actors' Laboratory, resumed teaching when she relocated to New York City in 1952. She gave classes at the American Shakespeare Festival in Connecticut and cofounded Theater in the Street, a group that toured neglected city neighborhoods with free outdoor performances of classic plays. She continued to teach acting techniques until a week before her death in 2004.

Many were not so resilient. Commenting on the psychological damage to the victims of McCarthyism, historian Ellen Schrecker noted that an entire generation of law-abiding men and women found it devastating to be suddenly transformed into social and political pariahs.[16] Supporters of charitable groups organized to aid European refugees and exiled writers and celebrities who entertained at benefits for the victims of fascism did not consider that they were engaged in subversive activities. When American Business Consultants struck with the publications of *Red Channels* and *Counterattack*, it came as a surprise to many that they had been singled out and censured for well-meaning activities during wartime. Since childhood, Margaret Webster had been a joiner and fundraiser for charitable causes; Judy Holliday and Mady Christians entertained for wartime relief efforts; and Kim Hunter took part in peace marches. When attacked by conservative forces, they were naïve in their belief in the protections of the First and Fifth Amendments, both under assault by the anti-Communist crusaders. Although the constitutional amendments protected witnesses from self-incrimination and possible jail terms for contempt, there were no constitutional protections against anonymous informants, innuendoes, unsubstantiated headlines, and punishing controversiality policies.

The shadow-boxing extended to private correspondence and books on the shelves of personal libraries. Margaret Webster's friends advised her to burn her letters written to her parents during a trip to Russia in 1935 and get rid of such incriminating books as John Reed's *Ten Days That Shook the World*. Not only was reading self-censored but so were conversations in public. Most important in this time of political repression, voices were silenced. Following her appearance before HUAC, the usually volatile Lillian Hellman became more circumspect when expressing her political views in public. Only Dorothy Parker, among this group of artists and writers, continued publicly to excoriate HUAC. By the time she called the men of HUAC a bunch of fools, the FBI considered her a harmless crank.[17]

No matter how culpable, well-meaning, or innocent their intentions, the public opprobrium fostered by *Red Channels, Counterattack,* and *Aware* created self-loathing in some victims and outrage in others. Nevertheless, the climate of accuse-and-denounce resulted in an outbreak of fear, paranoia, and somatic distress that took its toll on individuals before the blacklisting ended sometime in the mid-sixties. In their study of Hollywood's "inquisition," Larry Ceplair and Steven Englund estimated that only 10 per cent of the people forced out of the film industry ever returned to work.[18] Those who did return often found their careers, if not their talents, damaged by the enforced hiatus.

In the climate of accuse-and-denounce, there were major and minor variations on the theme of victimization. Crank calls, hate mail, and other forms of harassment tormented the victims of McCarthyism.[19] Mady Christians and Margaret Webster received notes accusing them of affiliations with Communist-front organizations followed by threats to boycott their shows. Moreover, Webster became convinced that her telephone was tapped. When she complained to Louis Nizer, he cheerfully answered, "Why not? We know there are about 56,000 telephones unofficially tapped in New York City alone."[20]

It was not uncommon for labor struggles to end in violence against pro-Communist strikers, but the film and theatrical trade unions were not prone to physical violence. Instead, the Hollywood craft unions failed to speak out against the political repression and blacklisting of their members. Hollywood's division of the International Alliance of Theatrical and Stage Employees did not oppose the blacklist, nor did the Screen Actors Guild denounce the industry's smear campaigns and witch-hunts. Neither union opposed the sanctions imposed on members by the studios.

In contrast, Actors' Equity took a braver stand by adopting a resolution that condemned blacklisting as a form of anti-union discrimination and unfair labor practices: "Now, Therefore, Be It Resolved: That this Association again condemns the practice of 'blacklisting' in all its forms, and that this Association will act to aid its members in their right to obtain a fair and impartial hearing of any charges that may be brought against them."[21] Moreover, Equity reached an agreement with the League of New York Theatres (today the League of American Theatres and Producers), a trade organization representing Broadway theater owners and producers, to keep "blacklisting out of theatres."

True to its word, Equity acted to condemn the blacklist as "iniquitous" when General Foods and NBC fired actress Jean Muir. Although Equity stood by its condemnation of blacklisting, the organization proceeded in June 1953 to implement the non-Communist loyalty oath to its members and by September voted to expel any member proven "by due process of law" to belong to the Communist Party or affiliated groups, or to be guilty of "any subversive act."[22]

Two years later, the American Federation of Television and Radio Artists passed a national referendum against unfriendly witnesses (meaning, in this instance, a member who refused to answer the question whether or not he or she was or ever had been a Communist) and declared that individuals "shall be subject to the charge that he is guilty of conduct prejudicial to the welfare of AFTRA." Local boards were granted the authority to "fire, censure, suspend or expel the accused from membership" at their discretion.[23] Recently, the president of AFTRA's Los Angeles local called the blacklist of the fifties the "saddest chapter in our union's history."[24]

Although many were harmed by the various actions of their unions, Congress, beginning in the late thirties, initiated more effective forms of political repression. The congressional committees were empowered by Congress to root-out Communists from government, entertainment, and education. Along the way, the anti-Communist nets ensnared a variety of suspects, ranging from spies to do-gooders. For example, Judy Holliday, Kim Hunter, and foreign-service officer John Fremont Melby, Hellman's sometime lover, were ensnared in a governmental dragnet similar to the one that swept up Judith Coplon and Alger Hiss.

In this atmosphere of political repression, gender sometimes played to the women's advantage. In general, gender and/or sexual orientation were not factors in the FBI investigations and subpoenas of the fifties. *Celebrity* was the overriding factor but only if the artist was associated with subversive or un-American activities. In some respects gender was a safeguard for the women against the wrath of the committeemen. The Hollywood Ten went to jail along with board members of the Civil Rights Congress, including Dashiell Hammett, but women in the entertainment industry were curiously safeguarded by the male chauvinism of the period. As HUAC's chairman explained to a reporter in reference to Lillian Hellman's contemptuous prevarications, she was not cited because "she's a woman."[25]

The second most effective government mode of containment was the U.S. Passport Division presided over by Ruth B. Shipley, a fervent anti-Communist who endorsed the work of the McCarran and un-American committees. With good contacts in Congress, she was the final authority on applications for travel abroad, and all petitioners, regardless of gender, had to pass through the gates of Shipley's "passport barony," as her fiefdom was called.[26]

In the early days of the anti-Communist crusade, emigration was still an option that permitted scientists, writers, and filmmakers to travel, work, and

relocate abroad.[27] By the mid-fifties there were clusters of Hollywood expatri-
ates in Europe and Mexico. Donald Ogden Stewart and his wife, Ella Winter,
departed for England; *Salt of the Earth* screenwriters Paul Jarrico and Michael
Wilson moved to France. Lillian Hellman, Arthur Miller, and Margaret Webster
struggled to convince Ruth Shipley to sanction their work-related travels abroad
and were eventually successful. Nevertheless, as a leading political dissenter,
Paul Robeson was denied a passport for eight years for his outspoken views on
race relations in America and his unrestrained expressions of friendship for the
peoples of the Soviet Union. In 1956, Robeson endured a brutal session before
the Committee, chaired by Francis E. Walter, who viewed Robeson as part of
an international conspiracy.

By the mid-fifties, Chairman Walter had seized the opportunity to extend
his interests to emigration—or at least to foreign travel by U.S. citizens. In 1956,
he held hearings on the "Unauthorized Use of United States Passports." Among
his targets were liberal clergy, playwrights, and concert singers. The Committee
tried the actor-singer and political activist Paul Robeson for passport violations "in furtherance of the objectives of the Communist conspiracy." Robeson refused to comply with the Committee's questions and invoked the Fifth
Amendment's protections of free speech and conscience. He was summarily
dismissed without guarantee of a new passport but not before he denounced
the gentlemen as non-patriots, un-Americans, and shameful human beings.[28]

When the State Department finally granted Robeson a passport in 1958,
he went abroad and did not return for five years. By then, he was in ill health,
his career was non-existent, and his history of political activism on behalf of
black Americans was ignored by a new generation of black activists. In his
isolation, he experienced clinical depression and spent years in and out of hos-
pitals. When he died of a stroke at age seventy-six, he had been a non-person
for twenty-five years.

McCarthyism Revisited

As viewed from the vantage point of millennial America, the individual histories of stage and film actors, directors, and playwrights in the fifties are further
nuanced in a post–9/11 world. Neoconservative agendas and new abridgements
of civil liberties in the name of national security have again, to a degree not seen
since the early fifties, seized the political and cultural landscape.

In a climate of paranoia, distrust, and fear brought on by the terrorist attack
by Islamic fundamentalists on U.S. cities, the dormant McCarthyite legacy had
resurfaced with national and international consequences. The U.S.A. Patriot
Act, enacted by Congress shortly after September 11, 2001, expanded the powers
of the U.S. Department of Justice. The attorney general (then John Ashcroft)
was empowered to detain and imprison resident and illegal aliens without legal

representation and due process. So-called "credible" allegations, along with anonymous tips, have been used to detain persons of Middle Eastern origins, namely Muslims and Arabs, under the new provisions of the Patriot Act.[29] In a resurgence of activity, the FBI and other federal agencies have investigated Internet communications, telephone records and conversations, libraries and bookstores without regard for the privacy rights of citizens, evidence of suspected criminal activity, or court-issued subpoenas or warrants.

As Ted Morgan asserted in *Reds: McCarthyism in Twentieth-Century America*, "In the post–9/11 emergency, with America at war first in Afghanistan and then in Iraq, the McCarthyite strain in American political life reemerged with a vengeance—the politics of fear, the politics of insult, and the politics of deceit."[30]

In an echo of things past, postmillennial dissenters have been accused of a lack of patriotism, and those who disagree with the new emergency measures branded as disloyal. Protesters, many of them artists and writers, demonstrating in the streets of New York City against the war in Iraq were arrested in the spring of 2003. In a reminder of the protest marches of the Cold War and Vietnam eras, New York City police arrested marchers, charged them with disorderly conduct, and placed them in holding cells at central booking in lower Manhattan. Asked by police to name their political affiliations, their answers were entered into a database for further use by authorities.[31]

On the popular entertainment front, the Federal Communications Commission, in an unrestrained act of censorship, fined multiple radio and television stations for broadcasting lewd behavior and offensive language by entertainers and public figures, most notoriously the networks that showed singer Janet Jackson's breast during a "wardrobe malfunction," broadcast talk show host Howard Stern's provocations, or Nascar driver Dale Earnhardt Jr.'s verbal indiscretions before television cameras. The FCC's indecency policy was later expanded to include "fleeting expletives," characterized as slips of the tongue resulting in coarse language and the use of offensive words, even though they were isolated events. The New York–based United States Court of Appeals for the Second Circuit struck down in 2007 the FCC's fleeting expletives policy as a breach of the First Amendment.

Independent of the FCC, conservative radio stations blacklisted the Dixie Chicks, a popular singing group, for unpatriotic behavior during a London concert where they made antiwar statements and denigrated the president of the United States.[32] A number of country music radio stations stopped playing their music and some organizations sponsored bonfires to destroy the group's CDs in a millennial version of book burning. In the new climate of censorship, television journalist Ted Koppel's recitations of the names of American casualties in Iraq were cancelled by ABC affiliates of the conservative network Sinclair Broadcast Group.

In the first years of the new century, journalists and historians writing about government policies have not hesitated to call attention to parallels with the McCarthy era. They point to a resurgence in political repression that disregards the privacy rights of individuals, asserts constitutional limitations on the First Amendment right to free speech, and uses government agencies and the mass media to silence dissent. In his weekly column on popular culture for the *New York Times*, critic Frank Rich called attention to the national media's creative manipulations of facts. The term *infoganda*, coined to define the creation of fake or faux news, has become a new and creative means of adjusting facts to fit political agendas.[33] Gone are *Counterattack* and *Aware*, but in their place are more sophisticated, insidious, and far-reaching means of manipulating world events to conform to special interests.

This book on creative artists compelled as reluctant witnesses before federal and state committees investigating un-Americanism has focused on the mid-twentieth century encounters of film and stage artists with Red-baiting, witch-hunting, and blacklisting. These key Hollywood and Broadway women did not escape punishment in varying degrees for their radical politics and liberal beliefs and for their support of political groups and humanitarian causes declared subversive during the Cold War. Moreover, the collective experiences of Mady Christians, Anne Revere, Judy Holliday, Kim Hunter, Phoebe Brand, Gale Sondergaard, Margaret Webster, Dorothy Parker, Uta Hagen, and Lillian Hellman, along with their male cohorts, remind us today of a *not too distant past* during which careers of creative women and men were stifled and lives destroyed by unrestrained congressional investigations into "un-Americanism."

Playwright Arthur Laurents, author of *The Time of the Cuckoo* and the musical books for *West Side Story* and *Gypsy*, revisited this era in his memoir of Broadway and Hollywood. He set out to present a balanced view of the participants and concluded, "no one on either side who was touched by the hunters escaped undamaged."[34] The reign of terror that was known as McCarthyism damaged the informers and the informed-against and brought harm to America's artists on both sides of the political divide during the mid-twentieth century, and subsequent events, reminiscent of Cold War politics in American life, portend a continuing legacy of McCarthyism in life and culture in millennial America.

Appendixes
Notes
Selected Bibliography
Index

Appendix 1
Chronology of Women on the Left, 1919–1976

1919	Founding of the American Communist Party.
1933	Franklin Delano Roosevelt becomes U.S. president.
1934	
November 20	*The Children's Hour* opens on Broadway.
1936	Anti-Nazi League founded in Hollywood.
July	Spanish Civil War begins.
1936–38	Moscow purge trials, U.S.S.R.
1938	
August	Special U.S. House of Representatives Un-American Activities Committee established with Martin Dies as chairman.
December 6	Hallie Flanagan Davis testifies before HUAC on behalf of the Federal Theatre Project.
1939	U.S. House of Representatives Appropriations Committee denies funding to the Federal Theatre Project.
February 15	*The Little Foxes* opens on Broadway.
August 24	Nazi-Soviet Pact creates Soviet alignment with Germany.
September 1	The Second World War begins in Europe.
1940	Hallie Flanagan publishes *Arena: The History of the Federal Theatre Project.*
June 28	Smith Act(also known as the Alien Registration Act) prohibits teaching or advocating the overthrow of the U.S. government.
1941	Hollywood Actors' Laboratory founded by Roman Bohnen and others.
April 1	*Watch on the Rhine* opens on Broadway.
	Actors' Equity Association disputed election.
June 22	Hitler invades the Soviet Union and the Soviets become U.S. allies.
	California Joint Fact-Finding Committee on Un-American Activities (better known as the Tenney committee) established.
December 7	Japanese attack Pearl Harbor. The U.S. enters the war.
1942	Joint Anti-Fascist Refugee Committee formed by merging three committees.

1943

October 19   *Othello* with Paul Robeson opens on Broadway.

1944   American Communist Party becomes Communist Political Association under the leadership of Earl Browder.

October 19   *I Remember Mama* opens on Broadway.

1945   HUAC becomes a permanent committee with J. Thomas Parnell as chairman.

March 31   *The Glass Menagerie* opens on Broadway.

April 12   Franklin Roosevelt dies; Harry S. Truman becomes president.

May 8   Germany surrenders.

July   Potsdam Conference settles postwar boundaries of Poland and divides Germany into four Allied zones.

August 6   United States drops atomic bomb on Hiroshima.

August 13   Japan surrenders.

1946   President Truman appoints Temporary Commission on Employee Loyalty that formulates loyalty-security program.

February 4   *Born Yesterday* opens on Broadway.

1947   CIA established.

January 29   *All My Sons* by Arthur Miller opens on Broadway.

March 12   Executive Order 9835 creates loyalty-security program for federal employees.

June   Marshall Plan proposed for postwar economic rehabilitation in Western Europe.

June 18   Taft-Hartley Act curtails unions' power and Communist leadership in unions.

July 21   Walter S. Steele testifies before HUAC.

October 27–30   HUAC begins Hollywood Ten hearings of screenwriters and directors.

    Committee for the First Amendment Hollywood Ten cited for contempt of Congress

November   Attorney general prepares list of subversive groups.

December 3   Motion Picture Association of America meeting at the Waldorf-Astoria Hotel, NYC. Endorses the Waldorf Statement and fires the Hollywood Ten.

    A Streetcar Named Desire opens on Broadway.

1948   Henry Wallace campaigns for president on the Progressive Party ticket.

February   Communists take over Czechoslovakia.

June   Berlin blockade begins.

August   Alger Hiss–Whittaker Chambers hearings begin HUAC's pursuit of Communists in government.

November	Harry S. Truman wins reelection.
December 2	Whittaker Chambers gives "Pumpkin Papers" to HUAC.
December 15	Alger Hiss indicted for perjury.
1949	Peekskill Riots, NY
February 10	*Death of a Salesman* opens on Broadway.
August	Soviet Union detonates atomic bomb.
	Dashiell Hammett testifies as president of the Civil Rights Congress and jailed for contempt.
1950	
January 21	Alger Hiss convicted of perjury in second trial.
February 9	Joseph R. McCarthy makes a speech in Wheeling, West Virginia, alleging presence of 205 Communist agents in the U.S. State Department.
June 22	Publication of *Red Channels* creates a blacklist of alleged Communists in entertainment industry.
June 25	Korean War begins.
July 17	Julius Rosenberg arrested for espionage (and his wife Ethel Rosenberg arrested in August).
September 22	Internal Security Act (McCarran Act) passes Congress and forces registration of Communist organizations.
December	Edward G. Robinson testifies before HUAC.
December 18	*An Enemy of the People* opens on Broadway.
1951	
March 6	Trial of Julius and Ethel Rosenberg begins.
March 7	*The Autumn Garden* opens on Broadway.
March 8	Second HUAC hearings (82nd Congress) begin with John S. Wood as chairman.
April 5	Judge Irving Kaufman sentences Rosenbergs to death.
April 10–13	Larry Parks testifies before HUAC.
April 17	Anne Revere testifies before HUAC.
April 23	John J. Garfield Jr. testifies before HUAC.
April 24	Morris Carnovsky testifies before HUAC.
May 22–25	José Ferrer testifies before HUAC.
May 30	*Variety* announces that HUAC is focusing on Broadway.
June 26	J. Edward Bromberg testifies before HUAC.
June	Uta Hagen subpoenaed by HUAC.
September	Film version of *A Streetcar Named Desire* released.
September 19	Martin Berkeley testifies before HUAC.
October 4	*Saint Joan* opens on Broadway.
October 28	Mady Christians dies.
December	Edward G. Robinson testifies a second time before HUAC.

1952

March 20	Kim Hunter awarded an Oscar for best supporting role in *A Streetcar Named Desire.*
April 10–30	Elia Kazan testifies before HUAC.
May 19	Lillian Hellman sends her famous letter to HUAC.
May 21	Lillian Hellman testifies before HUAC.
May 26	Judy Holliday testifies before McCarran Senate Internal Security subcommittee.
November	Dwight D. Eisenhower elected president.
December 18	Revival of *The Children's Hour* opens on Broadway.

1953

January 22	*The Crucible* opens on Broadway.
March	Joseph Stalin dies.
March 24	Dashiell Hammett testifies before McCarthy's subcommittee.
May 25	Margaret Webster testifies before McCarthy's subcommittee.
June 2	Lee J. Cobb testifies before HUAC.
June 15	Jean Muir testifies before HUAC.
June 19	Julius and Ethel Rosenberg executed.
July 7	Eslanda Goode Robeson, writer and wife of Paul Robeson, testifies before McCarthy's subcommittee.
July 27	Korean War ends.
October 21	*The Ladies of the Corridor* opens on Broadway.
	Film version of *Salt of the Earth* released.

1954

April-June	Army-McCarthy hearings: The U.S. Senate investigates McCarthy for alleged improprieties.
May 17	Supreme Court rules against segregated schools in *Brown vs. Board of Education.*
December 2	U.S. Senate censures Joseph R. McCarthy.

1955

February 25	Dorothy Parker testifies before New York legislative hearings.
March	Controversial AFTRA election for board members.
April 21	*Inherit the Wind* opens on Broadway.
August 15	Madeleine Lee Gilford testifies before HUAC.
September 29	*A View from the Bridge* opens on Broadway.
October 14	Zero Mostel testifies before HUAC.

1956

June 12	Paul Robeson testifies before HUAC on passport violation.
June 21	Arthur Miller testifies before HUAC on passport violation.
August	FBI launches COINTELPRO (an FBI secret program of political sabotage against the Communist Party).

November 4	Soviet Union invades Hungary.
1957	
April 1	Joseph Papp testifies before HUAC.
May 2	Joseph McCarthy dies.
June 17	Supreme Court limits HUAC power.
1960	
February 25	*Toys in the Attic* opens on Broadway.
1962	*Faulk v. AWARE, Inc., Laurence Johnson, and Vincent Hart-nett* tried. Kim Hunter testifies for John Henry Faulk.
October 13	*Who's Afraid of Virginia Woolf?* opens on Broadway.
1964	John Henry Faulk publishes *Fear on Trial*.
1965	
June 7	Judy Holliday dies.
1967	Lillian Hellman publishes *An Unfinished Woman*.
June 7	Dorothy Parker dies.
1972	Margaret Webster publishes *Don't Put Your Daughter on the Stage*.
November 13	Margaret Webster dies.
1976	Lillian Hellman publishes *Scoundrel Time*.
	Amendments to the Freedom of Information Act allow access to previously unavailable government documents.

Appendix 2

Excerpts from *Red Channels: The Report of Communist Influence in Radio and Television*, 1950

Red Channels, published on June 22, 1950, by American Business Consultants (a group made up of the professional anti-Communist Vincent Hartnett and three former FBI agents), was a compilation of 151 names of allegedly subversive writers, directors, and performers. The 213-page booklet became the official blacklist of the entertainment industry. The individual entries contained citations of alleged subversive activities and were annotated to indicate the source of the incriminating information. Sources were gleaned from left-wing newspapers and magazines (the *Daily Worker* and *New Masses* were favorites), conservative newsletters (*Counterattack* and *Hollywood Now*), letterhead used by front groups, and proceedings of the House Committee on Un-American Activities.

Forty women were listed in *Red Channels*, among them Broadway and screen artists Mady Christians, Uta Hagen, Lillian Hellman, Judy Holliday, Dorothy Parker, Anne Revere, and Margaret Webster. Their listings are appended here to show the kind of information that producers and other employers in the entertainment industry were handed in what was called "the blacklisters Bible."

Roster of 151 Names Listed in *Red Channels*

Asterisks indicate Broadway artists at the time of the publication of *Red Channels*.

The Men

Larry Adler	True Boardman
Luther Adler*	John Brown
Howard Bay*	Abe Burrows*
Ralph Bell	Morris Carnovsky*
Leonard Bernstein*	Edward Chodorov*
Walter Bernstein	Jerome Chodorov*
Michael Blankfort	Lee J. Cobb*
Marc Blitzstein*	Marc Connelly*
Himan Brown	Aaron Copland*
Oscar Brand	Norman Corwin
J. Edward Bromberg*	Howard Da Silva*
Millen Brand	Roger De Koven*

Dean Dixon
Olin Downes
Alfred Drake*
Paul Draper
Howard Duff
Clifford J. Durr
Richard Dyer-Bennett
José Ferrer*
Martin Gabel*
Arthur Gaeth
William S. Gailmor
John Garfield*
Will Geer*
Jack Gilford (Guilford)*
Tom Glazer
Lloyd Gough*
Morton Gould
Ben Grauer
Mitchell Grayson
Howard Grenell
Dashiell Hammett
E. Y. ("Yip") Harburg*
Robert P. Heller
Nat Hiken
Roderick B. Holmgren
Langston Hughes*
Leo Hurwitz
Charles Irving
Burl Ives*
Sam Jaffe*
Leon Janney*
Joe Julian
Garson Kanin*
George Keane*
Alexander Kendrick
Felix Knight
Howard Koch*
Tony Kraber
Millard Lampell*
John La Touche*
Arthur Laurents*

Ray Lev
Philip Loeb*
Alan (Allan) Lomax*
Avon Long*
Joseph Losey*
Peter Lyon
Paul Mann*
Myron McCormick*
Paul McGrath*
Burgess Meredith*
Ben Myers
Arthur Miller*
Henry Morgan
Zero Mostel*
Lynn Murray
Arnold Perl*
Samson Raphaelson*
Bernard Reis
Kenneth Roberts
Earl Robinson
Edward G. Robinson*
William N. Robson
Harold Rome*
Norman Rosten
Coby Ruskin*
Robert St. John
Pete Seeger
Artie Shaw
Irwin Shaw*
Robert Lewis Shayon
William L. Shirer
Allan Sloane
Howard K. Smith
Lionel Stander*
Johannes Steel
Paul Stewart*
Elliot Sullivan*
William Sweets
Louis Untermeyer
J. Raymond Walsh
Sam Wanamaker*

Theodore Ward
Orson Welles*
Josh White

Martin Wolfson*
Richard Yaffee

The Women

Stella Adler*
Edith Atwater*
Vera Caspary
Mady Christians*
Louise Fitch
Ruth Gordon*
Shirley Graham
Uta Hagen*
Lillian Hellman*
Rose Hobart*
Judy Holliday*
Lena Horne*
Marsha Hunt*
Donna Keath*
Pert Kelton*
Adelaide Klein*
Gypsy Rose Lee*
Madeline Lee*
Ella Logan*
Aline MacMahon*

Margo*
Jean Muir*
Meg Mundy*
Dorothy Parker*
Minerva Pious
Anne Revere*
Selene Royle*
Hazel Scott
Lisa Sergio
Ann Shepherd*
Gale Sondergaard*
Hester Sondergaard*
Helen Tamiris*
Betty Todd
Hilda Vaughn
Fredi Washington*
Margaret Webster*
Ireene Wicker
Betty Winkler
Lesley Woods

Seven Listings from *Red Channels*

Mady Christians

ACTRESS	Reported as:
American Committee for Protection of Foreign Born	Guest of Honor, "United Nations in America" dinner. *House Un-Am. Act. Com., Appendix 9*, p. 347
Exiled Writers Committee of League of American Writers	Sponsor. Dinner, 10/9/41. Also jointly sponsored by American Committee to Save Refugees and United American Spanish Aid Committee. *House Un-Am. Act. Com., Appendix 9*, p. 362.
Russian War Relief	Signer. Advertisement, *NY Times*, 10/10/41. *House Un-Am. Act. Com.*, Appendix 9, p. 475.
American Committee to Save Refugees; United American Spanish Aid Committee	Sponsor. Dinner-forum. Program. 10/9/41.
National Citizens Political Action Committee	Vice-chairman, Womens Division. Official invitation, 11/4/46.
American Friends of the Chinese People	Entertainer. *New Masses*, 11/4/41, p. 30.
Daily Worker	Subject of article. Portrayed as "Foe of Tyranny." *Daily Worker*, 4/27/45, p. 11.
Independent Citizens Committee of the Arts, Sciences and Professions	Participant, meeting. *The Worker*, 4/29/45, Honorary Vice- Chairman, Connecticut State Division. *The Independent*, publication of Independent Citizens of the Arts, Sciences and Professions, 6/45, p. 15. Sponsor. *The Worker*, 12/24/44, p. 14.

Uta Hagen

ACTRESS	Reported as:
American Committee for Protection of Foreign Born	Signer. Open Letter condemning Justice Department's deportation drive. *The Lamp*, published by American Committee for Protection of Foreign Born, 6/48, p. 3. Sponsor. National Conference Against Deportation Hysteria, Michigan, 12/3–4/49. Official Call. Sponsor. Letterhead, 3/4/49.

American Relief for Greek Democracy	Sponsor. Letterhead, 1947.
Artists' Front to Win the War	Sponsor. *House Un-Am. Act. Com., Appendix 9*, p. 576.
Citizens' Committee To Defend Representative Government	Member. Committee in favor of seating Simon Gerson, Communist, as member on New York City Council. *New York Times*.2/19/48, p. 13.
Committee for First Amendment	Sponsor. *Hollywood Reporter*, 10/24/47, p. 5; *Un-Am. Act. in California, 1948*, p. 210.
National Council of the Arts, Sciences and Professions	Signer. Advertisement "We Are for Wallace." *New York Times*, 10/20/48.
National Wallace for President Committee	Member. *Citizen,* 4/48, p. 12.
Win the Peace Conference	Sponsor. *Daily Worker*, 6/22/46, p. 5.
Scientific and Cultural Conference for World Peace	Sponsor. Official program, 3/49.
May Day Parade, 1946, 1947	Affiliated. Un-Amer. Act. Com. *Review of Scientific and Cultural Conference for World Peace*, 4/19/49, p. 54.
American Council for a Democratic Greece	Affiliated. Un-Amer. Act. Com. *Review of Scientific and Cultural Conference for World Peace*, 4/19/49, p. 22.
Committee for a Democratic Far Eastern Policy	Affiliated. Un-Amer. Act. Com. *Review of Scientific and Cultural Conference for World Peace*, 4/19/49, p. 24.
Progressive Citizens of America	Affiliated. Un-Amer. Act. Com. *Review of Scientific and Cultural Conference for World Peace*, 4/19/49, p. 33.
Moscow Art Theatre	Sent greetings. Un-Amer. Act. Com. *Review of Scientific and Cultural Conference for World Peace*, 4/19/49, p. 49.
American Continental Congress for Peace	Member, Continental Committee. Mexico City, 9/5–10/49. *Daily Worker*, 7/29/49, p. 5; Official Call.
Civil Rights Congress	Sponsor, Bill of Rights Conference, Henry Hudson Hotel, New York City, 7/16–17/49.Official program.
Amicus Curiae Brief	Signer. Petition to Supreme Court to review the conviction of Lawson and Trumbo.

National Non-Partisan Committee to Defend Rights of 12 Communist Leaders	Member. Letterhead, 9/9/49.
Joint Anti-Fascist Refugee Committee, Spanish Refugee Appeal	Speaker. Dinner in honor of Dr. Edward K. Barsky, Hotel Astor, New York City, 3/20/50. *Daily Worker*, 3/23/50, p. 4.

Lillian Hellman

PLAYWRIGHT, AUTHOR   Reported as:

Independent Citizens Committee of the Arts, Sciences and Professions	Speaker, Theatre Panel, Conference of the Arts, Sciences and Professions, 6/22, 23/45. *Daily Worker*, 6/10/45, p. 14.
Progressive Citizens of America, National Arts, Sciences and Professions Council	Participant, Cultural Freedom Conference,10/25, 26/47. *Daily Worker*, 10/27/47, p. 2.
National Council of American-Soviet Friendship	Signer. Women's Committee. Greetings to women of Soviet Union in celebration of International Women's Day. *Daily Worker*, 3/9/48, p. 5.
National Wallace for President Committee	Member. *Daily Worker*, 3/26/48, p. 7.
Harlem Women for Wallace	Speaker, 6/9/48; gave forceful tribute to Wallace. *Daily Worker*, 6/10/48, p. 6.
"New Party" (Wallace)	Member, Platform Committee, 7/23/48. *Daily Worker*, 7/19/48, p. 5.
Writers for Wallace	Member, Initiating Committee. *Daily Worker*, 9/21/48, p. 7.
Moscow Art Theatre	Sent greetings to directors and members. Celebration of Moscow Art Theatre's 50th Anniversary. *Daily Worker*, 11/1/48, p. 13.
Progressive Party	Attended three-day conference. *Daily Worker*, 11/16/48, p. 5.
National Council of the Arts, Sciences and Professions	Signer. Statement calling for abolition of House Committee on Un-American Activities. *Daily Worker*, 12/29/48, p. 2.

Scientific and Cultural Conference for World Peace	Signer. Invitation to conference. *Daily Worker*, 1/10/49, p. 11. Member, Program Committee. *Daily Worker*, 2/28/49, p. 9.
Amicus Curiae Brief	Signer. Petition to Supreme Court to review the conviction of Lawson and Trumbo.
Moscow Theatres	Plays, "The Watch on the Rhine," "The Little Foxes," performed in Moscow theatres. *Soviet Russia Today*, 10/45, p. 32.
American Committee for Democracy and Intellectual Freedom	Signer. Petition to discontinue Dies Committee: *House Un-Am. Act. Com., Appendix 9*, p. 331.
American Committee to Save Refugees; Exiled Writers Committee of the League of American Writers; United American Spanish Aid Committee	Chairman, "Europe Today" dinner forum,10/9/41. *House Un-Am. Act. Com., Appendix 9*, p. 357.
American League for Peace and Democracy	Sponsor, Refugee Scholarship and Peace Campaign, 8/3/39. *House Un-Am. Act. Com., Appendix 9*, p. 410.
Russian War Relief, Inc.	Signer. Advertisement asking for help on behalf of the Russian people, 10/10/41. *House Un-Am. Act. Com., Appendix 9*, p. 475.
Artists' Front to Win the War	Participant. Meeting, 10/16/42. *House Un-Am. Act. Com., Appendix 9*, p. 575.
Citizens Committee for Harry Bridges	Member and sponsor, 1941. *House Un-Am. Act. Com., Appendix 9*, p. 599.
Equality	Member, Editorial Council, 12/39. *House Un-Am. Act. Com., Appendix 9*, p. 698.
Friends of the Abraham Lincoln Brigade	Sponsor, 6/11/38. *House Un-Am. Act. Com., Appendix 9*, pp. 753–756. Sponsor. Disabled Veterans Fund, 3/22/39. *House Un-Am. Act. Com., Appendix 9*, pp. 753–756.
Joint Anti-Fascist Refugee Committee	Sponsor. Dinner, 10/27/43. *House Un-Am. Act. Com., Appendix 9*, p. 941.
The League of Women Shoppers, Inc.	Vice-president. *House Un-Am. Act. Com., Appendix 9*, pp. 1007–1010.

National Emergency Conference for Democratic Rights	Signer. "Open Letter to the United States Senate." *House Un-Am. Act. Com., Appendix 9*, p. 1212.
Progressive Committee to Rebuild the American Labor Party	Member, Executive Committee. *House Un-Am. Act. Com., Appendix 9*, p. 1500.
Statement by American Progressives on the Moscow Trials	Signer, 5/3/38. *House Un-Am. Act. Com., Appendix 9*, p. 1617.
Theatre Arts Committee	Member, Executive Board. *House Un-Am. Act. Com., Appendix 9*, p. 1626.
Frontier Films	Member, Advisory Board, 4/6/37. *Un-Am. Act. in California, 1948*, p. 96.

Judy Holliday
ACTRESS—SCREEN,
STAGE, RADIO AND TV   Reported as:

National Council of the Arts, Sciences and Professions	Signer. Advertisement in support of Hollywood Ten. *Variety*, 12/1/48. Nominee for office, Theatre Division Rally, Hotel Woodstock, NYC, 9/20/48. Handbill. Signer. Advertisement "We Are for Wallace." *NY Times*, 10/20/48.
People's Songs	Member, Board of sponsors. *Bulletin of People's Songs*, May, 1947. Sent birthday greetings. *Bulletin of People's Songs*, 2–3/47, p. 19.
Stop Censorship Committee	Speaker by recording. Rally at Hotel Astor, NYC, 3/23/48. *NY Herald-Tribune*, 3/24/48; *Daily Worker*, 3/26/48, p. 13.
Scientific and Cultural Conference for World Peace	Sponsor. Official program, 3/49.
World Federation of Democratic Youth	Sponsor. Un-Am. Act. Com. *Review of Scientific and Cultural Conference for World Peace*, 4/19/49, p. 36.

Moscow Art Theatre	Sent greetings, 1948. Un-Am. Act. Com. *Review of Scientific and Cultural Conference for World Peace*, 4/19/49, p. 49.
Save the Voice of Freedom Committee	Vice-chairman. Dinner program, 3/5/47.
Council on African Affairs	Participant at rally. *Daily Worker*, 5/23/46,p. 5.
Civil Rights Congress	Supporter. *Counterattack*, 10/28/49, p. 4.
New York Council of the Arts, Sciences and Professions	Entertainer. Carnival and Dance, Hotel Capital, 3/25/50. *Daily Worker*, 3/21/50.

Dorothy Parker
WRITER, VERSIFIER

Reported as:

Joint Anti-Fascist Refugee Committee	Speaker. Rally for Spanish Refugee Appeal at Manhattan Center. *Daily Worker*, 3/23/48, p. 12 Sponsor, 1943. *House Un-Am. Act. Com., Appendix 9*, p. 942
Scientific and Cultural Conference for World Peace	Sponsor. Official program, 3/49.
Amicus Curiae Brief	Signer. Petition to Supreme Court to review the conviction of Lawson and Trumbo.
American Continental Congress for Peace	United States Sponsor. Congress held in Mexico City, 9/5–10/49. *American Legion Summary*, 9/49, Vol. III, #9; Special Report #3, p. 6.
Voice of Freedom Committee	Chairman. *American Legion Summary*, 7/48, Vol. II, #5, p. 3.
American Relief Ships for Spain	Sponsor, 9/3/38. *House Un-Am. Act.Com., Appendix 9*, p. 489.
Artists' Front to Win the War	Sponsor. *House Un-Am. Act. Com., Appendix 9*, p. 577.
Citizens Committee for Harry Bridges	Sponsor, 9/11/41. *House Un-Am. Act. Com., Appendix 9*, p. 599.

Coordinating Committee to Lift the Embargo	Affiliated. *House Un-Am. Act. Com., Appendix 9*, p. 668.
Equality	Member, Editorial Council of magazine, *Equality*. *House Un-Am. Act. Com., Appendix 9*, p. 696.
Abraham Lincoln Brigade, Fund Drive for Disabled Vets	Sponsor. *House Un-Am. Act. Com., Appendix 9*, p. 754.
Hollywood Anti-Nazi League	Sponsor. *House Un-Am. Act. Com., Appendix 9*, p. 784.
New York Tom Mooney Committee	Sponsor. *House Un-Am. Act. Com., Appendix 9*, p. 1372.
Medical Bureau and Committee to Aid Spanish Democracy	Sponsor, 2/2/39. *House Un-Am. Act. Com., Appendix 9*, p. 1611.
Civil Rights Congress	Affiliated. Un-Amer. Act. Com. *Review of Scientific and Cultural Conference for World Peace*, 4/19/49, p. 25.
International Workers Order	Affiliated. Un-Amer. Act. Com. *Review of Scientific and Cultural Conference for World Peace*, 4/19/49, p. 27.
Progressive Citizens of America	Affiliated. Un-Amer. Act. Com. *Review of Scientific and Cultural Conference for World Peace*, 4/19/49, p. 33.
Stage for Action	Affiliated. Un-Amer. Act. Com. *Review of Scientific and Cultural Conference for World Peace*, 4/19/49, p. 34.
Statement of American Progressives on the Moscow Trials	Signer. Un-Amer. Act. Com. *Review of Scientific and Cultural Conference for World Peace*, 4/19/49, p. 47.

Anne Revere
ACTRESS—SCREEN,
STAGE   Reported as:

Committee for a Free Political Advocacy	Signer. *Daily Worker*, 2/28/49, p. 9.
National Council of the Arts, Sciences and Professions	Signer. Advertisement "We Are For Wallace." *NY Times*, 10/20/48.

156

Progressive Citizens of America	Member, Actors Division. *Hollywood Reporter*, 11/3/47, p. 15; *Un-Am. Act. in California, 1948*, p. 355. Candidate, Executive Board, 1947. *Un-Am. Act. in California, 1947*, p. 239.
Committee for First Amendment	Speaker. "Hollywood Fights Back" broadcast, 11/2/47 *People's Daily World*, 11/8/47, p. 5.
Amicus Curiae Brief	Signer. Petition to Supreme Court to set aside conviction of Lawson and Trumbo, 9/12/49.
Committee for Admission of World Peace Delegation	Member. *Daily Worker*, 3/1/50, p. 2.

Margaret Webster
AUTHOR, DIRECTOR,
PRODUCER

Reported as:

American Committee for Protection of Foreign Born	Sponsor. "United Nations in America" Dinner, 4/17/43. *House Un-Am. Act Com., Appendix 9*, p. 347.
American Relief for Greek Democracy	Sponsor. Letterhead, 11/19/49.
American Russian Institute	Speaker. American-Soviet Post-War Relations Dinner. *House Un-Am. Act. Com., Appendix 9*, p. 1096.
American Society for Russian Relief, Inc.	Member, Executive Council. Letterhead, 4/12/46.
Artists' Front to Win the War	Participant. Meeting, 10/16/42. *House Un-Am. Act. Com., Appendix 9*, p. 575.
Citizens Committee for the Re-election of Benjamin Davis	Sponsor. Artists, Writers and Professional Division. *Daily Worker*, 9/25/45, p. 12.
Civil Rights Congress	Sponsor. Conference on Civil Rights, 11/21/47. *People's Daily World*, 10/28/47, p. 4.
Open Letter to Members of 81st Congress	Signer. Letter urging abolition of House Un-American Activities Committee. *Daily Worker*, 1/3/49, p. 7.
Council on African Affairs	Signer. Leaflet.

National Council of American-Soviet Friendship	Speaker. Committee of the Arts, "First Conference on American-Soviet Cultural Cooperation." Official program. Sponsor. Committee of Women. *Daily Worker*, 2/10/44, p. 3; *House Un-Am. Act.Com., Appendix 9*, p. 480. Chairman, Theatre Committee. *Daily Worker*, 8/14/45, p. 11.
Independent Citizens Committee of the Arts, Sciences and Professions	Speaker. Theatre panel of Conference of the Arts, Sciences and Professions, 6/22, 23/45.*The Worker*, 6/24/45, p. 1.
Joint Anti-Fascist Refuge Committee	Sponsor. Dinner, "The Century of the Common Man," 10/27/43. *House Un-Am. Act. Com., Appendix, 9*, p. 942.
People's Radio Foundation, Inc.	Stockholder. *Daily Worker*, 7/1/46, p. 11.
Russian War Relief, Inc.	Sponsor. Appeal on behalf of Russian people. *NY Times*, 10/10/41; *House Un-Am. Act. Com., Appendix 9*, p. 477.
Soviet Russia Today	Sponsor. Dinner celebrating 25th anniversary of Red Army. *House Un-Am. Act.Com., Appendix 9*, p. 1604.
Spanish Refugee Appeal	Sponsor. Leaflet.

Notes

Preface

1. "Meeting-Goer," *Time,* June 2, 1952, 74.
2. Quoted in McClellan, *Anne,* 20.
3. *New York Daily News,* June 13, 1947.

1. McCarthyism

1. McCarthy's Wheeling speech was delivered on February 9, 1950, in West Virginia. In the version of the senator's speech inserted in the *Congressional Record* on February 20, 1950, the number of subversives in the State Department changed to fifty-seven. See Schrecker, *The Age of McCarthyism,* 238–41.
2. Lowenthal, 449.
3. Morgan, xiii.
4. Quoted in Bryer, 196.
5. *Testimony of Aaron Copland,* May 26, 1953. *Executive Sessions of the Senate Permanent Subcommittee on Investigations of the Committee on Operations.* U.S. Senate. 83rd Congress. 1st sess. 1953. *State Department Teacher-Student Exchange Program.* Vol. 2 (Washington, D.C.: U.S. Government Printing Office, 2003), 1267–90. See also Morgan, 446.
6. *Testimony of Aaron Copland,* 1267–90.
7. Schrecker, *Many Are the Crimes,* 85.
8. Morgan, 544.
9. Morgan, 544.
10. Eric Bentley, *Thirty Years of Treason,* 542–44.
11. *Testimony of Hallie Flanagan,* December 6, 1938. *Hearings on the Investigation of Un-American Propaganda Activities in the United States.* Special House Committee on Un-American Activities. 75th Congress. 2nd sess. Vol. 4 (Washington, D.C.: U.S. Government Printing Office, 1939). See also Eric Bentley, *Thirty Years of Treason,* 6–47.
12. Flanagan, 345.
13. Flanagan, 345. See also Joanne Bentley, 324.
14. Flanagan, 346.
15. Flanagan, 347.
16. Flanagan, 345.
17. Flanagan, 346.

2. Billie Dawn Goes to Washington: Judy Holliday

1. Griffith, 116–19.
2. See Ybarra.

3. Carey, 5.

4. Carey, 12, 16.

5. Holtzman, 94.

6. Quoted in Carey, 66–67.

7. Carey, 68.

8. Carey, 69.

9. See *Red Channels*, 78–79.

10. Kanfer, 76.

11. Vaughn, 170.

12. *Hollywood Life*, March 31 and July 13, 1951. See also Eric Bentley, *Thirty Years of Treason*, 306.

13. Eric Bentley, *Thirty Years of Treason*, 303.

14. *Red Channels*, 54, 56, 78–79; *Hollywood Life*, March 21, 1951. See also Foley.

15. FBI file cited in Holtzman, 142.

16. *Counterattack: Facts to Combat Communism*, letter number 127, (October 28, 1949): 4.

17. FBI file cited in Holtzman, 143.

18. Holtzman, 147.

19. See Faulk, 149, 156–57.

20. Lauren Kessler, 227.

21. Carey, 141.

22. Holtzman, 162–63.

23. *Testimony of Judy Holliday*, March 26, 1952. *Hearings before the Subcommittee to Investigate the Administration of the Internal Security Act and Other Internal Security Laws of the Committee on the Judiciary.* U.S. Senate. 82nd Congress. 2nd sess. *Subversive Infiltration of Radio, Television, and the Entertainment Industry.* Part 2. 1952 (Washington, D.C.: U.S. Government Printing Office, 1952), 141–86.

24. The United American-Spanish Aid Committee was one of several groups formed to support the Loyalists during the Civil War in Spain and merged in 1942 with the American Committee to Save Refugees and the Exiled Writers Committee of the League of American Writers to become the Joint Anti-Fascist Refugee Committee. Cited as a Communist front by the California Committee on Un-American Activities Report, Fourth Report, 1948, 270, 353.

25. The Committee for the Negro in the Arts was an organization founded to stimulate job opportunities for blacks in the arts, particularly in the theater, and to negotiate between the artists and the managers who sought to hire them for substandard salaries.

26. Carey, 145.

27. Holtzman, 13.

28. Holtzman, 155–56.

29. Attributed to K. Kevyne Baar, project archivist for the Tamiment Library, Robert F. Wagner Labor Archives, New York University.

30. Quoted in Carey, 147.

31. Carey, 148.

32. Quoted in Holtzman, 124.

33. Holtzman, 156.

34. Quoted in Carey, 138.

35. *Testimony of Sam Levenson*, March 20, 1952. *Hearing before the Subcommittee to Investigate the Administration of the Internal Security Act and Other Internal Security Laws of the Committee on the Judiciary.* U.S. Senate. 2nd sess. *Subversive Infiltration of Radio, Television, and the Entertainment Industry.* Part 2. 1952 (Washington, D.C.: U.S. Government Printing Office, 1952), 127–140. Also, Kanfer described Levenson as a "bland, ingratiating raconteur," 187.

36. *Testimony of Burl Ives*, March 20, 1952. *Hearings before the Subcommittee to Investigate the Administration of the Internal Security Act and Other Internal Security Laws of the Committee on the Judiciary.* U.S. Senate. 2nd sess. *Subversive Infiltration of Radio, Television, and the Entertainment Industry.* Part 2. 1952 (Washington, D.C.: U.S. Government Printing Office, 1952), 205–28.

37. *Testimony of Philip Loeb*, April 23, 1952. *Hearings before the Subcommittee to Investigate the Administration of the Internal Security Act and Other Internal Security Laws of the Committee on the Judiciary.* U.S. Senate. 2ns sess. *Subversive Infiltration of Radio, Television, and the Entertainment Industry.* Part 2. 1952 (Washington, D.C.: U.S. Government Printing Office, 1952), 187–204.

38. See Navasky, 112–43.

3. Death by Innuendo: Mady Christians

1. Morgan, 526.

2. Kanfer, 107.

3. Kanfer, 148. See also "Facts about the Blacklist," *Equity News*, November 1952, 2–3.

4. *New York Times*, April 22, 1951.

5. *Testimony of Philip Loeb*, April 23, 1952. *Hearings before the Subcommittee to Investigate the Administration of the Internal Security Act and Other Internal Security Laws of the Committee on the Judiciary.* U.S. Senate. 2ns sess. *Subversive Infiltration of Radio, Television, and the Entertainment Industry.* Part 2. 1952 (Washington, D.C.: U.S. Government Printing Office, 1952), 187–204.

6. *Red Channels*, 113.

7. Kanfer, 112.

8. FBI file number 100-63757. Subject Mady Christians, 1942–1951.

9. The birth date of Mady Christians is open to question. Records of the U.S. Immigration and Naturalization Service show that she was born January 19, 1896, in Vienna. *Who's Who in the Theater* (1947 edition), edited by John Parker, notes her birth date as January 19, 1900

10. Brooks Atkinson, *New York Times*, April 2, 1941.

11. *Daily Worker*, October 15 and 26, 1941.

12. "Recalls How Nazis Heckled Movies: Mady Christians Deplores Senate Inquiry," *New York World-Telegram*, September 20, 1941.

13. *New York Newspaper PM*, October 10, 1944.

14. *New York Times,* October 10, 1941.

15. *Daily Worker,* April 27, 1945, 11.

16. Quoted in Webster, *Don't Put Your Daughter,* 244.

17. Quoted in Webster, *Don't Put Your Daughter,* 244–45.

18. Webster, *Don't Put Your Daughter,* 244–45.

19. FBI file, letter from Mady Christians to FBI director J. Edgar Hoover, dated December 26, 1941; and letter from J. Edgar Hoover to Mady Christians, dated February 13, 1942. Christians file number 100-63757.

20. Webster, *Don't Put Your Daughter,* 245.

21. *New York Journal-American,* October 3, 1945.

22. "Equity Faces Internal Snarls of Race-Animosity, Red Charges," *Variety,* October 3, 1945. See also Webster, *Don't Put Your Daughter,* 246.

23. *Peoples World,* March 1, 1946, 6; see also Christians FBI file number 100-63757.

24. Webster, *Don't Put Your Daughter,* 247–48.

25. FBI memorandum from Special Agent in Charge, New York Office, to FBI director, dated August 8, 1950. Christians file number 100-63757.

26. *Daily Worker,* April 27, 1945.

27. See *Red Channels,* 202.

28. FBI memorandum from J. P. Coyne to D. M. Ladd, dated July 17, 1947. Christians file number 100-63757.

29. FBI memorandum, Los Angeles office, April 2, 1943. Christians file number 100-63757.

30. FBI memorandum, Los Angeles office, April 2, 1943. Christians file number 100-63757.

31. Typescript, dated November 28, 1943, in Mady Christians Papers, Billy Rose Theatre Collection, New York Public Library for the Performing Arts, New York City.

32. Slide, 6.

33. Schrecker, *Many Are the Crimes,* 124.

34. FBI memorandum from Special Agent in Charge, New York office, to FBI director, dated April 4, 1951. Christians file number 100-63757.

35. Schrecker, *Many Are the Crimes,* 98.

36. FBI memorandum from Special Agent in Charge, New York office, to FBI director, dated April 4, 1951. Christians file number 100-63757.

37. FBI memorandum, New York office, dated April 4, 1951. Christians file number 100-99584.

38. *New York Times* April 17, 1947; *New York Herald Tribune,* April 17, 1947; *New York Newspaper PM,* April 18, 1947.

39. *New York Times,* November 17, 1949; *New York Herald Tribune,* November 17, 1949.

40. FBI, letter to the New York office, dated June 30, 1950, and from the New York office, dated July 7, 1950. Christians file number 100-63757.

41. Ormsbee, 2.

42. Kanfer, 155.

43. Sien, 13.

44. Quoted in Kanfer, 155.

45. FBI memorandum from FBI director to Special Agent in Charge, New York office, dated January 16, 1951. Christians file number 100-63757.

46. The Security Index was originally called the Custodial Detention List until U.S. attorney general Francis Biddle ordered an end to the program. FBI director J. Edgar Hoover ignored the order, changed the name to the Security Index, and failed to inform the Justice Department of the transformation. For a more complete discussion, see Schrecker, *Many Are the Crimes*, 106–7. See also FBI memorandum, New York office, dated April 4, 1951; and memorandum from Special Agent in Charge, New York office, to FBI director, dated April 4, 1951. Christians file number 100-63757.

47. FBI memorandum from FBI director to Special Agent in Charge, New York office, dated June 5, 1951. Christians file number 100-63757.

48. Author interview with Gina Shields, July 1, 2004.

49. *New York Times*, October, 1941.

50. FBI letter from Special Agent in Charge, New York office, to FBI director, dated October 17, 1951. Christians file number 100-63757.

51. FBI letter from Special Agent in Charge, New York office, to FBI director, dated October 30, 1951. Christians file number 100-63757.

52. FBI letter from Louis Nichols to Clyde Tolson, dated November 14, 1951. Christians file number 100-63757.

53. Committee Report, dated February 19, 1952, in Actors' Equity Association Library, Robert F. Wagner, Labor Archives, Tamiment Library, New York.

54. Navasky, 340.

55. Kanfer, 155.

4. Unfriendly Witness: Anne Revere

1. *Variety*, May 30, 1951.

2. Brooks Atkinson, *New York Times*, November 21, 1934.

3. *New York Herald-Tribune*, August 24, 1935. During the run of *The Children's Hour*, Revere quietly married theatrical director and acting coach Samuel Rosen in a ceremony in Brooklyn's Borough Hall on April 11, 1935. She remained devoted to her husband until his death in 1984; she died on December 20, 1990, at her home in Locust Valley, Long Island.

4. McClellan, *Anne*, 20. See also McClellan, *The Unkindest Cuts*.

5. *Daily Peoples World*, May 2, 1947.

6. See FBI memorandum, Los Angeles office, dated December 5, 1944. Revere file number 100-22606. The book numbers recorded by the FBI for Anne Revere's Communist Party—USA membership cards were numbers 25098 (dated 1943) and 48951 (dated 1944); the number assigned to her membership in the Los Angeles section of the Communist Political Association was number 46937. In May 1944, Earl Browder dissolved the Communist Party—USA and replaced it with the Communist Political Association to achieve the left wing of a broad coalition within the two-party system. Anne Revere was issued a

membership card in the Communist Political Association that same year. See Ceplair and Englund, 232.

7. FBI memorandum from FBI director to Special Agent in Charge, Los Angeles office, dated July 21, 1945. Revere file number 100-33672

8. FBI memorandum from D. M. Ladd to FBI director, dated September 2, 1947. Revere file number 100-22606.

9. FBI memorandum from Special Agent in Charge, Los Angeles office, to FBI director, dated January 5, 1954. Revere file number 100-22606.

10. *Daily Peoples World*, May 2, 1947. See also FBI memorandum, dated September 12, 1947. Revere file number 100-336762.

11. FBI memorandum from D. M. Ladd to FBI director, dated September 12, 1947. Revere file number 100-336762.

12. FBI memorandum from Special Agent in Charge, New York office, to FBI director, dated September 20, 1950. Revere file number 100-22606.

13. FBI memorandum from FBI director to Special Agent in Charge, Los Angeles office, dated October 13, 1950. Revere file number 100-336762.

14. FBI memorandum, Los Angeles office, dated January 29, 1951. Revere file number 100-22606.

15. FBI memorandum, Los Angeles office, dated March 28, 1951. Revere file number 100-22606.

16. Quoted in FBI memorandum, Los Angeles office, dated March 28, 1951. The dinner was held on March 21, 1951. Revere file number 100-22606.

17. Quoted in FBI memorandum, Los Angeles office, dated November 11, 1951. Revere file number 100-22606.

18. FBI memorandum, Los Angeles office, dated November 13, 1951. Revere file number 100-22606. Samuel Rosen had been named a Communist to the FBI prior to 1945; he was assigned FBI file number 100-40318.

19. FBI memorandum, Los Angeles office, dated October 12, 1951. Revere file number 100-22606.

20. Larry Parks testified before HUAC on March 21, 1951.

21. *Los Angeles Times*, March 7, 1951.

22. *Testimony of Anne Revere*, April 17, 1951. *Hearings Regarding Communist Infiltration of Hollywood Motion-Picture Industry*. Part 1. U.S House of Representatives. 82nd Congress. 1st sess. (Washington, D.C.: U.S. Government Printing Office, 1951), 318–21.

23. "Anne Revere," *Screen Actor* (Summer 1979): 16–17.

24. See Roman Bohnen Papers, series 6, New York Public Library for the Performing Arts, New York City.

25. See Pollitt.

26. The alleged Communist Party card numbers did not correspond to Revere's Communist Political Association number or to her Communist Party—USA book numbers reported in her FBI file, dated December 5, 1944. Revere file number 100-33672. See also "Anne Revere, Two Hollywood Writers Balk at Red Questions, *Washington Post*, April 18, 1951.

27. The spelling of Samuel Rosen's name is incorrect in Revere's FBI file and in HUAC documents. The correct spelling is Rosen—Samuel Rosen. The confusion most likely resulted from the spelling of Robert Rossen's name, a writer-director-producer who was a key political activist in Hollywood in the thirties and forties.

28. *New York Daily News*, April 18, 1951.

29. *New York Times*, May 31, 1951.

30. *New York Times*, December 19, 1990.

31. *Hollywood Variety*, May 31, 1951. See also FBI memorandum, Los Angeles office, dated October 12, 1951. Revere file number 100-22602.

32. See Web site http://www.spartacus.schoolnet.co.uk/USArevere.htm, April 15, 2002.

33. Quoted in Navasky, 178.

34. *Testimony of Gale Sondergaard*, March 21, 1951. *Hearings Regarding Communist Infiltration of Hollywood Motion-Picture Industry*. Part 1. U.S. House of Representatives. 82nd Congress. 1st sess. (Washington, D.C.: U.S. Government Printing Office, 1951), 121–25.

35. *Testimony of Lee J. Cobb*, June 2, 1955. *Hearings Regarding the Investigation of Communist Activities in Hollywood.* . Part 2. U.S. House of Representatives. 84th Congress. 2nd sess. See Eric Bentley, *Thirty Years of Treason*, 653–66.

36. *Sunday News*, April 27, 1975.

37. McCelland, 21.

38. *Sunday News*, April 27, 1975.

39. Schrecker, *Many Are the Crimes*, 335.

40. *Daily Worker*, December 17, 1953.

41. FBI Memorandum, Los Angeles office, dated September 14, 1954. Revere file number 100-22606.

42. FBI memorandum from Special Agent in Charge, Los Angeles office, to FBI director, dated February 16, 1955. Revere file number 100-22606.

43. FBI memorandum, Los Angeles office, dated January 17, 1957. Revere file number 100-22606.

44. *Daily Variety*, November 7, 1956.

45. *Daily Variety*, June 12, 1956.

46. FBI memorandum from Special Agent in Charge, Los Angeles office, to FBI director, dated February 12, 1958. Revere file number 100-22606.

47. FBI memorandum, New York office, dated April 20, 1960. Revere file number 100-101399.

48. FBI memorandum from Special Agent in Charge, New York office, to FBI director, dated April 24, 1958. Revere file number 100-101399.

49. FBI memorandum, New York office, dated April 20, 1960. Revere file number 100-101399.

50. FBI memoranda, New York office, dated February 17, 1958, April 20 and 24, 1959. Revere file number 100-101399.

51. FBI memorandum from FBI director to Special Agent in Charge, New York office, May 9, 1960. Revere file number 100-336762. See also FBI memorandum from Special Agent in Charge, New York office, to FBI director, dated April 17, 1961. Revere file number 100-101399.

52. Author interviews with Joseph Hardy, May 12, 2002, and July 19, 2003.

53. Undated typescript, circa 1965; Anne Revere's sworn affidavit State and County of New York. Courtesy of Joseph Hardy.

54. McClellan, *Anne*, 8.

55. *Testimony of Larry Parks*, March 21, 1951; *Testimony of Sterling Hayden*, April 10, 1951; *Testimony of José Ferrer*, May 22 and 25, 1951.

5. The Defiant Ones: Lillian Hellman and Dorothy Parker

1. Hellman, *Scoundrel Time*, 345; see also Mead, 345.

2. *New York Times*, May 22, 1952.

3. Quoted in "Where'd the Money Go?" *Newsweek*, March 7, 1951, 25.

4. Hellman, *Unfinished Woman*, 218. Dorothy Rothschild married Edwin Pond Parker II in 1917; they divorced in 1928.

5. See *Testimony of Dorothy Parker*, February 25, 1955. *Hearings before the New York State Joint Legislative Committee Investigating Charitable and Philanthropic Agencies and Organizations*. Vol. 2 (Albany: Parsons Reporting Service, 1955), 300–414.

6. Hellman, *Unfinished Woman*, 218.

7. Hellman, *Unfinished Woman*, 218–19.

8. See Wright, 115–16. See also Layman, 65.

9. Keats, 192.

10. Frewin, 213.

11. Mellen, 115.

12. Kinney, 37.

13. Mellen, 169.

14. "The Moscow Trials: A Statement of American Progressives," *New Masses*, May 3, 1938, 19.

15. Clurman, 201–2.

16. Parker, 16.

17. Ceplair and Englund, 109.

18. Mellen, 80. See also "Lillian Hellman, Playwright, Author and Rebel, Dies at 79," *New York Times*, July 1, 1984, 1, 22.

19. Quoted in Schloss, 40.

20. Stark Young, *New York Times*, December 2, 1924.

21. Frewin, 236.

22. See FBI memorandum, dated June 16, 1941, file number 100-28760. Subject: Lillian Florence Hellman.

23. FBI memorandum from FBI director to Special Agent in Charge, New York office, dated October 23, 1943. Hellman file number 100-28760.

24. FBI memorandum, New York office, dated February 4, 1944. Hellman file number 100-25858.

25. FBI memoranda from Special Agent in Charge E. E. Conroy, New York office, to FBI director, dated March 30 and April 22, 1944. Hellman file number 100-28760.

26. Kinney, 43.

27. J. Donald Adams, "Speaking of Books," *New York Times Book Review*, June 11, 1944, 2.

28. Interview with Dorothy Parker, Popular Arts Project, Part 2 (audiotape, 1959), Columbia University Oral History Research Office, New York. See Transcript 11, courtesy of Joan Franklin, Cinema Sound Ltd., New York.

29. Keats, 259.

30. Meade, 342.

31. *New York Daily News*, June 13, 1947.

32. *New York Daily News*, June 13, 1947.

33. *New York Herald Tribune*, November 3, 1947.

34. Barrett, 216, 355–60.

35. Florence Eldridge testified on February 18, 1948. See Barrett, 376; see also *Fourth Report [on Un-American Activities in California] 1948: Communist Front Organizations.* California Legislature. Senate. (Sacramento, California, 1948).

36. *United States of America v. Judith Coplon, Defendant.* Washington, D.C., District Court, 1949 (microfilm ed. Fund for the Republic, New York). See also Kessler. Coplon was arrested, tried, and convicted in 1949, but her conviction was overturned on appeal.

37. Cited in Meade, 342.

38. FBI memorandum from Special Agent in Charge, Los Angeles office, to FBI director, dated April 11, 1951. Parker file number100-56075. As a person of interest to the FBI, Parker was assigned three file numbers: file number 100-56075 (Washington Bureau file, or Bufile), file number 100-32635 (Los Angeles office), and file number 100-98708 (New York office).

39. FBI memorandum from Special Agent in Charge, Los Angeles office, to FBI director, dated April 11, 1951. Subject: Interview with Dorothy Parker in West Los Angeles.

40. *Daily Worker*, July 28, 1951.

41. FBI memorandum, Los Angeles office, dated May 8, 1951. Parker file number 100-56075.

42. Wright, 244.

43. Mellen, 300.

44. Hellman, *Scoundrel Time*, 88–89.

45. Rollyson, 319.

46. Quoted in Mellen, 300.

47. *Testimony of Lillian Hellman*, May 21, 1952. *Hearings Regarding Communist Infiltration of Hollywood Motion-Picture Industry.* Part 8. U.S. House of Representatives. 82nd Congress. 2nd sess. (Washington, D.C.: U.S. Government Printing Office, 1952), 3541–49. See also papers of Joseph L. Rauh Jr., on deposit in the Library of Congress, Washington, D.C. Hellman's papers are housed in the Harry Ranson Humanities Research Center of the University of Texas at Austin.

48. *Testimony of Lillian Hellman*, 3545–46.

49. *Testimony of Lillian Hellman*, 3545–46.

50. Wright, 251.

51. Author interview with Daniel H. Pollitt, January 24, 2003.

52. Rollyson, 329. See also Miller, *Timebends*, 449–56.

53. Mellen, 300.

54. *New York Times*, May 22, 1952. See also "Lillian Hellman Says She's No Red Now but Refuses to Discuss Past," *New York World Telegram and Sun*, May 21, 1952.

55. Schickel, 270–72. See also Elia Kazan, "A Statement," *New York Times* (advertisement), April 12, 1952.

56. See Navasky, 255. See also *Testimony of Isobel Lennart*, May 20, 1952. *Hearings Regarding Communist Infiltration of Hollywood Motion-Picture Industry.* Part 8. U.S. House of Representatives. 82nd Congress. 2nd sess. (Washington, D.C.: U.S. Printing Office, 1952), 3512–29.

57. Interview with Dorothy Parker, Popular Arts Project.

58. *New York Times*, March 27, April 2 and 3, 1953.

59. Dashiell Hammett testified on March 24, 1953; Eslanda Goode Robeson and Arnaud d'Usseau testified on July 7, 1953. See *Executive Sessions of the Senate Permanent Subcommittee on Investigations of the Committee on Government Operations.* U.S. Senate. 83rd Congress. 1st sess. 1953. Vol. 1 (Washington, D.C.: U.S. Government Printing Office, 2003), 945–48, 1223–30.

60. Ward Morehouse, *New York World Telegram and Sun*, October 18, 1953.

61. Capron, 82–83.

62. Cited in FBI memorandum, dated February 28, 1955. Parker file number 100-56075.

63. FBI memorandum, FBI director to Special Agent in Charge, New York office, dated February 23, 1955. Parker file number 100-56075.

64. "Investigations: Where'd the Money Go?" *Newsweek*, March 7, 1955, 25. See also Charles Grutzner, "Red Fronts Face Fund Appeal Ban," *New York Times*, February 26, 1955, 1, 5; "Dorothy Parker Mum on Red Ties at Fund Probe," *New York Daily News*, February 26, 1955; "Dottie Parker Didn't Ask Where $$ Went," *New York News*, February 26, 1955.

65. *Testimony of Dorothy Parker*, February 25, 1955.

66. Charles Grutzner, "Red Fronts Face Fund Appeal Ban," *New York Times*, February 26, 1955, 1, 5. The refusal of the Joint Anti-Fascist Refugee Committees executive secretary and board of directors to comply with a subpoena to hand over the group's records resulted in contempt citations. See Ellen Schrecker, *Many Are the Crimes*, 128.

67. Quoted in Layman, 233.

68. FBI memorandum from Special Agent in Charge, New York office, to FBI director, dated April 25, 1955. Parker file number 100-56075. Even though the Bureau initiated no further memoranda of investigations into Dorothy Parker's activities after 1955, the New York office maintained file number 100-98708 until May 1956. The final entry is dated May 4, 1956.

69. Hellman, *An Unfinished Woman*, 222–23.

70. Moody, 339.

71. Alden Whitman, "Dorothy Parker, 73, Literary Wit, Dies, " *New York Times*, June 8, 1967, 1, 38; "Dorothy Parker Recalled as Wit," *New York Times*, November 10, 1967, 33.

72. Quoted in Moody, 340.

73. Meade, 341.

74. Eric Bentley, *Thirty Years of Treason*, 789.

75. *Testimony of Arthur Miller*, June 21, 1956. *Hearings Regarding the Investigation of Communist Activities, Hollywood. Unauthorized Use of United States Passports.* U.S. House of Representatives. 84th Congress. 2nd sess. (Washington, D.C.: U.S. Government Printing Office, 1956), 4686. See also Miller, *Timebends*, 411–12.

76. Hellman, "Reading Again," in *Three*, 9.

77. Irving Howe, "Lillian Hellman and the McCarthy Years," *Dissent* 23, number 4 (Fall 1976): 378–82; Sidney Hook, "Lillian Hellman's *Scoundrel Time*," *Encounter* 68, number 2 (February 1977): 82–91; Hilton Kramer, *New York Times*, October 3, 1976; Alfred Kazin, "Books: The Legend of Lillian Hellman," *Esquire* 88, number 2 (August 1977): 28, 30, 34.

78. *Conversations with Mary McCarthy*, ed. Carol W. Gelderman (Jackson: University Press of Mississippi, 1991), 250–51. See also Mellen, 443.

79. Quoted in Feibleman, 361.

6. Guilt by Association: Margaret Webster

1. Webster, *Don't Put Your Daughter*, 332.

2. Webster, *Don't Put Your Daughter*, 244.

3. See *Variety*, October 3, 1945 and *Peoples World*, March 1, 1946.

4. Webster, *Don't Put Your Daughter*, 252.

5. Webster, *Don't Put Your Daughter*, 245.

6. *Variety*, October 17, 1945.

7. Webster, *Don't Put Your Daughter*, 247–48.

8. *Red Channels*, "Margaret Webster," 154–55.

9. Webster, *Don't Put Your Daughter*, 248.

10. Ceplair and Englund, 386–97.

11. Laurents, 29; Vaughn, 270; K. Kevyne Baar quoted in "Equity Hosts Panel on Broadway and the Blacklist," *Equity News* (June 2005), 4.

12. Mostel and Gilford, 139.

13. Atkinson, *Broadway*, 434.

14. Author interview with Nancy Da Silva, date August 29, 2003.

15. Atkinson, *Broadway*, 434.

16. Webster, letter to Louis Nizer, April 23, 1951, Library of Congress.

17. The FBI activated file number 100-370937, Subject: Margaret Webster, on March 2, 1951.

18. FBI memorandum from Special Agent in Charge, New York office, to FBI director, dated August 8, 1950. Webster file number 100-37937.

19. *Testimony of Walter S. Steele*, July 21, 1947. *Hearings Regarding Communist Activity in the United States*. U.S. House of Representatives. 80th Congress. 1st sess. (Washington, D. C: U.S. Government Printing Office, 1947), 110.

20. *Testimony of Walter S. Steele*, 99.

21. *Testimony of Walter S. Steele*, 66.

22. *Testimony of Edward G. Robinson*, October 27, 1950. *Hearings Regarding Communist Infiltration of the Motion-Picture Industry*. U.S. House of Representatives. 81st Congress. 2nd sess. (U.S. Government Printing Office, Washington, D.C., 1951), 3325.

23. Webster, *Don't Put Your Daughter*, 257.

24. FBI memorandum from Special Agent in Charge, New York office, to FBI director, dated April 9, 1951. Webster file number 100-370937.

25. FBI memoranda, New York office, April 9, 1951, and September 21, 1951. Webster file number 100-99747.

26. *Testimony of José Ferrer*, May 22, 1951. *Hearings Regarding Communist Infiltration of Hollywood Motion-Picture Industry*. Part 3. U.S. House of Representatives. 82nd Congress. 1st sess.. (Washington, D.C.: U.S. Government Printing Office, 1951), 573.

27. *Testimony of José Ferrer*, 662.

28. Webster, *Don't Put Your Daughter*, 257. See also *Testimony of José Ferrer*, 662.

29. Margaret Webster, "One Word More, *New York Times*, November 25, 1951.

30. Margaret Webster, letter to Lawrence Langner, June 14, 1951, Library of Congress.

31. Brooks Atkinson, *New York Times*, October 5 and 14, 1951. Hagen, *Sources*, 111.

32. Author interview with Uta Hagen, October 12, 2000. See also Webster, *Don't Put Your Daughter*, 259.

33. Webster, *Don't Put Your Daughter*, 263.

34. Webster, *Don't Put Your Daughter*, 263.

35. Webster, *Don't Put Your Daughter*, 263–64.

36. Webster, *Don't Put Your Daughter*, 265.

37. Unpublished statement by Margaret Webster prepared for Senate Subcommittee on Investigations, undated, Library of Congress. See also FBI memorandum, Washington D.C. office, dated November 3, 1953. Webster file number 100-370937.

38. Webster, letter to Louis Nizer, April 23, 1951, Library of Congress.

39. Webster, *Don't Put Your Daughter*, 261.

40. FBI memorandum, Washington, D.C. office, dated November 13, 1953. Webster file number 100-370937.

41. Webster, *Don't Put Your Daughter*, 261.

42. Quoted in Webster, *Don't Put Your Daughter*, 262.

43. FBI memorandum, Washington, D.C. office, dated November 13, 1953. Webster file number 100-370937.

44. FBI memorandum, Washington, D.C. office, dated November 13, 1952. Webster file number 100-370937.

45. Quoted in Webster, *Don't Put Your Daughter*, 262.

46. Griffith, 213.

47. Griffith, 214.

48. *Testimony of Eslanda Goode Robeson*, July 7, 1953. *Executive Sessions of the Senate Permanent Subcommittee on Investigations of the Committee on Government Operations. State Department Information Service—Information Centers*. Vol. 2. U.S. Senate. 83rd Congress. 1st sess. 1953 (Washington, D.C.: U.S. Government Printing Office, 2003), 473–82.

49. *Testimony of Dashiell Hammett*, March 26, 1953. *Hearings Before the Permanent Subcommittee on Investigations of the Committee on Government Operations. State Department Information Program—Information Centers*. U.S. Senate. 83rd Congress. 1st sess. 1953. Part 1. (Washington, D.C.: U.S. Government Printing Office, 1953), 83–88. See also *Testimony of Dashiell Hammett*, March 24, 1953. *Executive Sessions of the Senate Permanent Subcommittee on Investigations of the Committee on Government Operations*. Vol. 2. U.S. Senate. 83rd Congress. 1st sess. 1953 (Washington, D.C.: U.S. Government Printing Office, 2003), 945–49.

50. *Testimony of Arnaud d'Usseau*, July 7, 1953. *Executive Sessions of the Permanent Subcommittee on Investigations of the Committee on Government Operations. State Department Information Service—Information Centers*. Vol. 2. U.S. Senate. 83rd Congress, 1st sess. 1953 (Washington, D.C.: U.S. Government Printing Office, 2003), 1227–28.

51. *Testimony of Eslanda Goode Robeson*, 1223–27.

52. *Testimony of Margaret Webster*, May 25, 1953. *Executive Sessions of the Senate Permanent Subcommittee on Investigations of the Committee on Government Operations. State Department Teacher-Student Exchange Program*. Vol. 2. U.S. Senate. 83rd Congress. 1st sess. 1953 (Washington, D.C.: U.S. Government Printing Office, 2003), 1259–65.

53. Frederick Graham, "Professor Loses Fulbright Award after Wife Balks at Red Inquiry," *New York Times*, June 20, 1953.

54. Webster, *Don't Put Your Daughter*, 273.

55. Webster, *Don't Put Your Daughter*, 273; see also Atkinson, *Broadway*, 435.

56. Miriam Howell, letter to Webster, July 2, 1954, Library of Congress.

57. Webster, *Don't Put Your Daughter*, 271.

58. FBI memorandum from Special Agent in Charge, New York office, to FBI director, dated August 10, 1953. Webster file number 100-99747.

59. FBI memorandum from Special Agent in Charge, New York office, to FBI director, dated November 3, 1953. Webster file nos. 100-370937 and 100-99747.

60. Webster, *Don't Put Your Daughter*, 269.

61. FBI from Special Agent in Charge, New York office, to FBI director, dated November 3, 1953. Webster file number 100-99747. The first interview took place on September 29, 1953.

62. FBI memorandum from Special Agent in Charge, New York office, to FBI director, dated November 23, 1953. Webster file number 100-370937.

63. FBI memorandum, from Special Agent in Charge, New York office, to FBI director, dated January 15, 1954, Webster file number 100-99747. See also FBI memorandum, dated April 20, 1954. Webster file number 100-37093.

64. FBI memorandum from Special Agent in Charge, New York office, to FBI director, dated February 20, 1957. Webster file number 100-99747.

65. Paul Martinson, letter to Webster, July 26, 1954, Library of Congress.

66. Webster, *Don't Put Your Daughter*, 274.

7. The Blacklist Is On Fire: Kim Hunter

1. Faulk, 135.

2. Schrecker, *Many Are the Crimes*, 411.

3. *Los Angeles Times*, September 12, 2002.

4. *Counterattack*, January 11, 1952. See also *New York Times*, May 17, 1952.

5. Faulk, 137.

6. Hunter, 3.

7. Hunter, 21.

8. Hunter, 25.

9. Kazan, 343. See also Staggs, 37.

10. Quoted in Hunter, 25–26.

11. Ward Morehouse, *New York World Telegram and Sun*, December 4, 1947; Brooks Atkinson, *New York Times*, December 14, 1947.

12. *New York Post*, December 19, 1952; *New York Herald-Tribune*, December 19, 1952; *New York Times*, December 19, 1952.

13. Kanfer, 215.

14. Kanfer, 211. See also Belfrage, 148. See also *New York Times*, May 17, 1962.

15. Faulk, 258.

16. Morgan, 526–27.

17. Morgan, 527.

18. Quoted in Kanfer, 216.

19. *Counterattack*, February 8, 1952, 3–4.

20. Kanfer, 216.

21. Belfrage, 148.

22. Quoted in Faulk, 141, and *New York Times*, May 17, 1962.

23. *Counterattack*, January 11, 1952, 4. Actors Uta Hagen and Mildred Dunnock and choreographer Helen Tamiris were the other three women cited in the bulletin.

24. *Counterattack*, January 4, 1952, 3.

25. *Counterattack*, January 25, 1952, 4.

26. Kanfer, 224.

27. Kanfer, 227.

28. Mostel and Gilford, 39–40.

29. *Testimony of Zero Mostel*, October 14, 1955. U.S. Congress. House Committee on Un-American Activities. 84th Congress. Part 8. *Hearings Regarding Investigation of Communist Activities, New York Area.* See Eric Bentley, *Thirty Years of Treason*, , 711, 722.

30. *New York World Telegram and Sun*, August 16, 1955; *New York Herald Tribune*, August 19, 1955; and Millard Lampell, "I Think I Ought to Mention I was Blacklisted," *New York Times*, August 21, 1966.

31. Eric Bentley, *Thirty Years of Treason*, 684. See *Hearings Regarding the Investigation of Communist Activities, Hollywood.* U.S. House of Representatives. 84th Congress. 1st sess. (Washington, D.C.: U.S. Government Printing Office, 1955).

32. Faulk, 1–3.

33. *Aware: News Supplement to Membership Bulletin*, number 16 (February 10, 1956), 6–7.

34. Faulk, xiv.

35. Quoted in Faulk, 1.

36. Faulk, 22–23.

37. Quoted in Faulk, 23. John Henry Faulk signed the affidavit on April 13, 1956.

38. Burton, 142.

39. Quoted in *Los Angeles Times*, September 12, 2002.

40. Quoted in *New York Times*, September 12, 2002.

41. Author interview with Melvin Bernhardt, August 24, 2004.

42. Faulk, 67.

43. Tennessee Williams, *A Streetcar Named Desire. Tennessee Williams Plays 1937–1955* (New York: The Library of America, 2000), 511. See also *New York Times*, May 17, 1962.

44. *Testimony of John Henry Faulk*, April 22–June 28, 1962. *John Henry Faulk v. Aware, Inc., Laurence Johnson, and Vincent Hartnett*, New York Supreme Court, 1962.

45. *Testimony of Thomas Murray*, May 14, 1962. *John Henry Faulk v. Aware, Inc., Laurence Johnson, and Vincent Hartnett*, New York Supreme Court, May 1962.

46. *Testimony of Kim Hunter*, May 15–16, 1962. *John Henry Faulk v. Aware, Inc., Laurence Johnson, and Vincent Hartnett*, New York Supreme Court, 1962. See also Faulk, 149–51.

47. Faulk, 142.

48. *Testimony of Mark Goodson*, April 28, 1962. *John Henry Faulk v. Aware, Inc., Laurence Johnson and Vincent Hartnett*, New York Supreme Court, 1962. See also Faulk, 149–51.

49. Faulk, 150. See *New York Times*, April 28, 1962.

50. *New York Times*, May 26, 1962, and June 28, 1962. Louis Nizer's summation in *John Henry Faulk v. Aware, Inc., Laurence Johnson, and Vincent Hartnett* took place on June 27, 1962, New York Supreme Court.

51. *New York Times*, June 26, 1962. See also Kanfer, 283.

52. Faulk, 51.

53. Burton, 167.

54. *New York Times*, September 12, 2002.

55. Morgan, 523–24.

56. *New York Times*, September 12, 2002. See also Schickel, 447, 448–54.

57. Author telephone interview with Kathryn Emmett, July 5, 2007.

58. *Los Angeles Times*, September 12, 2002.

Postscript

1. Author interview with Phoebe Brand, May 7, 2003. Phoebe Brand Carnovsky was ninety-six when she died on July 12, 2004.

2. Murphy, 4.

3. Laurents, 285.

4. Author interview with Leticia Ferrer, January 26, 2006. Also, author interview with Hagen biographer Jesse Feiler, March 21, 2006.

5. *New York Times*, March 18, 1951. See also Uta Hagen clippings file in the New York Performing Arts Library at Lincoln Center.

6. Uta Hagen, "Ideals Don't Bend," 63. See also "Uta Hagen," 173–75.

7. Hellman, *Scoundrel Time*, 113.

8. Quoted in Kanfer, 156.

9. *New York Times*, November 4, 1951.

10. *New York Times*, November 11, 1951.

11. Webster, *Don't Put Your Daughter*, 260.

12. Schrecker, *Many Are the Crimes*, 360.

13. Webster, *Don't Put Your Daughter*, 259.

14. Wright, 259–60.

15. Author Interview with Ann Shepherd, April 26, 2001.

16. Schrecker, *Many Are the Crimes*, 365.

17. Meade, 342.

18. Ceplair and Englund, 418–22.

19. Schrecker, *Many Are the Crimes*, 362.

20. Quoted in Webster, *Don't Put Your Daughter*, 268.

21. From the Council Minutes of Actors' Equity Association, November 13, 1951, 10,751–56. Actors' Equity Association Archives, Robert F. Wagner Labor Archives, Tamiment Library, New York. See also "Report of Equity Blacklisting Committee 1952," in Actors' Equity Association Archives.

22. *New York Times*, June 10, 1953, and September 30, 1953.

23. Navasky, 178–79.

24. "Equity Hosts Panel on Broadway and the Blacklist," *Equity News* (June 2005): 4.

25. "Meeting-Goer," *Time*, June 2, 1952, 74.

26. Newman, 253–54.

27. Schrecker, *Many Are the Crimes*, 364.

28. *Testimony of Paul Robeson*, June 12, 1956. *Hearings Regarding the Investigation of the Unauthorized Use of United States Passports—Part 3*. U.S. House of Representatives. Subcommittee of the Committee on Un-American Activities. 84th congress. 2nd sess.(Washington, D.C., U.S. Government Printing Office, 1956). See Eric Bentley, *Thirty Years of Treason*, 769–89.

29. *New York Times* April 21, 2003.

30. Morgan, 598.

31. *New York Times*, March 15, 2003.

32. *New York Times*, March 10, 2003 and July 8, 2003.

33. Frank Rich, "Watching Operation Iraqi Infoganda," *New York Times*, March 28, 2004.

34. Laurents, 299.

Selected Bibliography

This list omits specific FBI and other government files; informal interviews; and short, incidental, untitled and/or anonymous newspaper and magazine articles consulted in the preparation of this book. Full bibliographical information for these items can be found in the relevant notes.

Adams, John G. *Without Precedent: The Story of the Death of McCarthyism.* New York: Norton, 1983.

Adler, Thomas P. *American Drama, 1940–60: A Critical History.* New York: Twayne, 1994.

Arthur Miller, Elia Kazan, and the Blacklist: None Without Sin. American Masters Series. Public Broadcasting Company (September 3, 2003).

Atkinson, Brooks. *Broadway.* New York: Limelight, 1990.

Aware: News Supplement to Membership Bulletin. New York: Aware, 1954–56.

Barranger, Milly S. "Broadway's Women on Trial: The McCarthy Years." *The Journal of American Drama and Theatre* 15, no. 3 (Fall 2003): 1–37.

———. "Dorothy Parker and the Politics of McCarthyism." *Theatre History Studies* 26 (2006): 7–30.

———. *Margaret Webster: A Bio-Bibliography.* Westport, CT: Greenwood, 1994.

———. *Margaret Webster: A Life in the Theater.* Ann Arbor: University of Michigan Press, 2004.

Barrett, Edward L. *The Tenney Committee: Legislative Investigation of Subversive Activities in California.* Ithaca: Cornell University Press, 1951.

Bauland, Peter. *The Hooded Eagle: Modern German Drama on the New York Stage.* Syracuse: Syracuse University Press, 1968.

Belfrage, Cedric, *The American Inquisition 1945–1960.* Indianapolis: Bobbs-Merrill, 1973.

Bentley, Eric. *Are You Now or Have You Ever Been: The Investigation of Show Business by the Un-American Activities Committee, 1947–1958.* New York: Harper and Row, 1972.

———, ed. *Thirty Years of Treason: Excerpts from Hearings before the House Un-American Activities Committee 1938–1968.* New York: Viking, 1971.

———. *What Is Theatre? Incorporating The Dramatic Event and Other Reviews, 1944–1967.* 2nd ed. New York: Hill and Wang, 2000.

Bentley, Joanne. *Hallie Flanagan: A Life in the American Theatre.* New York: Knopf, 1988.

Bigsby, C. W. E. *Modern American Drama, 1945–1990.* New York: Cambridge University Press, 1992.

Bosworth, Patricia. "Memories of HUAC." *The Nation* 245 (October 24, 1987): 436–37.

Bryer, Jackson R., ed. *Conversations with Lillian Hellman.* Jackson: University Press of Mississippi, 1986.

Buhle, Mari Jo, Paul Buhle and Dan Georgakas, eds. *Encyclopedia of the American Left.* 2nd ed. New York: Oxford University Press, 1998.

Burton, Michael C. *John Henry Faulk: A Biography: The Making of a Liberated Mind.* Austin: Eakin Press, 1993.

Buttitta, Tony, and Barry Witham. *Uncle Sam Presents: A Memoir of the Federal Theatre, 1935–1939.* Philadelphia: University of Pennsylvania Press, 1982.

Calhoun, Randall. *Dorothy Parker: A Bio-Bibliography.* Westport, CT: Greenwood, 1993.

Capron, Marion. "Dorothy Parker." *Paris Review* 13, no. 4 (Summer 1956): 72–87.

Carey, Gary. *Judy Holliday, An Intimate Life Story.* London: Robson House, 1983.

Ceplair, Larry, and Steven Englund. *The Inquisition in Hollywood: Politics in the Film Community, 1930–1960.* Rev. ed. Urbana: University of Illinois Press, 2003.

Chinoy, Helen Krich, and Linda Walsh Jenkins. *Women in American Theatre: Careers, Images, Movements.* Rev. ed. New York: Theatre Communications Group, 2006.

Clurman, Harold. *All People Are Famous.* New York: Harcourt Brace Jovanovich, 1974.

———. *The Fervent Years: The Story of the Group Theatre and the Thirties.* New York: Da Capo Press, 1983.

———."Introduction." *Lillian Hellman Playwright,* by Richard Moody, New York: Bobbs-Merrill, 1972.

Cogley, John. *Report on Blacklisting.* 2 vols. New York: Arno Press, 1972.

Conrad, Christine. *Jerome Robbins: That Broadway Man, That Ballet Man.* London: Booth-Clibborn Editions, 2000.

Counterattack: Newsletter of Facts to Combat Communism and Those Who Aid Its Cause. New York: American Business Consultants, 1947–1973.

Crawford, Cheryl. *One Naked Individual: My Fifty Years in the Theatre.* Indianapolis: Bobbs-Merrill, 1977.

Dick, Bernard F. *Hellman in Hollywood.* Teaneck, NJ: Fairleigh Dickinson University Press, 1982.

Dilling, Elizabeth. *The Red Network: The "Who's Who" and Handbook of Radicalism for Patriots.* Kenilworth, IL: By the author, 1934.

Doherty, L. "The Art of Producing: The Life and Work of Kermit Bloomgarden." Ph.D. diss., City University of New York, 1989.

Doudna, Christine. "A Still Unfinished Women: A Conversation with Lillian Hellman." *Rolling Stone* 233 (24 February 1977): 52–57.

Duberman, Martin B. *Paul Robeson: A Biography.* New York: Knopf, 1989.

Epstein, Helen. *Joe Papp: An American Life.* New York: Little, Brown, 1994.

Fariello, Griffin. *Red Scare: Memories of the American Inquisition.* New York: Norton, 1995.

Faulk, John Henry. *Fear on Trial.* Austin: University of Texas Press, 1983.

Flanagan, Hallie. *Arena: The History of the Federal Theatre.* New York: Benjamin Blom, 1940.

Foley, Thomas J. "Probers List Ferrer, Judy on Red Ties." *Journal American,* April 5, 1951, 1–42

Freibert, Lucy M. "Dorothy Parker." *A Dictionary of Literary Biography: American Short-Story Writers 1910–1945.* 1st ser. vol. 86. Detroit: Gale, 1989, 223–33.

Frewin, Leslie. *The Late Mrs. Dorothy Parker.* New York: Macmillan, 1986.

Fried, Richard M. *Men against McCarthy.* New York: Columbia University Press, 1976.

Gelderman, Carol W. *Mary McCarthy: A Life.* New York: St. Martin's Press, 1988.

Goldston, Robert C. *The American Nightmare: Senator Joseph R. McCarthy and the Politics of Hate.* Indianapolis: Bobbs-Merrill, 1973.

Goodman, Walter. *The Committee: The Extraordinary Career of the House Committee on Un-American Activities.* New York: Farrar, Straus and Giroux, 1968.

Gottfried, Martin. *Arthur Miller: His Life and Work.* Cambridge, MA: Da Capo Press, 2003.

Grant, Thomas. "Dorothy Parker." *Dictionary of Literary Biography.* vol. 11. Detroit: Gale, 1982, 369–82.

Griffith, Robert. *The Politics of Fear: Joseph R. McCarthy and the Senate.* 2nd ed. Amherst: University of Massachusetts Press, 1987.

Gussow, Mel. *Edward Albee: A Singular Journey: A Biography.* New York: Simon and Schuster, 1999.

Hagen, Uta. "Ideals Don't Bend." In *This I Believe.* 2nd ed. Edward R. Murrow. New York: Simon and Schuster, 1954.

———. *Sources: A Memoir.* New York: Performing Arts Journal Publication, 1983.

Hellman, Lillian. *Pentimento: A Book of Portraits.* Boston: Little, Brown, 1973.

———. *Scoundrel Time.* Boston: Little, Brown, 1976.

———. *Six Plays by Lillian Hellman.* New York: Vintage Books, 1979.

———. *Three: An Unfinished Woman, Pentimento, Scoundrel Time.* Boston: Little, Brown, 1979.

———. *An Unfinished Woman—A Memoir.* Boston: Little, Brown, 1969.

Harbin, Bill J., Robert A. Schanke, and Kim Marra, eds. *The Gay and Lesbian Theatrical Legacy.* Ann Arbor: University of Michigan Press, 2005.

Henderson, Mary C. *Theater in America: Two Hundred Years of Plays, Players, and Productions.* New York: Harry N. Abrams, 1988.

Hersey, John. "Tribute to Lillian Hellman." *Proceedings of the American Academy and Institute of Arts and Letters*. 2nd ser., no. 35. New York: American Academy and Institute of Arts and Letters, 1984.

Hewitt, Barnard. *Theatre U.S.A. 1889 to 1957.* New York: McGraw Hill, 1959.

Hill, Holly, ed. *Playing Joan: Actresses on the Challenge of Shaw's Saint Joan.* New York: Theatre Communications Group, 1987.

Hirsch, Foster. *The Boys from Syracuse: The Shuberts' Theatrical Empire.* Carbondale: Southern Illinois University Press, 1998.

Holtzman, Will. *Judy Holliday.* New York: Putnam, 1982.

Houseman, John. *Front and Center.* New York: Simon and Schuster, 1979.

Hughes, Glenn. *A History of the American Theatre 1700–1950.* New York: Samuel French, 1951.

Hunter, Kim. *Loose in the Kitchen.* North Hollywood: Domina Books, 1975.

Interview with Dorothy Parker. Popular Arts Project, Part 2, Office of Oral History Research, Columbia University, New York, 1959.

Interview with Lillian Hellman. Televised interview conducted by Marilyn Berger, Public Broadcasting System, 1980.

Interview with Madeleine Lee Gilford. Conducted by Muriel Meyers, September 22, 1993. American Jewish Committee, Oral History, New York Public Library.

Interviews with Madeleine Lee Gilford and Sondra Gorney. Conducted by Lee Grant, November 1, 2005. New York Public Library for the Performing Arts.

Israel, Lee. "Judy Holliday." *MS* (December 1976): 72–74, 90–96.

Johnson, Diane. *Dashiell Hammett: A Life.* New York: Random House, 1983.

———. "Obsessed." *Vanity Fair* 48 (May 1985): 79–81, 116–19.

Kahn, Gordon. *Hollywood on Trial.* New York: Boni and Gaer, 1948.

Kanfer, Stefan. *A Journal of the Plague Years: A Devastating Chronicle of the Era of the Blacklist.* New York: Simon and Schuster, 1973.

Kazan, Elia. *A Life.* New York: Knopf, 1988.

Keats, John. *You Might As Well Live: The Life and Times of Dorothy Parker.* New York: Simon and Schuster, 1970.

Kempton, Murray. *Part of Our Time: Some Ruins and Monuments of the Thirties.* New York: Simon and Schuster, 1955.

———. "Witness: Review of *Scoundrel Time*." *New York Review of Books* 23, no. 10 (June 10, 1976): 22–25.

Kessler, Lauren. *Clever Girl: Elizabeth Bentley and the Dawn of the McCarthy Era.* New York: HarperCollins, 2003.

"Kim Hunter." *Current Biography 1952.* New York: H. W. Wilson, 1953, 281–83.

Kinney, Arthur F. *Dorothy Parker.* Rev. ed. New York: Twayne, 1998.

Krutch, Joseph Wood. *The American Drama since 1918.* New York: George Braziller, 1957.

Langner, Lawrence. *The Play's the Thing.* New York: Putnam, 1960.

———. "'Saint Joan'—A Play for Today." *New York Times*, September 30, 1951.

Laurents, Arthur. *Original Story By: A Memoir of Broadway and Hollywood.* New York: Knopf, 2000.

Lawrence, Greg. *Dance with Demons: The Life of Jerome Robbins.* New York: Putnam, 2001.

Layman, Richard. *Shadow Man: The Life of Dashiell Hammett.* New York: Harcourt Brace Jovanovich, 1981.

"Lillian Hellman." *Playwrights at Work: The Paris Review.* Ed. George Plimpton. New York: Modern Library, 2000, 23–49.

Lowenthal, Max. *The Federal Bureau of Investigation.* New York: William Sloane, 1950.

Lyon, James K. *Bertolt Brecht in America.* Princeton, NJ: Princeton University Press, 1980.

Mandelbaum, Ken. *Not since Carrie: Forty Years of Broadway Musical Flops.* New York: St. Martin's Press, 1991.

Mathews, Jane D. *The Federal Theatre, 1935–1939.* Princeton, NJ: Princeton University Press, 1967.

McClellan, Doug. "Anne Revere." *Film Fan Monthly* 96 (June 1969): 20–21.

———. *The Unkindest Cuts: The Scissors and the Cinema.* South Brunswick, NJ: A. and S. Barnes, 1972.

McConachie, Bruce. *American Theatre in the Culture of the Cold War: Producing and Contesting Containment, 1947–1962.* Iowa City: Iowa University Press, 2003.

Meade, Marion. *Dorothy Parker: What Fresh Hell Is This?* New York: Villard Books, 1988.

Mellen, Joan. *Hellman and Hammett: The Legendary Passion of Lillian Hellman and Dashiell Hammett.* New York: Harper Collins, 1996.

Miller, Arthur. *The Theater Essays of Arthur Miller.* Ed. Robert A. Martin. New York: Viking Press, 1978.

———. *Timebends: A Life.* New York: Harper and Row, 1987.

———. "The Year It Came Apart." *New York* (December 30, 1974): 43–44.

Mitgang, Herbert. *Dangerous Dossiers: Exposing the Secret War against America's Greatest Authors.* New York: Donald I. Fine, 1988.

Monaco, Pamela. "Lillian Hellman." *Dictionary of Literary Biography: Twentieth-Century American Dramatists.* Ed. Christopher Wheatley. 2nd ed. vol. 228. Detroit: Gale, 2002, 96–115.

Moody, Richard. *Lillian Hellman Playwright.* New York: Bobbs-Merrill, 1972.

Morehouse, Ward. *Matinee Tomorrow.* New York: McGraw-Hill, 1949.

Morgan, Ted. *Reds: McCarthyism in Twentieth-Century America.* New York: Random House, 2003.

Mostel, Kate, and Madeleine Gilford, with Jack Gilford and Zero Mostel. *170 Years of Show Business.* New York: Random House, 1978.

Murphy, Brenda. *Congressional Theatre: Dramatizing McCarthyism on Stage, Film, and Television.* New York: Cambridge University Press, 1999.

Navasky, Victor S. *Naming Names.* 3rd ed. New York: Hill and Wang, 2003.

Nesmith, N. Graham. "An Interview with Eric Bentley." *The Yale Review* 91, no. 3 (July 2003): 73–99.

Newman, Robert P. *The Cold War Romance of Lillian Hellman and John Melby.* Chapel Hill: University of North Carolina Press, 1989.

Ormsbee, Helen. "Mady Christians Recalls How Nazis 'Cleansed' the Theaters." *New York Herald Tribune,* July 13, 1941, 2.

Oshinsky, David M. *A Conspiracy So Immense: The World of Joe McCarthy.* New York: Free Press, 1963.

Parker, Dorothy. "Incredible, Fantastic . . . and True." *New Masses* 25 (November 23, 1937): 16.

Paxton, Robert O. *The Anatomy of Fascism.* New York: Knopf, 2004.

Phillips, John, and Anne Hollander. "Lillian Hellman: An Interview." *Paris Review* 9, no. 33 (Winter–Spring 1965): 65–95.

Point of Order: Documentary of the 1954 Army-McCarthy Hearings. Ed. and narr. Emile de Antonio. New Yorker Video, 1964.

Pollitt, Daniel H. "The Fifth Amendment Plea before Congressional Committees Investigating Subversion: Motives and Justifiable Presumptions—a Survey of 120 Witnesses." *University of Pennsylvania Law Review* 106, no. 8 (June 1958): 1117–37.

Red Channels: The Report of Communist Influence in Radio and Television. New York: American Business Consultants, 1950.

Reeves, Thomas C. *The Life and Times of Joe McCarthy: A Biography.* New York: Stein and Day, 1982.

Remembering the Entertainment Blacklist. Produced by New York Public Library for the Performing Arts, April 30, 1994.

Rice, Elmer. *Minority Report: An Autobiography.* New York: Simon and Schuster, 1963.

Robinson, Alice M., Vera Mowry Roberts, and Milly S. Barranger, eds. *Notable Women in the American Theatre: A Biographical Dictionary.* Westport, CT: Greenwood, 1989.

Rollyson, Carl. *Lillian Hellman: Her Legend and Her Legacy.* New York: St. Martin's Press, 1988.

Salvi, Delia Nora. *The History of the Actors' Laboratory, Inc., 1941–1950.* Ph.D. diss, University of California at Los Angeles, 1969.

Schanke, Robert A. *Shattered Applause: The Lives of Eva Le Gallienne.* Carbondale: Southern Illinois University Press, 1992.

Schanke, Robert A., and Kim Marra, eds. *Passing Performances: Queer Readings of Leading Players in American Theater History.* Ann Arbor: University of Michigan Press, 1998.

Schickel, Richard. *Elia Kazan: A Biography.* New York: HarperCollins, 2005.

Schloss, Leon. W. "Dorothy Parker Quits Her Role as Humorist." *Los Angeles Times,* January 7, 1939.

Schrecker, Ellen. *The Age of McCarthyism: A Brief History with Documents.* 2nd ed. Boston: Bedford Books of St. Martin's Press, 1994.

———. *Many Are the Crimes: McCarthyism in America.* Boston: Little, Brown, 1995.

Schwartz, Bonnie Nelson, and the Educational Film Center, eds. *Voices from the Federal Theatre.* Madison: University of Wisconsin Press, 2003.

Sheehy, Helen. *Eva Le Gallienne: A Biography.* New York: Knopf, 1996.

Sien, Max. "The Ordeal and Martyrdom of Mady Christians." *The Compass,* November 18, 1951, 13.

Slide, Anthony. *Actors on Red Alert: Career Interviews with Five Actors and Actresses Affected by the Blacklist.* Lanham, MD: Scarecrow Press, 1999.

Spector, Susan Jane. "Uta Hagen: The Early Years 1919–1951." Ph.D. diss., New York University, 1982.

Staggs, Sam. *When Blanche Met Brando: The Scandalous Story of "A Streetcar Named Desire."* New York: St. Martin's Press, 2005.

Steinberg, Peter L. *The Great "Red Menace": United States Prosecution of American Communists, 1947–1952.* Westport, CT: Greenwood, 1984.

Stone, Geoffrey R. *Perilous Times: Free Speech in Wartime from the Sedition Act of 1798 to the War on Terrorism.* New York: Norton, 2004.

Suber, Howard. "The Anti-Communist Blacklist in Hollywood Motion Picture Industry." Ph.D. diss., University of California at Los Angeles, 1968.

Swindell, Larry. *Body and Soul: The Story of John Garfield.* New York: William Morrow, 1975.

Tanenhaus, Sam. *Whittaker Chambers: A Biography.* New York: Random House, 1997.

Taubman, Howard. *The Making of the American Theater.* Rev. ed. New York: Coward-McCann, 1967.

Taylor, Tedford. *Grand Inquest: The Story of Congressional Investigations.* New York: Simon and Schuster, 1955.

Trumbo, Dalton. *The Time of the Toad: A Study of Inquisition in America.* West Nyack, NJ: Journeyman Press, 1982.

"Uta Hagen." *Current Biography 1962.* New York: H. D. Wilson, 1962, 173–75.

Vaughn, Robert. *Only Victims: A Study of Show Business Blacklisting.* New York: Putnam, 1972.

Watters, Pat, and Stephen Gillers. *Investigating the FBI.* Garden City, NY: Doubleday, 1973.

Webster, Margaret. *Don't Put Your Daughter on the Stage.* New York: Knopf, 1972.

———. *The Same Only Different: Five Generations of a Great Theatre Family.* New York: Knopf, 1969.

Wertheim, Albert. "The McCarthy Era and the American Theatre." *Theatre Journal* 34, no. 2 (May 1982): 211–22.

Witham, Barry. "Appropriately Wistful: Blacklisting and the American Theatre." *Exchange* (Winter 1981): 11–17.

———. *The Federal Theatre Project: A Case Study.* New York: Cambridge University Press, 2004.

Wright, William. *Lillian Hellman: The Image, The Woman.* New York: Simon and Schuster, 1986.

Ybarra, Michael J. *Washington Gone Crazy: Senator Pat McCarran and the Great American Communist Hunt.* Hanover, NH: Steerforth Press, 2004.

Zheutlin, Barbara, and David Talbot. *Creative Differences: Profiles of Hollywood Dissidents.* Boston: South End Press, 1978.

Government Hearings and Documents

Special House Committee 1938

Special House Committee on Un-American Activities. *Hearings on the Investigation of Un-American Propaganda Activities in the United States.* 75th Congress. 2nd sess. Washington, D.C.: U.S. Government Printing Office, 1939.

Standing Committees on Un-American Activities,
U.S. House of Representatives, 1945–1967

Hearings Regarding Communist Activity in the United States. 80th Congress. 1st sess. *Hearings Regarding Communist Infiltration of the Motion-Picture Industry.* 2nd sess. Washington, D.C.: U.S. Government Printing Office, 1947.

Hearings Regarding Communist Infiltration of the Motion-Picture Industry. 81st Congress. 2nd sess. Washington, D.C.: U.S. Government Printing Office, 1951.

Hearings Regarding Communist Infiltration of Hollywood Motion-Picture Industry. 82nd Congress. 1st sess. Part 5–8. 2nd sess. Washington, D.C.: U.S. Government Printing Office, 1952.

Hearings Regarding Communist Methods of Infiltration. 83rd Congress. *Investigation of Communist Activities in the New York City Area.* Part 3–4. Washington, D.C.: U.S. Government Printing Office, 1953.

Hearings Regarding the Investigation of Communist Activities, Hollywood, 84th Congress. Parts 6–8. *(Entertainment). Investigation of the Unauthorized Use of U.S. Passports.* Parts 1–4. Washington, D C: U.S. Government Printing Office, 1956.

Hearings Regarding the Investigation of Communists in the Metropolitan Music School, Inc. and Related Fields. 85th Congress. *Communism in the New York Area (Entertainment).* Part 5. Washington, D.C.: U.S. Government Printing Office, 1958.

Standing Committees, U.S. Senate, 1952–54

Hearings before the Subcommittee to Investigate the Administration of the Internal Security Act and Other Internal Security Laws of the Committee on the Judiciary. U.S. Senate. 2nd sess. *Subversive Infiltration of Radio, Television, and the Entertainment Industry.* Washington, D.C.: U.S. Government Printing Office, 1952.

Executive Sessions of the U.S. Senate Permanent Subcommittee on Investigations of the Committee on Government Operations. 83rd Congress. 1st sess. *State Department Information Service—Information Centers.* Vol. 1. *State Department Teacher-Student Exchange Program.* Vol. 2. Washington, D.C.: U.S. Government Printing Office, 2003.

Hearing before the Permanent Subcommittee on Investigations of the Committee on Government Operations. State Department Information Program—Information Centers. U.S. Senate. 83rd Congress. 1st sess. Part 1. Washington, D.C.: U.S. Government Printing Office, 1953.

California State Senate Committee Report, 1948

California Legislature. Senate. *Fourth Report [on Un-American Activities in California] 1948: Communist Front Organizations.* Sacramento, CA., 1948.

New York State Legislative Hearings, 1955

Hearings before the New York State Joint Legislative Committee Investigating Charitable and Philanthropic Agencies and Organizations. New York City. Vol. 3. Albany: Parsons Reporting Service, 1955.

Index

Biberman, Herbert, 60, 61, 72
Bierly, Kenneth, 17, 26
Big Sister (radio), 132
Bing, Rudolf, 113
Black, Ivan, 114
Black Chiffon (play), 47
blacklist, xiii, xv, 31, 34, 35, 46, 49, 50, 60,
  61, 64, 65, 85, 86, 87, 89, 90, 91, 105, 109,
  113, 124, 128, 129, 85, 137; end of, 123, 132;
  financial impact of, 104, 122, 123, 126; in
  Hollywood, 16, 34, 78, 91, 105, 111, 126,
  127, 131; on networks, 15–16, 30, 32, 34,
  35, 63, 88, 108, 111–12, 114, 116, 117, 119,
  122, 127, 128, 131, 136
Bloomgarden, Kermit, 77, 127
Body and Soul (film), 50
Bogart, Humphrey, 111
Bohnen, Roman, 51, 56, 57
Bolan, Thomas A., 118, 121–22, 123
Boleslavsky, Richard, 59
Born Yesterday (film), 12, 14, 15
Born Yesterday (play), xiv, 8, 12, 127
Brand, Phoebe, xi, 61, 124, 132, 137; on
  blacklisting, 126
Brando, Marlon, 108
Brandt, George, 47
Brecht, Bertolt, 38, 43
Brewer, Roy, 112, 122
British War Relief, 88
Broadway, 9, 13, 16, 32, 38, 45, 47, 49, 50,
  61, 64, 69, 70, 83, 87, 88, 105, 108, 109,
  110, 111, 113, 123, 127, 129, 130, 137; and
  blacklisting, 89–90. 95, 104, 114; and
  graylisting, 89–90, 128; theatres on,
  12, 40, 105
Bromberg, J. Edward, xiii, 48, 51, 56, 57, 78,
  124, 128, 147; as blacklisted, 88; in *Red
  Channels*, 147
Brooks, David, 41
Broun, Heywood, 69
Broun, Heywood Hale, 31
Browder, Earl, 68
Bryan, Helen, 92
Buchman, Harold, 55
Budenz, Louis F., 42, 44, 54, 72, 90–91
Burrows, Abe, 4, 14, 122
Burton, Michael, 123
Burton, Richard, 105

Caesar, Sid, 32
California Joint Fact-Finding Committee
  on Un-American Activities (Tenney
  committee), 35, 43, 49, 51, 66, 71–72,
  112, 112
Campbell, Alan, 66, 68, 69, 70, 79
Candide (Hellman and Bernstein), 77
Carey, Gary, 21
Carnovsky, Morris, 42, 51, 53, 56, 57, 61, 64,
  124, 126; in *Red Channels*, 147
Catholic War Veterans, 17, 24
Ceplair, Larry, 133
Chaplin, Charlie, 14, 91
Chase, The (Foote), 109, 111
Chekhov, Anton, 57
Children's Hour, The (Hellman), xiv, 50, 56,
  64, 65, 77, 109, 111, 113, 129
Choate, Edward, 92, 93
Christians, Mady, 33, 34–48, 52, 71, 80,
  83, 86–87, 88, 90, 93, 94, 127, 128, 129,
  130, 132, 133, 137, 147; actor training, 37;
  as blacklisted, 33, 34, 46, 94, 110, 128;
  Broadway career of, 33, 38, 45, 47, 87;
  citizenship, U.S., 37; as controversial,
  35–36; death of, 46, 47, 93; elected to
  Actors Equity Council, 39; FBI investigations of, 38, 42, 43, 45, 46, 71–72,
  73, 75, 86–87, 93; film career of, 38, 45,
  110; parents of, 37; political activism
  of, 38, 42–44, 46, 73–74, 82, 84, 88–89;
  radio career of, 46; in *Red Channels*,
  147, 149, 150–52
Christians, Rudolf, 36
Citizens Committee to Preserve American
  Freedom, 62
Civil Rights Congress, 12, 13, 14, 51, 53, 78,
  79, 80, 98, 103, 134
Clarence Derwent Award, 12
clearance services, 34, 35, 109, 111–12, 113,
  114, 119, 122, 131
Clift, Montgomery, 50, 51
Close Harmony (Rice and Parker), 69
Clurman, Harold, xv
Cobb, Lee J., xiv, 30, 49, 50, 51, 53, 57, 147;
  as friendly witness, 60–61
Coca, Imogene, 32
Cohn, Harry, 13, 16, 17
Cohn, Roy M., 95, 98, 100–103

Green, Robert L., 17
Griffith, Robert, 98
Group Theatre, 56, 57, 61, 64, 124, 126; communist cell in, 64
Gulf Playhouse: A Present from Cotton Mather (television show), 64
Gypsy (Laurents), 89, 137

Hagen, Uta, xiv, xv, 87, 94, 111, 113, 127, 128–29, 137, 147, 149, 155, 201, 202; as blacklisted, 14, 15, 154, 201–2; in *Red Channels*, 128, 147, 149, 150–52
Hamlet (Shakespeare), 38, 87
Hammer, Alvin, 10, 11, 17, 20
Hammett, Dashiell, 14, 49, 51, 65, 67, 68, 73, 78, 83, 86, 98–99, 103, 134, 148; death of, 83; as Marxist, 67, 68; as unfriendly witness, 98–99; writings of, 65, 98
Happiest Man, The (Parker and Campbell), 69–70
Harding, John, 78
Hardy, Joseph A., 63
Hart, Moss, 11
Hartnett, Vincent W., 12, 14, 34, 35, 108, 109, 111–13, 115, 116, 118, 119–20, 121, 122, 123, 147; as clearance consultant, 34, 35, 113, 116, 119
Harvey (play), 41
Hayden, Sterling, 53, 64, 93, 111, 112
Hellman, Lillian Florence, xiii, xiv, xv, 2, 7, 11, 33, 38, 40, 49, 50, 51, 52, 61, 63, 64, 65–69, 70–71, 73–77, 81–82, 83–84, 86, 88, 91, 92, 95, 96, 109, 111, 113, 126–27, 128, 129, 131, 132–33, 134, 137, 147; as blacklisted 77; Broadway career of, 33, 38, 65, 83; as CP member, 68, 74; death of, 84; FBI investigation of, 70–71; HUAC testimony of, 75–76; Jewish heritage of, 68; lawsuit against Mary McCarthy, 84; as legend, 84; passport difficulties of, 82, 96, 135; political activism of, 66, 67, 68, 83, 84; in *Red Channels*, 147, 149, 152–54; as unfriendly witness, 51, 74, 75–76; writings of, xiii, xv, 38, 50, 56, 63, 64, 65, 69, 74, 77, 81, 83–84, 109, 111, 113, 127, 128, 129
Henderson, Leon, 69, 72–73
Henreid, Paul, 53
Henry IV, Part 1 (Shakespeare), 38

Hepburn, Katharine, 12
Hersey, John, 84, 91
Hewitt, Alan, 39
Hiss, Alger, 134
Hobart, Rose, 57, 61, 149; in *Red Channels*, 149
Hochwalder, Fritz, 105–6
Holding, William, 12
Holliday, Judy, xiv, xvi, 2, 8, 9–33, 61, 88, 113, 122, 131, 132, 134, 137, 147; awards, 10, 12, 14; as blacklisted, 13, 15, 16, 30; Broadway career of, 12, 32; death of, 33; education of, 10; family of, 10; FBI investigation of, 15; film career of, 11, 12, 32; Hollywood makeover, 11; as Judy Tuvim, 10, 18; marriage of, 17, 18; parents of, 10; political activism of, 13–14, 25, 88–89; in *Red Channels*, 13, 14, 147, 149, 154–55; SISS testimony of, 17–30
Hollywood, 9, 16, 17, 34, 36, 38, 49, 56, 61, 65, 67, 68, 71, 111, 114, 124, 130, 137; and blacklisting, 13, 20, 34, 50, 51, 62, 78, 91, 104, 106, 108, 110, 111, 112, 123, 126, 133
Hollywood Actors' Laboratory, 43, 48, 50, 53, 56, 57, 59, 62, 72, 126, 132
Hollywood Anti-Nazi League (a.k.a. Anti-Nazi League), 35, 66, 69, 72, 73
Hollywood Nineteen, 51
Hollywood Now (newsletter), 147
Hollywood Ten, xv, 2, 13, 14, 15, 27, 29, 34, 49, 51, 54, 60, 61, 71, 78, 110, 112, 134
Holt, Stella, 24
Holtzman, Will, 15, 31
Hood, R. B., 52
Hook, Sidney, 84
Hoover, J. Edgar, 1, 36, 40, 47, 52, 54, 70, 106, 130,
Hopkins, Harry, 4
Hopper, Hedda, 14
Horne, Lena, 14, 35, 53, 149
Hot Spot (musical), 32
House Committee on Un-American Activities (HUAC), 1, 2, 13, 16, 21, 25, 31, 38, 43, 48, 49, 50, 52, 54, 55, 56, 57, 59, 60, 61, 62, 63, 66, 67, 71, 73–78, 79, 84, 85, 88, 89, 90, 92, 113, 114, 115, 126, 127, 131, 132, 133, 147; passport hearings, 82–83, 134–35
Houseman, John, 10

Milly S. Barranger is distinguished professor emerita at the University of North Carolina, Chapel Hill, where she has served as chairman of the Department of Dramatic Art and producing director of PlayMakers Repertory Company. She is the author of *Margaret Webster: A Life in the Theater; Theatre: A Way of Seeing; Understanding Plays;* and *Theatre: Past and Present* and coeditor of *Notable Women in the American Theatre: A Biographical Dictionary.*

THEATER IN THE AMERICAS

The goal of the series is to publish a wide range of scholarship on theater and performance, defining theater in its broadest terms and including subjects that encompass all of the Americas.

The series focuses on the performance and production of theater and theater artists and practitioners but welcomes studies of dramatic literature as well. Meant to be inclusive, the series invites studies of traditional, experimental, and ethnic forms of theater; celebrations, festivals, and rituals that perform culture; and acts of civil disobedience that are performative in nature. We publish studies of theater and performance activities of all cultural groups within the Americas, including biographies of individuals, histories of theater companies, studies of cultural traditions, and collections of plays.